Vulnerable MISSION

14-01-12

To
Colin & Rosemary,

I hope you enjoy the read. Appreciating your hospitality yet again in 2012.

Jim Harries

(Jim Harries)

Vulnerable Mission: Insights into Christian Mission to Africa from a Position of Vulnerability

Published by William Carey Library
1605 E. Elizabeth St.,
Pasadena, California 91104 | www.missionbooks.org

Kelley K. Wolfe, editor
Brad Koenig, copyeditor
Hugh Pindur, graphic designer
Rose Lee-Norman, indexer

William Carey Library is a ministry of the
US Center for World Mission
Pasadena, CA | www.uscwm.org

Printed in the United States of America
15 14 13 12 11 5 4 3 2 1 CH800

Library of Congress Cataloging-in-Publication Data
Harries, Jim.
Vulnerable mission : insights into christian mission to Africa from a position of vulnerability Jim Harries.
p. cm.
ISBN 978-0-87808-524-8
1. Missions--Africa. 2. Missions--Theory. I. Title.
BV3500.H29 2011
266.00967--dc23
2011022686

PREFACE

This compilation of articles, most already published in professional peer-review journals, presents a clear case in favour of VM (vulnerable mission). VM is, according to the AVM (Alliance for Vulnerable Mission), Christian mission work carried out by Westerners using the languages and resources of the community being reached. For the sake of the future health of church and society in Africa, I say unequivocally that there is an important need for some Western missionaries to operate in a "vulnerable way" in Africa, and beyond.

The practical nature of the insights provided in the pages of this book cannot be overemphasised. I began my time in Africa as an agriculturalist. My concern for the plight of the people I found myself working with, combined with my faith in God as a Christian, had me begin a search for answers to troubling questions in the African mission context from as early as 1988. I learned the Kaonde language of Zambia, then later moved to Kenya and became fluent in Kiswahili and Dholuo. I have lived in a Kenyan village since 1993, confining my interactions to the Luo language (Dholuo) and Kiswahili in my home and in key Bible training ministries. I have extensive experience of coal-face ministry (as against administrative roles and roles that are more set-apart from the people) in the African context. My experiences drove me to write my PhD, and before and after completing it (in 2007) to write articles expressing my heart in respect to relationships between the West and Africa, particularly in the context of mission and church.

Certain key threads run through these articles. They consider efforts at encouraging economic and social development as well as evangelistic and discipling ministries. They draw on the Scriptures and Christian teaching. They are linguistically informed; they draw particularly on pragmatics—the understanding that the meaning of language arises largely from its use. They challenge the status quo and the idealism that underlies much of the West's activities in Africa today. They are searching for a new radical commitment to the gospel. They often need to be followed systematically and carefully for the reader to grasp the sweeping new vision being presented. While specifically concerned with the church and with advocating for a reformation in the character of mission from the West, the articles point way beyond that to the political scene and have implications for international policy and for many academic and practical disciplines.

The articles included in this compendium were originally written as early as 1997, and as late as 2010. The observant reader may notice a progression in my thinking, and that allusions to the period of time that I have spent in Africa are increased for articles written latterly.

I continue to live in my rural African home, with up to a dozen local orphan children in my care. I teach in informal theological education programmes that are oriented especially to indigenous African churches. I have also taught part time at an American-based theological seminary eight miles from my Kenyan home since 1997. I am the Chairman of the AVM. I arranged conferences in the USA, UK, and Germany in 2009, and then made visits to seminaries and Christian universities in Europe and North America in 2010. I continue to promote "vulnerable mission" to Western missionaries to the best of my ability, given my rural African location.

Interested readers are encouraged to consult the website of the AVM (Alliance for Vulnerable Mission) at www.vulnerablemission.org. Please contact jim@vulnerablemission.org for more information. The introduction to the AVM as found on the website is as follows:

> The AVM (Alliance for Vulnerable Mission) seeks to encourage wider use of mission and development strategies that depend on locally available resources and local languages.
>
> These strategies are "vulnerable" in the sense that they do not have fringe benefits built into them, deliberately or otherwise. They will therefore fail unless or until there is strong local confidence in their spiritual or developmental value. The missionary or development worker will allow them to fail rather than prop them up with outside money.
>
> *"Vulnerable mission" may be seen as part of the movement toward contextualiz*ation of the gospel of Jesus, which we regard as the theory of many and the practice of few. We would like to see more people take the risks of contextualization and vulnerability in order to reap the

rewards that only come to those who value local resources and invest in local languages.

If local tools seem slow or weak by comparison with foreign money and English (Spanish etc.—European language), then we say with a wise missionary of long ago, “When I am weak, then I am strong” (2 Cor 12:10). While vulnerable mission may not be the only biblical approach to mission, it deserves much more attention than it has been getting. Let’s talk.

CHAPTER 1

"The Name of God in Africa" and Related Contemporary Theological, Development, and Linguistic Concerns[1]

1. INTRODUCTION

I recently asked an elder in a local church which we were visiting in western Kenya how his people's understanding of God today had changed from what it was one hundred years ago (that is, before the coming of the missionaries). "Not at all" was his confident response. "The way our forefathers understood God, is the way that we still understand him today. Nothing has changed." I was taken aback. If one hundred years of Bible-believing Christianity has not changed how some Christians consider that they understand God, what has gone wrong?

In this part of Africa, in both church usage and translated Scriptures, local African names for God are used. This implicitly assumes that the African people already knew God in advance of the coming of missionaries. Presumably that made, and/or makes, it difficult for outsiders to speak authoritatively about God.[2] How can one engage in Christian theological teaching when the people already know "God" on the basis of their own ancient extra-Christian oral tradition?

The industry recently built up around Third World "development" seems in some ways to have usurped what was once the role of Christian mission in

1 This chapter was originally published as follows: Harries, Jim. 2009. "The name of God in Africa" and related contemporary theological, development and linguistic concerns. *Exchange: Journal of Missiological and Ecumenical Research* 38/3: 271–91.

2 As it would be hard to correct a woman's understanding of a man she has been married to for forty years, so the choice of a name for God that a people already know makes it hard to convince them of anything new.

reaching out to non-European territories. This chapter is, in my view, as applicable to "development workers" of all kinds with an interest in Africa as it is to Christian mission.

Many of the examples given in this essay draw on the Luo people in Africa. The term Luo, meaning "follow" in the Luo language, arises from following after someone, like a leader (Atiga 2004). The Luo are a part of the larger Nilotic group that preferred low-lying areas, so are sometimes called "River Lake Nilotes." Luo people extend to what are now Uganda, Kenya, Tanzania, and Sudan. They are part of those identified by Butt as "*Jii* speakers," being those who use the name *jii* to mean "people" (Butt 1964, 15). In Kenya the Luo people are known simply as "the Luo," without reference to their subtribe. Unless specified otherwise, reference to "Luo" in this essay is to the "Kenya Luo."

The Luo have settled in what is now known as Nyanza Province, alongside the shores of Lake Victoria. As well as their love for fishing and cattle herding, the Luo are renowned for their proud, truculent behaviour (Butt 1964, 41). Despite an earlier reputation as intellectual elites (Morrison 2007, 120), Luo regions of Kenya have more recently come to be known for their economic backwardness (Morrison 2007, 118), a reputation apparently arising from their strong orientation to maintaining ancient customs and traditions. The latter include traditions of wife-inheritance (thought to be responsible for high levels of HIV in Luoland), rules regarding the design of homesteads, funeral rituals, etc.

This author has been a member of a rural Luo community since 1993 through having his home in a Luo village, rearing Luo children using the Luo language, and actively ministering in a great variety of Luo churches.

Use of terms such as "magical" and "superstitious" in this chapter arises from an understanding of language, expounded in section 2, as being inextricably linked to the lifestyle of a people. Terms emphasising difference are used to ensure accuracy in describing what goes on in Luoland and more broadly in Africa, to compensate for dissimilarity in the cultural foundations of Western and academic English as against African English.[3]

It has at times proved difficult to know in this essay when "God" (or translations of "God") should be capitalised. Please ignore the capitalisation of "God," which is anyway not an issue in oral societies.

---

3 For more on this language question, see Harries 2007a, here chapter 14. This is a radical departure from Platvoet and Van Rinsum's claim that Africa is "not incurably religious" (2008). I do not have the space in this chapter to address their article in more detail.

2. UNDERSTANDING OF LANGUAGE

Understanding of this chapter depends on an appreciation of some assumptions made in linguistics and pragmatics, which have been given in outline form below.[4] For more details, see my PhD thesis (Harries 2007c).

(1) The critical eye of non-Westerners reading Western languages is preventing Westerners from stating publicly that which is evidently true, because to do so would either:

a. offend the non-Westerner, or
b. cause the Westerner to consider the non-Westerner to have been offended according to the former's (sometimes false) perception of the nature of the non-Westerner.

(2) There is a limit to how foreign a thing can appear when the language used to describe it has to be familiar. The foreign, obscure, and incredible easily appears domestic and familiar when the only metaphors available to picture it are thoroughly commonplace (Venuti 1998, 67). Similarly, what is domestic and familiar must, at least initially, appear foreign and obscure when expressed in an unfamiliar language.

(3) The fact that people will interpret "in line with their experience of the way the world is" (Yule 1996, 141) cuts both ways. Wonderful truths, be they scientific, technological, social, or theological, are frankly grasped in a different way by many in Africa than is anticipated by Westerners. Explanations by Africans to Westerners do not reveal "what is," but an imagined middle world somewhere between reality on the ground in Africa, reality in the West, and Western mythology and fiction.

(4) Enormous context dependence of language unveiled in recent research in pragmatics and discourse analysis has shown that mutual understanding is possible only insofar as one has a mutual context (Gutt 1991, 97). The more distant the context of communicators, the lower the level of understanding. It is hard to imagine a more distant context than between some Western and African societies.

4 This section is very similar in content to chapter 9, first published as Harries 2007b.

(5) While misunderstandings occur in very simple day-to-day activities, these linguistic difficulties apply the most profoundly and intricately to the complexities of spiritual life, meaning, value, and purpose, which are the bread and butter of the work of the theologian and missionary.

The above introduce a particular obstacle to cross-cultural communication, which has caused difficulty in writing this chapter. That is, that every term used may (even if written in English) originate either from an East African or an English meaning or impact, or some other alternative. For example, because the word "life" in English when translated into Dholuo includes "prosperity," an important question is: Which of these meanings do I assume in this chapter when I use this word?[5] Similarly for the term "God" itself. With some exceptions, I attempt to use English meanings when writing in English, meaning that the arguments here contained may not be sensible to Kenyan English speakers if they assume English word meanings or impacts to be equivalent to those of Kenyan languages (including Kenyan English).

3. NAMES FOR GOD

Bediako's research has revealed a startling difference between ways of naming God that historically occurred in Europe as against those in more recent years in Christian Africa. According to Bediako, "The God of African pre-Christian tradition has turned out to be the God the Christians worship," whereas "no European indigenous divine name—whether Zeus or Jupiter or Odin or Thor—qualified to enter the Bible." The reason Bediako gives for this state of affairs is that the European gods were "merely the heads of pantheons of divinities, and were not elevated above them." Hence he concludes that "Africa had a higher and more biblical sense of God than Europeans ever had," which to him is why Europeans tend to underestimate Africans' knowledge of God (Bediako 2006, 9). He explains that in African languages the names of God are uniquely singular. Hence Tshehla tells us that "*Modimo* is ever one." According to Tshehla, *Badimo* are the living dead, but one such living dead would never be referred to as *Modimo* by the Sesotho people because this would be presumptuous, even though *mo-* is technically the prefix for singularity (Tshehla 2002, 20).

5 Non-English words are in the Luo people's language, Dholuo, unless otherwise specified.

This does not seem to apply to languages used by the Luo people of western Kenya. Speakers of Dholuo, the language of the Luo people, most commonly use *Nyasaye* to refer to God. This is the term that translates biblical words such as *El* (e.g., Gen 14:18), *Elah* (Ex 4:24), *Elohim* (Gen 1:1), *Yhwh* (when not translated as *Ruoth*, "Lord," as in Ex 3:2), *Theos* (Matt 5:9), and so on (Bible 1976).[6] Yet a human being or a ghost can also be referred to as *nyasaye*. I will make further reference to the identity of *Nyasaye* in Luo traditional and current usage below. First, however, I want to consider what appears to me to be a strong irony in the choice of languages used in discussing matters pertaining to God in Africa.

4. LANGUAGES USED IN THEOLOGICAL DEBATE IN AFRICA

A great irony in formal theological discussion in Africa is that while little-understood European languages[7] are often used to engage in theological debate, the nature of God himself is understood by African people to be already known (see above). That is, theological debate that ought to be the use of a known human tool (language) to elucidate the ultimately unknowable (God) is reversed—and God is known, but the language not. Surely debate on theology has to be a process of the discovery of the unknown using the known, where he of whom understanding is sought is God. But if God is known and the language not, then the debate going on is linguistic: Which terms in this foreign language are the most appropriate to describe what is already known in someone's mother tongue? Hence debates on African theology have become a process of explaining to the West what the African people already know about God—an explanation of a preexisting theology and not an exploration of new theological insights.

Few would question the value of helping the wider community to a better understanding of our African brothers and sisters.[8] But it is important also to ask: If "theological debate" in Africa is actually explaining things considered already to be *known about* God to foreigners, then where is the debate, rooted in the Scripture, that questions and considers the actual nature of God?

6 This applies to the more recent translation of the Luo Bible (1976). An older translation translated "God" as "Jehovah" (Bible 1968).

7 I am here assuming that appropriate use of a language is only possible insofar as someone is aware of the context of its origin. Hence even someone with a very good knowledge of English vocabulary and grammar can be deficient in their communication ability if they are unfamiliar with pragmatic rules pertaining to that language; that is, conventions of language usage in the UK or America (see Pohl 2004).

8 Although some may question how possible this actually is. The question of how one can translate between diverse traditions, given that the language of people A is rooted in a culture that is very different from that of people B, is both valid and important (Harries 2008, here chapter 8).

I suggest that very little of such formal debate is going on, and the reason for this is that almost all *formal* theological debate on the African continent happens in foreign languages, which have the problem mentioned above. This is more and more the case as increasing amounts of foreign funds swamp the continent to aid the theological process. In addition to the problem of the lack of understanding of how these European languages are used in their "home contexts" is the additional issue that theologies already exist in those languages. It is often said, and certainly true, that these theologies do not have a good fit, if any fit at all, to existing African contexts. Hence the widely prescribed need for genuine African theologies (e.g., see Nyamiti 1994, 73). Yet using these foreign (to Africans) languages in ways contrary to accepted orthodoxy will elicit protest from the owners of that orthodoxy; that is, "Western Christians." Hence in effect, again, theological debate in Africa using English is proscribed.

What would happen to theological deliberation in Africa if God was taken as having been *unknown* to African people? This could bring genuinely theological debate to the discussion table. There would be an evident gap in knowledge that needed to be filled. But, and I suspect that this underlies the reluctance of African scholars to concede that God may be unknown to them, the missing content would not be appropriate if the gap was to be filled using an unfamiliar (Western) language, with roots in an unfamiliar culture. God would be a stranger, and quite likely an unfriendly one at that.

If God's nature is taken as known before discussion commences, then debate cannot genuinely be on the nature of God. If he is unknown, and we are to define him using foreign categories, then he will turn out to be stranger. Hence for as long as we continue to use other than indigenous languages in theological debate in Africa, we are stuck.

The theological venture on the African continent seems to be in trouble. The recent, much-acclaimed "African Bible" is in English (The African Bible 1999). The highly publicised "Africa Bible Commentary" suffers from exactly the same problem (Adeyemo 2006). Theological texts are continually being shifted to Africa from Europe and America. Theological education, along with much if not all of formal education in sub-Saharan Africa, is in Western languages. (Some "lower level" courses are taught in mother tongue or regional languages such as Kiswahili. In many cases though, even then the material taught is a translation from English so does not use genuine, local African linguistic or cultural categories.) In fact almost the whole *formal* effort engaged in theologising in Africa is foreign-founded and/or foreign-rooted. Indigenous educational movements almost invariably sooner or later (and usually sooner) fall into line. Salaries, support, incentives, and inducements, coming as they do from the West, selectively favour what is "foreign" in Africa. The foreigners do not understand, so can scarcely be expected to appreciate—never mind fund—genuinely African theological discourse.

The effect that the above has of precluding the option of genuine theological debate has already been mentioned. There is another effect that runs in parallel and is perhaps even more pernicious. This is—that supposed theological debate in English can easily be interpreted to African cultures as akin to magic. Bediako shares: "To suggest that a considerable portion of the missionary transmission of the gospel in Africa in modern times may have erred, theologically . . . would be such a serious verdict to pass on a justly heroic enterprise, that one hesitates to entertain the idea. And yet, this may well be what happened" (Bediako 2006, 5).

Why should such theological erring be a promotion of magic? This is related to assumptions about causation. For many African people, causation is essentially magical (as I am defining magic). Alternative means of causation may be God or science. But if we assume that science is not recognised in traditional Africa (i.e., God or magic are given credit for all events[9]), then what is not caused by God must be caused by magic. Hence if we say that God is doing something when actually he is not, then that effect must be due to magic. For example, telling people that belief in God brings prosperity, when actually belief in God does not bring prosperity, means that the prosperity acquired seems to be brought on by magic, even if God is given the credit.

The background in superstition for which Africa is known contributes to this; taking "superstition" as a translation for *ushirikina* (Kiswahili), which Omari finds to be very widespread in Tanzania (1993). People build and understand from the known to the unknown. If God is unknown (and science is unknown, see above), then people will build in their understanding from what is known; that is, "superstition" (magic). Hence while the meaning of a term may in the West relate to God, its impact (or implicature—what it implies) can be very different in Africa. Until a hitherto unknown God is made known to them, people remain as they were, with their prior magical comprehension.

In practical terms, belief or faith in magic increases when what was once thought impossible has become possible. Achievements enabled through science

9 This is not to say that people believe God or magic to be directly involved in every physical event, such as a branch falling from a tree. But in the way that some divine force is likely to be considered responsible should that branch from a tree fall onto someone walking below it, the divine is integrally involved in what has in the West come to be known as "nature" or "science."

and technology can in Africa find themselves in the category of "magical," so that an increasing introduction of science and its products results in a rise in the perceived prevalence or power of magic.

The label often given to the positive side of the perpetuation of "superstition" is "prosperity gospel." Sometimes known as the gospel of health and wealth, this interpretation of the Scriptures proclaims success in life for all who truly believe (Chilongani 2006, 1). The wide spread of this misleading teaching through much of Africa surely shows that something is wrong. It appears to be a fulfillment of traditional conceptions that good ought to arise by default and that any lack of good results from the evil orientation of human hearts (Harries 2006, here chapter 11). Apart from promoting idleness and a less-than-productive (from a Western perspective) view of life, it results in a search for a witch—that is a person with an evil heart—every time misfortune arises (Harries 2007c, 207–45). Few would deny the damage done by such witchcraft beliefs to human society.[10] It is time to ask what has gone wrong theologically for such thinking to be so proliferating.

5. *NYASAYE:* GOD FOR THE LUO PEOPLE OF WESTERN KENYA

I will confine my discussion here to that with which I have some personal familiarity. I thus hope to avoid following misleading oversimplifications resulting from:

(1) Translation into European languages as if European words have equivalent impacts to African ones (see above).

(2) Theological debates that have hidden agendas. That is to avoid "the kind of oversimplifications and overgeneralisations which have bedevilled our [i.e., African] literature" (Ogot 1999c, 196), because according to Bethwell A. Ogot the African has seen himself as "a man more sinned against than sinning" (1999c, 189), one result of which has been the international academic community's bending over backwards in order to conceal "primitive" features of the life of African people from view (Platvoet and Van Rinsum 2008, 166). Section 2 of the present chapter gave more details of the underlying linguistic presuppositions made in it. The widespread use of English in Africa clearly conceals much of African Traditional Religion, because English does not have terms to substitute for all the African ones. So scholarship about Africa in English gives a deceptively anglicised view

10 For the prevalence of and damage done by witchcraft in Africa, see Ter Haar 2007.

of the continent,[11] which astute scholars need to counter by being proactive in highlighting "difference." Above, Ogot points out that the African people are attempting to conceal their guilt or emphasise their innocence by claiming to be more "sinned against than sinning"—a situation the reality of which Ogot denies.

Much has been written about God in Africa. Being in my sixteenth year of living in a Luo village in western Kenya, frequently using the Dholuo language, involved with a variety of indigenous and mission churches, I hope my readers will consider my effort justified at enlightening the English-speaking world a little about an African people's understanding of "God."

Okot p'Bitek (a Luo man from Uganda) has been one of the most controversial and provocative of postcolonial African scholars. His contemporary Ogot has at times been sharply critical of him (1999b). Yet it is hard to totally ignore his aggressive outbursts, including his claim that the Luo people in their pre-missionary history had no conception of one high God. According to p'Bitek this notion was brought to them, or forced onto them, by missionary propaganda (1971, 50). The names used for God by various Luo people today seem to support this. *Lubanga*, p'Bitek explains as originally being the "*Jok* that breaks people's backs" (1971, 45). *Jok*, used by the Acholi (Luo people of Uganda) to refer to God is the term referring throughout the Luo languages to mystical force or vital powers (Ogot 1999a). *Were*, used by the Jopadhola of Uganda, and *Nyasaye*, used by the Luo of Kenya, are both terms shared by their Bantu neighbours. There is much debate as to the origin of the term *Nyasaye*—both Bantu and Luo peoples claim it as their own.[12] Yet the history books tell us that Luo and Bantu people have a distinct origin—the Luo having reached Kenya five hundred years ago from Sudan (Ogot 1996, 76), whereas the Bantu originated from West Africa (Middleton 1985, 69). Someone had to have borrowed the term from their neighbour, and if it was the Luo borrowing from the Bantu, this suggests that they may, before meeting the Bantu, have had no belief that needed such a word.

The Luo have other names, less frequently used in Christian circles, for God. One such is *Obong'o Nyakalaga*. *Obong'o* is by Capen (1998) and Odaga (2003) given as "only son"—suggesting that this God is singular and unique.[13] *Nyakalaga* refers to a force (or "god") that "creeps" (from the root *lago*, "to creep").

11 See Venuti 1998 for details of the "scandals of translation."

12 Ogutu (1975, 68) for the Luo. The Luyia people can explain the origin of *Nyasaye* as being in their word *lisaye*, meaning human procreation, so *Nyasaye* is "the procreator."

13 The question must be asked as to whether this term or its usage has arisen since the missionary era. Interestingly however, the term frequently used to refer to Christ as the only Son of God is not *obong'o* but *miderma*.

Odaga and Capen both give the term as meaning "omnipresent." Paul Mboya, writing at a much earlier date refers to God as "creeping" (*lak*) within the bodies of people, reflecting the Luo belief that "God" lives in human bodies (1983, 25). Contained in this seems to be a notion of God as "life" or "life-force." The Luo term that can be used to translate the English "life," *ngima*, is much broader than its English "equivalent" as it includes health and prosperity in general.[14]

The term *juok* (or *jok*) is often used by the Luo to translate "witchcraft" (*uchawi* in Kiswahili). Its plural (*juogi*) are a type of spirit linked with ancestors or the dead. The popular name for the witch doctor or diviner in Dholuo is *ajuoga*, which implies something like "just *juok*" or "*juok* only." The person of *juok* (*jajuok*) is often translated into English as "night-runner"—a witch who runs around at night naked, frightening people by rattling windows or throwing stones onto them or their homes. I have already mentioned that this very term *Jok* was used by the Acholi people (a Luo tribe in Uganda) to translate "God" (Ogot 1999a, 1). The Shilluk people consider *Juok* to be spirit, God and body in one (Ogot 1999a, 2). Ogot has found *jok* to be the Luo equivalent of Placide Tempels' "vital force" (1999a, 7), which, Tempels found through his research amongst the Luba people of the Congo, forms the basis for African philosophy. Tempels explains of the African (Bantu Luba) people that this vital force "dominates and orientates all their behaviour" (1959, 21). The "Bantu speak, act, live as if, for them, beings were forces," he explains (Tempels 1959, 57). Because everything—including the animal, vegetable, and mineral—has "forces" (Tempels 1959, 63), the whole of African life is sacred; there is nowhere that *juok* ("vital force") is not found.

"The relationship between *Nyasaye* and *Juok* is difficult to explain," writes Ocholla-Ayayo (1976, 219). Paul Mboya takes *Nyasaye* and *juogi* (the plural for *juok*) as synonyms in the following passage: "*Giluongo wendo juogi; ka wendo ok wendi ionge juogi maber. Juogi tiende Nyasaye; ok ng'ato nyalo riembo Nyasaye; tiende, wendo ng'at Nyasaye*" (1983, 191). This can be translated (taking *Nyasaye* as "God") as: "Visitors are called *juogi*; so that if you do not get visitors they say that you do not have good *juogi*. *Juogi*, that means God; someone cannot chase God away, meaning that a visitor is a person of God." What underlies this passage seems to be the Luo people's belief that having visitors brings good fortune (*gueth*, "blessing"), here apparently brought by *juogi*.

"Spiritual churches" are amongst the Luo known as *Roho* churches, where *Roho* (originating in Arabic and reaching Dholuo through Kiswahili) is considered

14 This is one reason for the prosperity nature of the gospel in Luoland.

to be the Holy Spirit of the Scriptures. The predecessor to *Roho* is known as having been *juogi*—the object of attention of spiritual gatherings prior to the coming of current *Roho* practice across the border from Uganda before 1912 (Hoehler-Fatton 1996, 12) and the *Roho* church movement in 1932 (Ogot 1999d, 129).[15] In some senses then, *Roho* ("Holy Spirit"—known by Christians as God, as he is a member of the Trinity) is a translation of *juogi*—"spirits."

The Dholuo term *hawi* could be translated as "good fortune."[16] Odaga goes so far as to say in her dictionary that *hawi* is "interchangeable with the word god" (2003, 119). She said a similar thing in a lecture (2004). I have frequently experienced the same in people's use of Dholuo. A Luo translation of "good-bye" is *oriti*, which means something like "he keep you" or "he to protect you," where the "he" presumably refers to "god," however understood. It seems almost that what "he" (or "she" or "it," the Luo term is gender neutral and can refer to something inanimate) refers to is intentionally left ambiguous. An alternative farewell is *Nyasaye obed kodi* ("God be with you"), which seems to be interchangeable with *bed gi hawi* ("be with *hawi*"). *Jahawi* ("a person of *hawi*") is someone whose *nyasache ber* ("god is good").

The Luo can refer to *nyasache* ("his or her god"), often strongly implying that everyone has their own god, and that this god is like *hape* ("his *hawi*, or fortune"). So it can be said that *hape ber* ("he has good fortune"), which is interchangeable with *nyasache ber* ("his god is good"). This seems to correspond in some ways to the guardian angel conception found in some Christian theology. Having "good fortune," the Luo recognise, often arises through having a relationship with someone who is competent and is good to you. Hence, explains Odaga, "your fellow human being . . . is your god [i.e., *nyasachi*]" (2004). I have heard much the same thing said in various church circles.

One would expect the understanding of *Nyasaye* to affect the practices of churches in Luoland. If the Luo people take *Nyasaye* as being "vital force," then one would expect churches to be seen as sources of *ngima* ("life/prosperity"). Indeed this is what is happening. This "healing" orientation of African Christianity is known throughout the continent. See, for example, Oosthuizen (1992). In the course of working with churches in Luoland, it has become clear to me that people are attracted to church by the prospect of material and physical reward.

---

15 "Indigenous charismatic Christianity developed alongside—and borrowed heavily from—*juogi* spirit possession," says Hoehler-Fatton (1996, 206).

16 The term "luck" is often given as a translation of *hawi*, but I think misleadingly so because of the association of "luck" in Western English usage with statistical probability.

This can be the money and rewards carried by missionaries from Western churches, and/or *hononi* ("miracles") of various types by spirit- (*Roho*-) filled locals. Any Christian (or any other) movement without clear prospect of material reward (in which category I include miracles and healing) from one of these sources can get a minimal following.

Considering the above and many other uses of the term *Nyasaye* in Luoland, forces me to conclude that *Nyasaye* is in many ways accurately translated as the "vital force" of Tempels (1959), who is valued according to his (or her or its) manifest and immediate power. This is increasingly so, judging by the young generation's increasing attraction to Pentecostal denominations. Within Christian circles there can appear to be little *heartfelt* conception by the Luo of *Nyasaye* as a great high God. It is hard not to conclude that the perception of *Nyasaye* as a "High God" could be a foreign notion brought to the Luo from the outside that has barely penetrated many Luo people's orientation to their Christian faith.[17]

The identity of god as life-force is evident in the Luo understanding of God. God being the power of *ngima* ("life," including health and prosperity) means that *ngima* is what he is sought in prayer to provide.[18] Someone who does not have *ngima* does not have God.[19] God being the one who creeps in living bodies means that his release occurs when those living bodies are sacrificed, hence the shedding of animal blood is thought to bring blessing. The role of a missionary and that of a donor are barely distinct when the god being brought is the god of prosperity. Then the success of a missionary is defined by the material prosperity that he or she brings. I have discussed elsewhere how this role of "provider" has the additional affect of binding the missionary force to a position of ignorance of what is "actually going on" amongst the people they are serving (Harries n.d.).

A missionary to the Luo people is here faced with very real difficulties. The Scriptures make much reference to *Nyasaye*. Thus it is made clear to the Luo people that *Nyasaye* of the Luo and the God of the Hebrew people, who then is identified as the Christian God in the New Testament, are one and the same. It is as if the theological task has already been completed and the missionary is left with the role of bringing *ngima* ("prosperity"). The God whom the people want,

17 I suspect that the *Roho* movement is a reaction against some mission practices taking *Nyasaye* as resembling the English "God." This, not suiting African people, caused them to follow again their "African god," now called by the new international name of *Roho*. For the founding of the *Roho* movement, see Hoehler-Fatton 1996 and Ogot 1999d.

18 Note that the Luo term frequently used to translate "prayer" (*lamo*) is much broader than the English term and includes worship and other religious practices and rituals.

19 It is widely perceived that someone's becoming sick indicates that they have lost their salvation.

and the one whom they are implicitly and constantly being told that they already have, is the God who is *ngima* ("life"), who supplies all needs to those who worship him. Major efforts by the Western donor community, Christian and secular, to provide materially for the "poor" in Africa further substantiate this view. The foreign missionary (and "development") role has been captured by foundational African cosmologies and incorporated into that set of people's behaviours that seeks to fulfill ancient utopian ideals,[20] which can barely be considered to be Christian in the orthodox sense.

6. ENGLISH LANGUAGE MINISTRY IN AFRICA

Difficulties faced by European missionaries in communicating theologically with the Luo people are compounded because the Europeans' theology is based on an understanding of God in "retreat," sometimes known as God "of the gap," who requires apologetics to defend his very existence.[21] The Western theological understanding of God that informs its Christians has been weakened ("spiritualised") to the extent of being understood through metaphor, simile, and illustration.[22] Jesus' miracles were (according to Western biblical interpretation) carried out to teach us something and not primarily to demonstrate the power of God, because if it were the latter, yet in the present age miracles no longer occur, how could missionaries substantiate their claim to be his true followers? In the place of miracles, in the West there is science, planning, rationality, budgeting, engineering, banking, and telecommunications. The God worshipped in the UK can seem as different from the Luo god as pie is different from cheese. *But, as we have discussed above, such difference cannot formally be acknowledged*, because *Nyasaye* is legitimised by his presence in the Bible. To acknowledge it, to suggest that perhaps the understanding of God held by the Luo people is foundationally different to that of native-English speakers, is to invite accusations of racism, colonialism, and theological one-upmanship. All that one can do with this enormous difference is to ignore it. *Nyasaye* is simply taken as a translation of "God."[23]

---

20 In much the same way as Schumacher explains that anthropology has been "captured" by African people (2001).

21 Apologetics being the "reasoned defence, especially of Christianity"; see Sykes 1982.

22 I here write so as to be understood by my African or Luo readers, to help them to understand something of where Western missionaries are coming from.

23 See footnote 8.

Theological texts coming from the West carry implicit assumptions about the nature of God. Many of those assumptions are not shared by many African people. These assumptions are not accessible to be taught, to debate, or to critique, as they are officially no different from assumptions made in Africa. Yet the assumptions are profound and consequential.

The question as to what to do about this is as important for the field of "development" (and other areas of academics and life) as it is for theology.[24] If prosperity arises as a result of appropriate interaction with vital force (God), then how can it at the same time also arise from budgeting, planning, and the application of science? The assumptions about the relationship between God and the real world, the segments of life controlled by God and controlled by "natural processes," are an important part of theology. Much of Western theology inside and outside of the church appears (from an African point of view) to say that God does almost nothing.

Examples of miscomprehension are many and frequent. A member of staff at a secondary school in Zambia had reared broiler chickens, a process that takes at least seventy days. After his announcing that one hundred broilers were ready for purchase, a fellow African prayed, "Thank you, God, for this unexpected provision." Thus God was given credit for what was from a Western point of view a very straightforward human process of planning and implementation for success, for which (in Western thinking) God deserves no particular acclaim. Here in Gem constituency in Kenya we are privileged to be beneficiaries of the Millennium Project instigated and run by the United Nations. Should we thank God for this, or has it occurred because of certain key discussions having been made in our favour in New York City? Is the healing brought about through the removal of cancerous growth by a surgeon creditable to God, or to a surgeon's skill?

These are not empty questions, because the understanding of them will determine the responses made to them. For example, how should people respond to the absence of broilers, the end of free seed provision by Millennium Project workers, or the death of the doctor who knew how to remove cancerous growths? By prayers to God, or by an imitation and perpetuation of the desired processes? That depends on one's understanding of God, or one's theology. Here again we find vast differences between European and African theologies that are in need of serious attention but that current theological protocol renders out of bounds.

24 If the theology is wrong, I can be so bold as to say, then so also will everything else be. Other problems are as liable to the problem discussed above as is theology.

Western theological texts are increasingly accessible in much of sub-Saharan Africa. They come in via Book Aid and fill the shelves of theological institutions and pastors' libraries on the continent. Their being welcomed and valued however should not fool us into thinking that they are understood as their authors intended them to be. How could they possibly be, given the vastly different cultures underlying Western and African English language usages? What these English texts seem to present, when implicitly translated into African cultural frameworks, is too foreign for incorporation into an African people's own conceptual world. Instead, a separate conceptual world is constructed to accommodate the foreign insights with tenuous and often unhelpful connections to the theological realities underlying someone's actual way of life. But then, what happens when these foreign theological formulations actually "work"—that is, if articulating them results in *ngima* ("prosperity")? (Which typically happens if Western people are on hand to fund those African Christians who are following Western usages.) As these are incompatible with any sensible world of indigenous theology, the other option is that these things arise from other gods.[25]

African delegates at the Annual School of Theology in Butere were encouraged to *develop theory*. Bediako pointed out, in the course of plenary discussion, that theories which Westerners used to construct their academia (including their theologies) were not plucked out of the sky, but devised on the basis of their observation and experience. Such theory construction, we were told, is what African theologians (and presumably also nontheologians) should be engaged in today, to reduce current, enormous Western dependence in Africa (Bediako 2006).

While an admirable objective, I suggest it is also a very problematic one in Africa today. It is true that this is what European peoples have been engaged in for centuries, and that this is how they have gradually built up a vast resource of theological and other knowledge. (Note that reference to the Scripture and God's spiritual revelations are not alternatives to learning from observation and experience. Both are intertwined, as the very words of the Scripture or revelations received must be interpreted through language derived in interaction with people's physical and social context, and in turn influence their physical and social context.) But, in modern Africa, people's contexts are greatly influenced from the outside in ways that they do not understand. To try to ignore these outside influences would be to produce archaic theologies that are no longer relevant in the world

25 See Harries 2000, here chapter 12, for more comments on "magic" in Africa.

as it is today. To take account of those influences, given the starting point of many African peoples, is to create theologies in which Westerners are gods.

It is these theologies that are these days advertently and inadvertently being developed. While often functional for the African people, they are clearly problematic for Europeans! Taking Westerners—the instigators of amazing technological achievements that go way beyond much biblical precedent even on miracles—as gods raises questions of polytheism and idolatry. How should Europeans respond when they are the gods being worshipped; when the processes that they have devised through supposedly "human intelligence" are in Africa considered to be divine in origin? Theological systems always arise out of and in relation to contexts.

Theologies that are dovetailed to contexts such as aid provision, development projects, donated vehicles, and imported mobile phones that are, from the Western point of view artificial human constructs, seem to be a remystification of science. Is it appropriate to create theologies based on contexts produced by the indecipherable (by local people) actions of foreigners? Surely the repeated construction, destruction, and reconstruction of such theologies (that will inevitably arise as their foundations change; for example, as technology advances) will, if they are Christian, cause the recipients to begin to doubt the theological truths that they perhaps ought not to doubt—such as the deity of Christ.

The above are the popular theologies being constructed for indigenous consumption in Africa. Other theologies are also being constructed by African people in international languages for other reasons again related to *ngima* ("life/ prosperity"). There is a big market for foreign-language theologies in Africa. Salaries, facilities, prestige, and even fame are available for African lecturers at colleges and universities, authors of books, conference speakers, and even radio presenters, once they become adept at the use of English (or other European languages). The language used by these theologians on the international scene must not be offensive to their supporting donor community. Not understanding the basis for the rules of the game that these foreign-language theologians are following unfortunately again orients these theologies, in their attempts "to please," to a willingness to put aside their own people's understanding.

European peoples, as others around the world, once had the privilege of understanding God as he appeared in, through, and in contrast to "nature." Such an understanding is now considered to be "orthodox." The option of developing such theologies is not available to budding African theologians today, as they are facing not nature but a context dominated by incomprehensible foreign powers.

Hence it can be impossible for African people to achieve theological orthodoxy without committing intellectual suicide. Such a singular and unique predicament, brought about by vast, impersonal (enabled from a distance by technology) intrusion of Westerners onto African communities, has never before been faced by mankind on a comparable scale.

Empires today are uniquely "faceless." Different peoples have in the course of history frequently conquered, dominated, and oppressed each other. But technology now enables this to occur impersonally and from a distance. Never in the past has technology (printing, radio, Internet, TV, satellites, etc.) enabled one people to crush another's values and culture *without a personal presence*. This absence of "personal presence" means that those being imposed upon do not have the option of filling the gaps in their understanding through imitation and careful observation of the life of the "other." This serious epistemological tragedy denies "subject peoples" the means for ever attaining a deep understanding of that which encumbers them.

A major failing in previous efforts at overcoming some of the above difficulties is the assumption that it could be done through the use of a language whose foundations are unfamiliar to the listeners concerned. That is, attempts that originate in Europe to "educate" African people who continue to live in their own contexts, using languages whose contexts remain unfamiliar. The result is garbled at best, and all too often the construction of artificial (somewhat meaningless) conceptual islands only tenuously connected to "real life." The only way to "help" African people to build from their own foundations is for missionaries (and development workers) to build on what is already there. This requires operating in African languages, sufficiently profoundly understood as to be correctly used in relation to a people's foundational culture. This in practice requires a greater degree of adjustment to African ways than is these days common on the part of the European, or at the very least an opting out of those so-called development projects that are dependent on foreign funds.[26]

Theologically, I suggest that it is only appropriate for Christians to take African names for God, if theological debate about that God then continues to be in the very African languages. Only such is self-correction enabled on the understanding of God through the hermeneutical circle (Thiselton 1986, 90), in the reading of the Scriptures, and in people's experience of God. If this is not done, then people's understanding of "God" will remain unresponsive to formal theological debate.

26 Which is pretty much all "development projects." For more details see Harries n.d. and Harries 2007c.

7. CONCLUSION

What should be done? One option is to continue as we are. The implications of continuing with current practice are, in my view, serious. The brutal insensitivity of current levels of imposition of Western life onto the African continent is threatening to exterminate whole peoples, because "societies with ancient but eroded epistemologies of ritual and symbol . . . [are] knocked off balance . . . under the voracious impact of premature or indigestible assimilation" (Steiner 1998, 16). How can I as a Christian stand by and watch fellow human beings be reduced to the status of being victims of Westerners' ideological and sociological experiment? I suggest the following steps as essential to the missionary (and development worker's) task of the future:

(1) An admission of the mystery and unknownness of God. It is only when one is ready to have one's view of God questioned that true theological debate can occur.

(2) A prerequisite for number 1 above is that theological debate occurs in indigenous languages. It is unrealistic to expect heartfelt acceptance by genuine Christian people that God's character must be defined in terms that are foreign to them. To expect to be able to so contort the English language, as to make it fit into African categories, while the Westerner is looking on, is plainly impossible.

(3) The missionary task must be one of communicating Christ *across* cultural and linguistic divides. This requires a missionary force that is ready to "die to this world" so as to live for and be used by Christ in strange cultural contexts. It requires the same of those working in the field of development. It requires the dominant communication in a cultural context to be in a language that is rooted in that context.

(4) A prerequisite for number 3 is a discontinuation of the current enormous drive at imposing Western technologies, languages, and cultures by force around the world. If the secular world is not ready to stop, then at least the Christian missionary force must opt out of such practices, and begin to promote Christ and not Western culture.

(5) I do not perceive an easy solution to the current "facelessness" of the context being presented to African peoples mentioned above, apart from a "filling of the subject gap" by those who are prepared to take the time (i.e., spend their lives) in translating in more or less formal ways between African and historically Christian, European worlds. That is, missionaries who are ready to live close to the people.

REFERENCES

Adeyemo, Tokunboh, ed. 2006. *African Bible commentary: A one volume commentary written by 70 scholars*. Nairobi: Word Alive.

The African Bible. 1999. *Biblical text of the New American Bible*. Nairobi: Paulines Publications Africa.

Atiga, Ajos. 2004. Kar chakruok Luo. Luo. http://www.joluo.ch/luo.htm (accessed October 29, 2008).

Bediako, Kwame. 2006. Their past is also our present: Why all Christians have need for ancestors; Making a case for Africa. Lecture and discussion at the Annual School of Theology of the African Institute for Christian Mission and Research (AICMAR), August 1–4, in Butere, Kenya.

Bible. 1968. *Muma manyien mar ruodhwa gi jawarwa Yesu Kristo* [Bible in the Luo language]. Nairobi: Bible Society in East Africa.

Bible. 1976. *Muma Maler mar Nyasaye: Moting'o Muma Machon kod Muma Manyien* [Bible in the Luo language]. Nairobi: Bible Society of Kenya.

Butt, Audrey. 1964. *The Nilotes of Sudan and Uganda, East Central Africa*, Part 4. London: International African Institute.

Capen, Carole A. 1998. *Bilingual Dholuo–English dictionary*. Tucson, AZ: Carole A. Capen.

Chilongani, Dickson. 2006. Prosperity gospel in Africa: A response from the book of Job. Lecture presented at the Annual School of Theology of the African Institute for Christian Mission and Research (AICMAR), August 1–4, in Butere, Kenya.

Gutt, Ernst-August. 1991. *Translation and relevance: Cognition and context*. Oxford: Basil Blackwell.

Harries, Jim. 2000. The magical worldview in the African church: What is going on? *Missiology: An International Review* 28/4: 487–502.

———. 2006. Good-by-default and evil in Africa. *Missiology: An International Review* 34/2: 151–64.

———. 2007a. Language in education, mission and development in Africa: Appeals for local tongues and local contexts. *Encounters Mission Ezine* 19 (August), http://www.redcliffe.org/uploads/documents/Language_in_Education_19.pdf (accessed February 4, 2008).

———. 2007b. Mission to the South, words to the North: Reflections on communication in the church by a Northerner in the South. *Exchange: Journal of Missiological and Ecumenical Research* 36/3: 281–98.

———. 2007c. Pragmatic theory applied to Christian mission in Africa: With special reference to Luo responses to "bad" in Gem, Kenya. PhD thesis, Univ. of Birmingham. http://etheses.bham.ac.uk/15 (accessed January 2, 2010).

———. 2008. Intercultural dialogue: An overrated means of acquiring understanding examined in the context of Christian mission to Africa. *Exchange: Journal of Missiological and Ecumenical Research* 37/2: 174–89.

———. n.d. Power and ignorance on the mission field or the hazards of feeding crowds. http://www.jim-mission.org.uk/articles/power-and-ignorance.pdf (accessed April 15, 2011).

Hoehler-Fatton, Cynthia. 1996. *Women of fire and spirit: History, faith and gender in Roho religion in western Kenya*. Oxford: Oxford Univ. Press.

Mboya, Paul. 1983. *Luo kitgi gi timbegi*. Kisumu, Kenya: Anyange.

Middleton, John. 1985. Bantu. In *The world book encyclopedia*, vol. 2, 69–70. London: World Book.

Morrison, Lesa B. 2007. The nature of decline: Distinguishing myth from reality in the case of the Luo of Kenya. *Journal of Modern African Studies* 45/1: 117–42.

Nyamiti, Charles. 1994. Contemporary African Christologies: Assessment and practical suggestions. In *Paths of African theology*, ed. Rosino Gibellini, 62–77. London: SCM.

Ocholla-Ayayo, Andrev B. C. 1976. *Traditional ideology and ethics among the Southern Luo*. Uppsala, Sweden: Scandinavian Institute of African Studies.

Odaga, Asenath Bole. 2003. *Dholuo–English dictionary*. Kisumu, Kenya: Lake.

———. 2004. Christianity in the context of African cultural practices. Lecture presented at Kima International School of Theology, June 23, in Kima, Kenya.

Ogot, Bethwell A. 1996. *Economic adaption and change among the Jii-speaking peoples of Eastern Africa*. Kisumu, Kenya: Anyange.

———. 1999a. The concept of Jok. In *Re-introducing man into the African world: Selected essays 1961–1980*, ed. Bethwell A. Ogot, 1–11. Kisumu, Kenya: Anyange.

———. 1999b. Intellectual smugglers in Africa. In *Re-introducing man into the African world: Selected essays 1961–1980*, ed. Bethwell A. Ogot, 133–38. Kisumu, Kenya: Anyange.

———. 1999c. A man more sinned against than sinning: The African writer's view of himself. In *Re-introducing man into the African world: Selected essays 1961–1980*, ed. Bethwell A. Ogot, 189–96. Kisumu, Kenya: Anyange.

———. 1999d. Reverend Alfayo Odongo Mango 1870–1934. In *Re-introducing man into the African world: Selected essays 1961–1980*, ed. Bethwell A. Ogot, 109–31. Kisumu, Kenya: Anyange.

Ogutu, Gilbert Edwin Meshack. 1975. An historical analysis of the Luo idea of God c. 1500–1900. MA thesis, Univ. of Nairobi.

Omari, C. K. 1993. *Uchawi na ushirikina.* [Witchcraft and superstition.] Mwanza, Tanzania: Inland.

Oosthuizen, Gerhardus C. 1992. *The healer prophet in Afro-Christian churches.* Leiden, Netherlands: Brill.

p'Bitek, Okot. 1971. *Religion of the Central Luo.* Nairobi: East African Literature Bureau.

Platvoet, Jan G., and Henk van Rinsum. 2008. Is Africa incurably religious? Part 3: A reply to a rhetorical response. *Exchange: Journal of Missiological and Ecumenical Research* 37/2: 156–73.

Pohl, Gabriela. 2004. Cross-cultural pragmatic failure and implications for language teaching. *Second Language Learning and Teaching* 4, http://www.usq.edu.au/users/sonjb/sllt/4/Pohl04.html (accessed October 29, 2008).

Schumacher, Lyn. 2001. *Africanising anthropology: Fieldwork, networks and the making of cultural knowledge in Central Africa.* London: Duke Univ. Press.

Steiner, George. 1998. *After Babel: Aspects of language and translation.* 3rd ed. Oxford: Oxford Univ. Press.

Sykes, J. B., ed. 1982. *The concise Oxford dictionary of current English.* 7th ed. Oxford: Clarendon.

Tempels, Placide. 1959. *Bantu philosophy.* Paris: Presence Africaine.

Ter Haar, Gerrie, ed. 2007. *Imagining evil: Witchcraft beliefs and accusations in contemporary Africa.* Trenton, NJ: Africa World.

Thiselton, Anthony C. 1986. The new hermeneutic. In *A guide to contemporary hermeneutics: Major trends in biblical interpretation*, ed. Donald K. McKim, 78–107. Grand Rapids, MI: Eerdmans.

Tshehla, Samuel M. 2002. Can anything good come out of Africa? Reflections of a South African Mosotho reader of the Bible. *Journal of African Christian Thought* 5/1: 15–24.

Venuti, Lawrence. 1998. *The scandals of translation: Towards an ethics of difference.* London: Routledge.

Yule, George. 1996. *The study of language.* 2nd ed. Cambridge: Cambridge Univ. Press.

CHAPTER 2

The Immorality of Aid to the "Third World" (Africa)[1]

1. INTRODUCTION

This chapter points to the immorality of aid provision as practiced today from the West to the "poor world," especially Africa. The unpredictability of quantities and channels of funding results in donor-driven activities encouraging a "lottery" mentality. Offers of loans are traps that are hard to evade. Windfalls into the formal sector of an economy discourage investment into the critical truly indigenous informal sector. Donor funds' unpredictability can underscore superstitious beliefs, discourage forward thinking and planning, distract people from local but less "lucrative" means for helping themselves, cause disputes and fighting and perhaps most importantly take away people's responsibility for their own lives. Meanwhile attention by the West is withdrawn from intelligent consideration of how to assist other people in their struggles, and invested instead into exploring ever more ways of using donor money. Donor activities create dependence. Overseas funds come with access to immoral Western lifestyles. The position of Westerners as controllers of funds giving Westerners an almost divine status in Africa is idolatrous. This chapter encourages interpersonal fellowship, mutual assistance, and sharing of the Christian faith without donor roles for at least a part of the Western Christian mission force.

---

1 This chapter was originally published as follows: Harries, Jim. 2003. The immorality of aid to the "Third World" (Africa). Jim Harries' Mission. http://www.jim-mission.org.uk/articles/The-Immorality-of-Aid-to-the-Third-World.pdf. A version of this paper was presented by Fred Lewis at the annual conference of the Evangelical Missiological Society, March 20, 2009, in Los Angeles, CA.

The debate as to the true impact and value of aid and development assistance to so-called Third World countries continues. I would like to add to it by suggesting that often the provision of "aid and development" assistance is not only not helpful; it is also immoral. (Note that I use the term "man" in the generic sense in this essay that is not exclusive of the female gender.)

2. THE JUSTIFICATION OF AID AND DEVELOPMENT INTERVENTION

People in the aid and development business rarely take account of the "counterfactual argument."[2] They look at a condition at the beginning and end of their intervention. Then they try and explain all changes according to the impact of their intervention. They rarely consider what might have been had they not intervened, or had there been no option for their kind of intervention.

For example, a development plan may be drawn up for a country or region. Various economic indicators are chosen that are thought to show the presence of economic advance. Policy makers take credit for the advances made and find excuses for their failures. Their underlying assumption is that an economy is somewhat like a machine that ought to behave predictably according to their rules. Their other assumption is that without their intervention things would not have changed.[3]

This rather crude way of treating peoples as parts in a machine enables those carrying out interventions to take credit for whatever changes are occurring while rarely taking sufficient account of what might have been the case if they had not been there. (Never mind whether the indices that they use are really appropriate, or whether radically different interventions may have been more helpful.)

---

2 The counterfactual argument is that which looks at what might have been had things not have been done as they were done. In terms of the provision of aid and development, what would the position of countries have been if they had not been provided with aid and development assistance? I am grateful for Deryk Belshaw for my awareness of this notion of "the counterfactual."

3 This could of course mean that rates of change would not have changed. That is, if there was already a state of economic deterioration, then the assumption is that this would not have been halted without the provision of the outside aid or intervention. Baseline surveys provide the foundation for future evaluations. These may be distorted to prove that progress has been made. The author has found an enormous discrepancy between official, local government statistics and those found by researchers of the Millenium Development Project (MDP) in Siaya District of Kenya. Government figures give an average life expectancy in Siaya District of 52.6 years in the 2002–2008 year report (Ministry of Finance and Planning n.d., 8). Millenium statistics in 2004 give the life expectancy in the same area as 37–43 years (Millenium Villages Project 2005, 1). Has this been done so as to provide justification for the MDPs?

Such is just one basis on which relief and development aid continues to be justified. It can also be justified on the basis that:

(1) Western people value "equality." To achieve a theoretical equality, someone should not have what someone else does not have. The greater the difference between what person X has and what person Y has, the greater the effort required to give Y more.

(2) Donor countries have aid budgets that are drawn in advance and then must be spent. The same applies to voluntary groupings such as churches which consider it appropriate to give away a certain proportion of their income. Then there are charities whose whole existence depends on the continuation of the aid/development machine.

(3) There are those who for various reasons make it their business to present guilt traps to people in wealthier nations so as to create moral pressure for them to contribute finances to aid and development initiatives.

I am often asked about the value or otherwise of aid and development initiatives. Those who promote them use simple arithmetic to demonstrate how advantageously such resources are utilised. They frequently fail to grasp some of the broader and frequently disadvantageous consequences of the use of aid and development funding. I am attempting in this paper to examine these so as to show just how deleterious the overall impact of outside interventions into the Third World (specifically Africa) can be.

I am considering these under three headings: firstly, the problems of wealth; secondly, destabilising distractions; and thirdly, situations created.

I have lived and worked in Zambia, Tanzania, and Kenya from 1988 to date. When referring to the "Third World" or to "Africa," I do so on the basis of my experience in these three countries, supplemented by some broader reading. I consider that what I write has much wider application across Africa, and the Third World in general.

3. PROBLEMS OF WEALTH

While wealth itself may not be a bad thing, the way it is acquired is important.

3.1 The African lottery?

While there is little doubt as to the popularity of lotteries around the world, their helpfulness to human society is more questionable. Very few people come to win a lottery, while very many put their hope and much time and energy into participating in it. The prospect of a big win draws attention out of all proportion to its actual size. Those who do succeed and win vast amounts of money often meet many problems.

Such is the nature of Western money and how it reaches Africa. There are just a few people who hit the jackpot, but they come to be well known in a "poor" community. They manage to convince a Westerner to be a major donor to their interest or project. The story they tell in order to achieve this may or may not be true. Large amounts of money received create many problems (what may seem to be little money in the West can be vast in a place where a month's full-time wage can be £15.00/$25.00). Vast numbers of people are distracted from or lose the motivation to engage seriously in their day-to-day activities, choosing instead to orient themselves to this "lottery."

3.2 Dubious loans

The offer of large loans of money, especially if there is little to pay back in the early period, is too much to resist for many people around the world. Many are tempted to take out loans to satisfy immediate needs or to invest in businesses that later prove questionable. The paying back of loans later proves to be an enormous burden. In some cases a bailiff can enforce the taking of property as repayment. People can be deeply troubled and sometimes pauperised by such thoughtless loan taking.

There is always a question in such a situation as to who is actually guilty. The one who has accepted such a loan is on principle asked to repay. But the offering of such a loan can also be considered immoral. Interest rates may be incredibly high. Such loans aim to trap the gullible. The African cultural scene adds extra pressure for people to take such options. Extended family networks put enormous pressure on people to take available "quick fixes."

I suspect that recipients of loans in the Third World rarely understand how repayment is to be achieved. Even if they do understand, there is a good chance that they doubt as to its likelihood. In African ways of life, loans are repaid when the donor becomes poorer than the recipient, not when due dates are reached (Maranz 2001, 143–70). (I *highly* recommend Maranz's book to those interested in aid and development as well as mission in Africa.) There are many reasons why people will not, or even cannot, refuse a loan, including:

a. Repayment can often be delayed and is sometimes cancelled altogether.
b. Even should a key leader responsible for accepting a loan perceive its problematic nature, if others come to know that the loan is being offered they will probably not understand this and will pressurise them to accept.
c. A person accepting a loan is rarely personally liable for its repayment. They will use various means—such as other loans—to repay if need be. An organisation such as a government or a church can be left to repay.
d. Repayment seems to be a long way off when a loan is taken out.

Loans have been used over many years to keep a stranglehold on Third World economies. This forces the countries concerned, and to a lesser extent the organisations or people concerned, to follow close instructions and thus effectively be under the thumb of wealthy beneficiaries. It is time to acknowledge that there should be an acceptance of responsibility on the part of the giver of a loan and not only its recipient. The offering of a loan is indeed often immoral.

3.3 The brain drain

Brains usually follow money. The encroachment of the West into many Third World countries means that these countries have two sectors. The international (sometimes called formal) and then the local (or informal) sector. The latter represents the indigenous people's genuine efforts at helping themselves. But the most capable of the local people jump into the international arena. In this sector earnings are in a far higher league. In this sector also corruption and misunderstandings are rife. The appropriation of the best and most able people into the international sector perpetuates the poverty of the indigenous sector. Sadly the scale and nature of operation of this formal sector is usually so out of proportion to that of the informal sector that those who have succeeded in it have little useful wisdom to share with those left "at home." That is, the vast gap between the two means that management and operational techniques learned by people who have functioned in the formal sector are of little help to them in their interaction with the informal sector. (This principle extends widely, certainly as far as theological education available on the African continent.)

4. DESTABILISING DISTRACTIONS

Large and/or unpredictable inputs into any system easily have a destabilising affect. The development of an effective indigenous system of operation is hindered or entirely prevented by large, ill-placed, unpredictable bombshells or windfalls. This applies to businesses, voluntary associations such as churches, and even governments.

4.1 Perpetuating "superstition"

Ongoing poverty in the Third World is often ascribed to people's being primitive or superstitious. It is less often realised that the policy of the West in dealing with such contexts can be responsible for perpetuating (or even creating) such "superstition."

Superstitious people are those who ascribe phenomena to spiritual rather than physical agencies, especially ancestral spirits and witchcraft forces. Such happens and is perpetuated in circumstances beyond the normal reasonable grasp of people's understanding. Hence rural people are said to be particularly superstitious due to the unpredictability of the rainfall and climate that they depend upon.

One effect of "civilisation," according to some theorists, is that more of life is made predictable as people's lives are further removed from dependence on elements of nature such as vagaries of weather. Superstition is not necessitated to the same extent as an explanatory theory in such a predictable environment.

It is extremely difficult for any such predictable system to develop in the Third World today. People do not understand how things that have a great impact on their lives are done, as they are done by foreigners and in foreign ways. Local innovations are swamped by the intrusion of foreign ideas with financial backing. Those who succeed are not diligent and hard-working people who follow well-thought-out plans, but the "lucky" who know how to sweet-talk outsiders.

Significant amounts of income are achieved only through corruption. Finance comes either in trickles or in windfalls.

Such erratic and unpredictable events are of no help to the development of consistent and productive ways of life. They substantiate and accentuate superstitious beliefs of causality. They all too easily reward the charlatan. Foreigners' ways remain mysterious, and to a people historically steeped in witchcraft, are interpreted as being magical. Promoting this kind of belief is a contradiction to Christianity, which sets out to teach monotheism. It is certainly a roadblock to many kinds of social progress.

4.2 Distraction from "real" issues

Development initiatives are demanding of local people's time and efforts. They make it difficult for people to prioritise what is important in their lives. Often the possibilities of financial and material reward arising from a "new" project being introduced from abroad are too high to resist. Vast amounts of effort are put into getting a share of the cake, to the neglect of other important life concerns. As a result, problems that "should" be solved with careful discussion, planning, or wisdom are instead solved with donor money.

Numerous examples of this that are happening in the Third World today could be cited. The proliferation of child sponsorship schemes seems to do away with the need for family planning. The availability of loans for agricultural inputs obviates the need for budgeting. Finances that might have brought business growth are invested in education (a means of helping one's children get a share of the pie by teaching them how to imitate the West). Hospital bills eat up capital that may have been invested in productive activities (dying can be very expensive when a family feels obliged to take even terminally ill people to die in an expensive hospital, as happens in some parts of Africa). Children who may have been learning useful things from their grandparents are instead stuck in classrooms waiting for poorly motivated teachers to drone on about things that are meaningless to their everyday lives, in a language that they barely understand. Late-teenage girls, who should have husbands and homes, instead have boyfriends and abortions.

In today's Third World, those who work hard to help themselves in honest ways find themselves near the bottom of the social heap and despised or mocked by those who succeed in milking the aid machine. Things that require order and genuine effort to be held together are falling apart.

4.3 Destabilising

It is not an enormous exaggeration to say that whatever a foreign donor touches falls apart. The king who found that everything he touched turned to gold, discovered that this was not always a good thing (Child Story Hour 2004). The foreigner's hand that always carries money has a similar impact.

Voluntary groups such as churches or self-help initiatives thrive until someone puts in outside money, at which stage infighting, jealousy, suspicion, and witchcraft accusations take over. Someone's productive small business is destroyed by the importation of cheap foreign products. A relationship between husband and wife turns to arguing and fighting, resulting in both turning to drink, when the wife gets involved in a foreign-funded women's project for making money independently of her husband. A community leader accustomed to serving his people radically reorients his behaviour when he realises that those he needs to serve in order to enrich himself are foreigners who have little clue as to his people's problems. Those insisting on the imposition of unfamiliar moral codes are not there to see their impact. For example, the ruling that was brought banning corporal punishment in schools so as to continue to acquire donor funds, that caused chaos in Kenya in 2001.[4]

People revert to telling lies and half-truths in order to protect their well-being and that of their families. A foreign intervention promises X on the condition of Y. Y is clearly impractical, and the foreigner would realise as much if he were to hang around long enough. There are two options. The first is telling the truth and watching the money go somewhere else, which makes you look to be a fool. Better to hide the truth, get the money to feed your family, and hope that the things that fall apart in the process will somehow come right in the end.

Once hiding things in communication with foreigners has begun, it soon gains respectability and becomes the norm. From here on, the foreigner no longer realises that his activities are destabilising. What he has in view is the formal sector, which gradually grows as a foreign implant rife with corruption. The local sector on which most people depend limps along in its shadow.

---

4 I was in Kenya at this time and saw this happening. The Kenyan media announced that corporal punishment in schools had been declared illegal. There followed a widespread spate of extremely destructive strikes by schoolchildren up and down the country. To my understanding, corporal punishment has been recontinued. Hence we have yet another example of the separation of the legal system from practice, for the sake of the continued acquisition of foreign aid. Corporal punishment is declared illegal in Kenya so as to please foreign donors, but continues unabated in many schools, so as to prevent chaos.

4.4 *Taking responsibility from people*

From time immemorial, children have been the responsibility of their parents, or other adults under whose protection they fall. This is no longer universally the case. Child sponsorship schemes have proliferated in Africa. One centre alone may adopt hundreds of children. Details vary, but the overall aim is to ensure that a child gets a good education and upbringing despite the poverty of the parents.

Parents now find themselves beneficiaries of a small windfall through having children. Whole families can seek to live off the "relationship" this child has developed with a white donor seen in a photograph. A small team of locally recruited, salary-earning people become foster parents on behalf of donors from many miles away. The African parents are no longer left to bring up their own children, and the child learns to despise his parents, as he knows from early on that his well-being is dependent not on them but on that image of his sponsors that he sees on a photograph. He has achieved the peculiar status of being African through and through, yet also being American, Swedish, or British while living in a mud hut with his parents. Projects that take in orphan children giving them Western "perks" can have some children realise that they could be economically advantaged through the death of their parents.

The implications of this kind of upbringing in an age when African countries are apparently "independent" are hard to imagine. Is a child not being taught from the beginning that he is unfortunate to be born in Africa, but that all good things come from abroad? Is there not a risk that such children will never come to value their own country or people until they have first learned to despise those who gave them a hope, that later dwindled and died?[5] These child sponsorship schemes certainly save lives and give someone a "quality" of life that they otherwise wouldn't have had. But I am dubious as to the long-term effects of the unnatural mind-set that they impart to children.

---

5 The child sponsorship schemes often focus strongly on providing children with education. The education that is provided is invariably rooted in foreign languages and countries, so is hard for local children in Africa to understand. They are only likely to benefit from it through corruption or by coming to be employed in the formal or international sector. Mushrooming education may leave its students frustrated, if there are only the same numbers of jobs available in the international sector. A sponsored child has two options: either to despise his own people or to wonder why someone has paid for them to be brought up in a way that gives false hope. What other parent rears a child and then says, "Don't ever come near my home"?

4.5 *Inappropriate relinquishing of donor responsibility*

The counterfactual must here be considered. Development/aid activities relieve the rich man's guilt burden. When he (or she) sees and hears of "the poor," he assures himself that he is playing his part through having given some money. Now he can sit back, relax, and enjoy life. Focusing on finance as the "only" means of helpfully intervening in the Third World precludes other thought and action that may otherwise be very helpful.

The alternative to these kinds of projects need not be seen as "doing nothing" (as is suggested by Wolf 2005). Should such an easy way of relieving one's guilt by passing on the surplus of one's economy not have been found, alternative courses of action could have been established to bring disparate ends of the human race together. In the current state, both sides conveniently relinquish themselves of responsibility: Third World parents because someone else is looking after their children, and donor nations because they are already "doing something."

Thinking people in donor nations perceive these problems. Because this is the way work in poor countries is defined, they may choose not to get involved with the "poor" at all. Even should they go to the "poor," they have enormous standards of charitability to live up to just to gain an audience. They will have an enormous task of breaking through their (Western) people's reputation of only being interested in providing money.[6] They can be left standing aside, in tears. Is it surprising that there are not more people interested in long-term commitments to Third World nations these days when short-term projects are buying up all the attention?

In reality there are many ways of contributing to life in the Third World apart from giving out money. These ways need urgent opening and exploration for the sake of the gospel of Jesus Christ and the future unity (and sanity) of the human race. One of these ways is "vulnerable Christian mission." There is an urgent need for Christian missionaries whose ministry is engaged using local, and not foreign, languages and resources.

6 Nearly every white man who goes to Africa these days seems to do so with the intention of spending money. This makes it extremely difficult for someone not intent on spending money to be understood or valued in any other role.

5. SITUATION CREATED

Continuous preoccupation with foreign donor funding "creates" artificial circumstances. Many of these may be extremely unhelpful to general social progress.

5.1 Creation of dependence

Enormous international trade has in recent years brought great interdependence of peoples in distant corners of the world. Given the advantages of trading and the benefits that accrue to all when specialisation of task is allowed, this interdependence is generally seen as a good thing that brings a net gain in economic standing of the world's people. In other words, cooperation has many advantages over the alternative scenario in which every family provides for all their own needs from a small piece of land. Nations these days depend on one another, so why is this not a good thing for Africa?

Trading is not only of physical goods. It can also be affective. Africa trades its poverty. It is the poverty of Africa that brings a high proportion of its income. This peculiar kind of dependence can force Africa to remain poor in order to maintain its revenue.

"Guilt relief" is of course one of the least pressing items for trade. Should the rest of the world be beset with more serious problems (such as the 2008 financial crash), the first trading partner they will drop is the one that gives them no benefits in return except for clearing of conscience. Hence one problem of dependence in the African case is its great vulnerability.

Why has Africa become "dependent" in this unique way? An important foundational reason is that the African way of life does not give prosperity a physical cause. Prosperity is seen as arising as a result of "blessing." The receipt of such blessing may not result in increase in productivity on the part of the African people if they do not perceive that increased economic activity is correlated to increased economic prosperity.

The above paragraph may appear presumptuous. This is not something I have learned from the scholarly literature. It is a working conclusion that I have drawn after many years of living and working in Africa, mostly in an African village with local people, following their lifestyle.

5.2 Access to immoral life

Much of what is "normal" life in the West comes across as highly immoral in Africa. African people love clothes, and when they become available they like to cover their bodies. Thus a modesty in dress has developed across the continent. Westerners often like to wear few clothes when they reach warm climes. Hence they, and those who set out to imitate them, appear to be immoral.

The freedom that Western women and girls have in relating to men has a similar impact. In traditional African societies the drinking of beer was carefully regulated and restricted. Youth had little access to it. The advent of the use of money for exchange in African society has made it easy for many who so desire to acquire alcohol. Disincentives to premarital sex, such as the damaging of the reputation of a girl who is not a virgin on marriage, have been eroded in today's Westernising culture. When money is available, televisions and radios follow in its wake. Television especially exposes young people to styles of immorality previously strictly taboo or that they had perhaps never even thought of. Then there is education. "Higher education is the hotline that connects all the dirt of Western culture from its point of origin there to here [Kenya]. We [the educated in Kenya] are the rubbish tips of that dirt," says Mbatiah (1999, 52–53, my translation).

Without entering into the debate on absolutes in rights or wrongs, my point is that the coming of the West to African society is often perceived as an intrusion of immorality. The impact is perceived as an immoral impact. The predominance of teenage unmarried pregnancy, youth alcoholism, etc., these days seems to show the same. Aid and development assistance (and unfortunately Christian mission) invariably being harbingers of the West, bring immorality in their wake.

A community's resources are usually carefully controlled in particular ways. These resources include food, houses, wives, alcohol, farmland, etc. In traditional Africa (as elsewhere), old men control these for the benefit of all. Outside aid and development quickly bypass such channels for the control of resources, thus making them available in immoral ways for immoral uses. Even should the resources pass through regular channels (i.e., through the elders), their nature and quantity is easily such as to defeat what was an effective system for control and distribution. For example, large quantities of resources of nondescript origin cause infighting and jealousy between elders, as well as between communities.[7]

7 I am here suggesting that all money is not equal. Finance and aid that has come from outside of one's community is perceived and understood differently from funds generated from the inside. Someone who makes $1,000 through his own sweat and toil or through traditional means is considered to have obtained this finance legitimately. Someone who receives it from a foreign donor is immediately suspected of having lied to the donor and is in the possession of funds that are not truly, rightfully his, and are therefore "up for grabs."

5.3 Perpetuation of pointless institutions and activities

Resources coming into a community earmarked for particular uses have a very complex impact on that community. A "normal" community is largely responsible for how it uses its resources according to certain guidelines and the decision makers' comprehension of what is good, right, and appropriate. Sometimes a government may intervene, be it forcefully or by propaganda, thus distorting the original set of priorities in resource use. This does relatively little damage if the government of a country is aware of people's inherent inclinations and at least to some extent representative of, locally informed about, and speaking the same language as the people.

Foreign institutions involving themselves in a community through provision of tied resources of whatever form are typically much less aware of local conditions and difficulties. The kind of scenarios that can then develop are perhaps best illustrated by taking an example of a clearly useless "project," such as a project of painting white spots on the backs of flies, from hereon referred to as "spotting flies."

People's initial reaction on being told of this practice, if they can control their laughter and if it is being seriously proposed, is to acknowledge its value so as to please their visitor. The visitor may encourage them to undertake spotting. He may explain that spotted flies carry less disease than unspotted flies. People will be happy to accept this—as it is always a good thing to protect oneself from disease and it is not good to offend a visitor. Yet after spotting a few flies, especially once the visitor has left, people may lose interest.

Per-fly payments combined with training courses on spotting methodologies will have to come from outside for the practice to continue. This will require phones, administration, secretaries, teachers, classrooms, vehicles, electricity, food provision, road construction, housing and thus craftsmen, government approval (licenses), burning of bricks, and other boosts to the local economy. Maintaining a fly-spotting training centre in the hope that the practice may eventually become indigenous is therefore resulting in an inflow of thousands of dollars annually into the local community. Soon the community becomes dependent on this. Then there is a tacit agreement made that no one is to speak against fly-spotting, because any interference with this new industry would spell disaster to the local economy.

Thus institutions and activities that are dependent on outside support are perpetuated and come to gain a normative existence in a society, even if the activity engaged in is totally useless—such as putting paint spots onto flies.

The existence and continuity of such institutions is only extremely, minimally, and precariously related to any usefulness of their stated aim.

It is in this way that numerous practices these days in the Third World continue. They may be totally inappropriate, but no one will say this. They may be useless or even damaging, but unless *extremely* damaging will still continue as long as money keeps coming to support them. People's time and effort can be invested in numerous such useless activities oriented to pleasing outsiders, so that little or none remains for truly relevant and locally useful occupations. The success of a "project" has almost nothing to do with the desirability of its intended outcome(s).

Much of "education" in Africa may fall under this category. It is perpetuated—not because of its value to the local people, but because of the side benefits in its enabling someone to link up with the international community. It then comes to be accepted as a "ritual" with inherent "power," much as many temple rituals are considered around the world. The people themselves become convinced of its value, even though they do not know why, as sometimes even a perpetrator of lies may do his job so well as to be convinced by his own inventions.

5.4 Idolatry of the white man

The understanding of the "white man" is in much of Africa these days incredible. While in some ways despised or even hated for the damage he has done to people's cultures and ways of life, he is at the same time held in enormous awe and esteem. After my years of living with African people, I do not always "feel" like a white man (although looking at a mirror is a crude reminder), but I all too often come to be treated as one.

The white man is in a sense all that the African aspires but always falls short of being. He is so far "up" as to be out of reach to most. His participation in an activity adds great respectability and power to it. Some things are considered useless without his presence. He is considered capable of building aeroplanes and being able to communicate instantaneously all around the world—the mechanics of which defeat the African people. (I don't understand them either, but that is beside the point.) He is always loaded with as much money as he wants and floats to the top of any social pile. His efforts at passing on his great powers are valiant though flawed, as many devoted Christians in Africa, who despite imitating missionaries fail to reach their high echelons of wealth and grandeur, have discovered. (So there is talk of the white man's secret knowledge, that he has so far not shared with the African people.)

Every new money-intensive project (and this they all seem to be) adds to this same image. Given the holistic religious worldview of the African, the white man is worshipped like a god. This constantly perpetuated idolatry (every time a white man on the scene is shown to have money) is extremely damaging in numerous ways. Anything like "normal relationship" between black and white is rendered almost impossible. The powerful (but ignorant) white man is the last to hear the truth on a matter.

Africa is known to be corrupt. This state of affairs perpetuates corruption. Much money comes through the white men's hands. The continuity of the financial flow is maintained by a continual pretence or telling of half-truths. The outsider is thus in a state of enforced ignorance, so unable to make wise decisions as to resource use and allocation. This must be compensated for by local people, through the process widely known as corruption.

5.5 *Numerous conflicts and divisions*

The above state of art is not conducive to unity and cooperation. Instead it constantly produces conflict and division.

The ownership of resources plus the moral right to their use are carefully defined in "traditional" societies around the world. That which someone has acquired through their own sweat and toil is legitimately theirs. The same applies to something that is acquired or inherited through acceptable, traditional avenues. Things quickly become unclear when resources come as "aid" for "development."

Legitimate ownership of aid funds is much less easy to define. Suspicions quickly arise that a beneficiary of large amounts of foreign money has used immoral means of acquisition; for example, that he indicated to a donor that the aid he receives would be for everybody, but then has gone on to consume a large part of it alone.

As indicated above, access to aid money is enabled by a close association with white people. Those with a good knowledge of foreign tongues and the ability to be at ease with and socialise with Westerners are the ones who are ahead in this game. Such access being the key to unlocking the floodgates is itself greatly coveted and even fought over. People will go to great efforts to protect "their" white man to ensure that funds they anticipate do not end up going in the "wrong" direction—that is, to someone else. Little may a new visitor from the West realise just how coveted a prize he is. Conflicts over privileged access to his benevolence easily result in the destruction of what may have been long happy relationships, now replaced by extended feuds.

The patron-client system, in which many people come to be under the rule and guidance of him who has resources, continues to be very common in Africa (Maranz 2001). But today there is a question over the legitimacy of the way wealth is acquired. Division quickly results, should someone who has been a follower (i.e., other than the head of a church or other organisation) get his own funds (e.g., his own link to the West or friendship with a white man). It is very likely that he will quickly pull out "his" people, cease to respect the authority of his previous patron, and become a law unto himself. (This frequently occurs in churches. For a bishop to continue to be respected as overall leader of his church, he may need to ensure that his juniors not have direct contact with whites. In these days of the Internet and widespread knowledge of English, it is becoming more and more difficult to ensure this, thus churches are more and more liable to splitting.)

Westerners who realise that this is happening, and just how much damage is being done to local relationships through contact with the West, try to minimise the number of people who gain access to the West (and Western people). Hence the move to try and ensure that (Western) education can as far as possible be accessed outside of the West. (It is widely accepted by Westerners to be better to have African people participate in theological education on the African continent in preference to their travelling to get it in a Western country such as the UK or USA.) This reluctance to send "good men" to visit the West through fear that they thus be spoiled results in "scarcity value" for those who do make it, meaning that they can get a hero's welcome and an enormous slice of any available financial cake, further substantiating the view that the West is really only about money. This is hardly an influence to morality.[8]

5.6 Machine and technology graveyards

The presence of machine and technology graveyards is just one well-known side effect of the current tendency to try to promote development through aid. Recipients of resources reason that it is best on principle to say "yes" to whatever is

8 I am here referring to those African people who do manage to get to visit and be welcomed to Western nations. The reluctance of people to send Africans from Africa to the West means that the few who do arrive have a scarcity value that increases the prospects of their self-enrichment. In some Western people's view, these few are the key ones that Western Christians should work with! (For example, see Finley 2005.) Indeed whoever makes a decision to send an African person to the West is like a distributor of the crown jewels.

offered, through fear that saying "no" may discourage the giver, which would mean a loss of the side benefits that almost invariably arise with whatever resources are concerned, and possibly further future donations. The decision to accept machines is typically not based on any economic or rational reasoning as to their specific advantage, but a desire for spin-off benefits and an obligation to the perpetuation of aid on the part of the donor (for example, to keep the machine running).

Sometimes machines of various sorts from tractors to computers have little more than scrap value in the country of origin. Transportation may however be expensive. The distraction produced by these new devices from people's normal tasks may be great. Much frustration easily arises if those who have taken the trouble to donate find themselves responsible to pay for the upkeep and maintenance of the introduced machines, so that they do not end up lying unrepaired and idle (although all too often they very soon do). The effect of imported machines is to distract and draw local people from their normal productive activities and to tie Westerners to expensive follow-ups to avoid embarrassment.

6. CONCLUSION

I have attempted to point out some aspects of the immorality associated with aid practices. Some questions remain.

Why is this not more widely known? There are many reasons for this. One that I have alluded to frequently is that aid interventions are desired and considered beneficial by people in the Third World through their spin-off effects regardless of whether or not they "work" as intended. It is thus hard to speak against them.

Initiatives that are taken up time and time again from the West that are supposedly in the interests of the African people have here been seen frequently to be extremely damaging to the prospects of development on the continent. The solution to these difficulties, that I have mentioned elsewhere,[9] lies in interventions that minimise the use of funds and Western languages and are based on "religious faith" and vulnerability and not materialist or secular ideologies of social change or development.

The saddest aspect of the whole aid/development enterprise of the last fifty years is that it has occluded all sorts of other options. The identity of the West in the Third World is so strongly tied to money and Western superiority as to dwarf

9 See, for example, Harries 2002.

and distort other aspects of international relationships such as religious exchange and the building of friendships across ethnic and international boundaries.

REFERENCES

Child Story Hour, 2004. King Midas' Golden Touch. http://www.childstoryhour.com/story22.htm (accessed April 15, 2011).

Finley, Bob. 2005. *Reformation in foreign missions: A call for change in the way foreign missionary work is carried on by evangelical Christians*. Longwood, FL: Xulon.

Harries, Jim. 2002. *Jim's Journal* (December), http://www.jim-mission.org.uk/journal/index.html (accessed April 15, 2011).

———. 2009. "The name of God in Africa" and related contemporary theological, development and linguistic concerns. *Exchange: Journal of Missiological and Ecumenical Research* 38/3: 271–91.

Maranz, David. 2001. *African friends and money matters: Observations from Africa*. Dallas: SIL International.

Mbatiah, Mwenda. 1999. *Upotevu*. Nairobi: Standard Textbooks.

Millenium Villages Project. 2005. Annual report: Millennium research villages. http://www.millenniumpromise.org/pdf/MVP_Annual_Report_05.pdf (accessed April 15, 2011).

Ministry of Finance and Planning. n.d. *Siaya District development plan, 2002–2008: Effective management for sustainable economic growth and poverty reduction*. Nairobi: Rural Planning Department, Ministry of Finance and Planning.

Wolf, Martin. 2005. How to Help Africa Escape Poverty Trap. *Financial Times*, January 11, 2005. http://www.ft.com/cms/s/1/d28aa0cc-6405-11d9-b0ed-00000e2511c8.html (accessed April 15, 2011).

CHAPTER 3

Heart-led Development: An East African Study[1]

"What does your church do to promote development (*maendeleo*—Kiswahili, *dongruok*—Dholuo)?" asked the theological student. "Well, we arrange to have coffins made for people," replied the church elder (Yala, Kenya, May 2004).

1. INTRODUCTION

"Development" activities originating from the West tend to be rooted in secularism. This is problematic for African Christians who in their lives are very spiritually oriented. I argue below that what is often known as spirituality could more accurately be known as heart orientation, and that such a heart orientation is needed for "development" in Africa to link in with where people are and hence to take root.

A translation of "Holy Spirit" back into English from prominent western Kenyan languages is "cleansed heart." For example, *Roho* that is used to translate "spirit" (Greek *pneuma*, Hebrew *ruach*) in the Scriptures is considered a synonym of *chuny* (Dholuo) or *omoyo* (Kiluyia), which can in turn be translated as the English "heart" (Ogutu 1975, 87).[2] Churches that are oriented to *Roho*, which are commonly known as "spiritual churches," are perhaps more accurately rendered in English as "heart-oriented churches."

The terms "holy" (Hebrew *qodes*) as against "cleansed" (Hebrew *tahor*) are not distinguishable in many African languages (Mojola 2003). "Holy" in the

1 This article is also to be published as follows: Harries, Jim. In press. Heart-led development: An East African study. In *The modern world reader*. Pasadena, CA: Institute of International Studies.

2 *Chuny* is strictly the liver and not the heart, but can be translated into English as "heart," as for the Luo people this is the seat of emotions and the core part of human life.

nonritual sense seems to be unknown, so a "holy state" is widely identified as being a "cleansed state" (hence the Kiswahili term for "holy" is *takatifu*, literally "cleansed"). Hence when considering what is "holy" in East Africa, we must understand this as being in people's minds, in part at least, as what has been "cleansed."

The seemingly ever-growing popularity of the Holy Spirit ("cleansed heart") in East Africa should be educative to us. Many Christians of this region, especially those in Pentecostal and indigenous churches, arduously follow teachings based on *Roho* ("spirit," "heart"). The Holy Spirit ("cleansed heart") is to very many the ultimate source of what is good—including development. Power that is widely recognised in Christian circles is that of the "cleansed heart" (Holy Spirit), hence also cleansing of people's hearts is considered vitally important.[3]

The "cleansing" referred to in this deeply rooted understanding is of ghosts (Luo *jochiende*, Luyia *ebitsieno*) that trouble people who do not adhere to ways of life laid out by their ancestors. This is why to many people funeral ceremonies and the maintenance of their ancient ways of life are a vital component to development. They are a part of the process of satisfying or pleasing the departed; in other words, cleansing the community of them, so as to avoid the activities of the troublesome ones.

In English we can therefore say that these African people are "people of heart." Much of what they do revolves around concern for the purity of hearts—dead and alive. As to be effective in working with people it is important to link in with their own interests and values, so development must be heart-led and oriented to "cleansing of hearts." Not to be "heart-led" is asking for confusion, misunderstanding, and all too often disaster. Matters of the heart are of concern to God. Hence how to do development is rightly the subject of theology and biblical studies, in fact the mission of the church.

Secular models of development, be they capitalist, socialist, functionalist, technological, educational, and so on, may not be "wrong," but still may not work. They may be correct on the supposition that the world is a physical entity within which people interact rationally. They fall down in a world that is "spiritual" or "holistic" and populated by people who are concerned for the cleansing of their hearts and interacting with gods and ancestors.

3 This is not to say that such understanding of the Holy Spirit is necessarily correct or orthodox. Whether orthodox or not, it is a widespread and significant understanding.

2. LANGUAGE

An oversimplistic understanding of language, I suggest, has been leading numerous mission and development scholars astray. It is hard to know where to begin in addressing this important issue, for this not to become a paper on pragmatics and linguistics. I suggest that the use of one language (English) internationally and cross-culturally is often not a help to the development enterprise. This is for *many* reasons, which I draw on heavily, but can in this paper only outline in barest detail:[4]

(1) The critical eye of non-Westerners who can read the Western language concerned prevents the Westerner from stating publicly that which is evidently true, because to do so would either:

(a) offend the non-Westerner or
(b) cause the Westerner to consider the non-Westerner to be offended according to the former's (often false) perception of the nature of the non-Westerner.

(2) There is a limit to how foreign a thing can appear when the language used to describe it has to be familiar. The foreign, obscure, and incredible easily appears domestic and familiar when the only metaphors available to picture it are thoroughly commonplace. Hence the above view of the non-Westerner.

(3) The fact that people will interpret "in line with their experience of the way the world is" (Yule 1996, 141) cuts both ways. Wonderful truths, be they scientific, technological, social, or even theological, are frankly grasped in a different way by those in the South than is anticipated by those in the North. Explanations by those in the South do not tell those in the North "what is," but an imagined middle world somewhere between reality on the ground in the South and Northern mythology and fiction.

(4) Enormous context dependence of language unveiled in recent research in pragmatics and discourse analysis has shown that mutual understanding is possible only insofar as one has a mutual context. The more distant the context

4 I refer readers to my PhD thesis (Harries 2007).

of communicators, the lower the level of understanding (Gutt 2008, 5). It is hard to imagine a more distant context than between some Northern and Southern societies.

(5) While misunderstandings occur in very simple day-to-day activities, the above applies the most profoundly and intricately to complexities of spiritual life, meaning, value, and purpose, which are the bread and butter of the work of the theologian and missionary.

The above brief preview of an enormous literature has to date been too little applied to development thinking. I hope it is making my readers aware of the importance of language and cultural learning as a prerequisite for understanding and engaging in cross-cultural mission and development, and thus by implication some weaknesses of scholarly work engaged in by those who have not passed through such learning.

3. THE PROBLEMS OF DEVELOPMENT AND THEIR RESOLUTION

3.1 Imitation of Christ

Imitation of Jesus is an essential part of Christian living. What this means is a question of interpretation. The church or branches of the (universal) church have at times in history considered this to mean to dress as he desired (for example, many indigenous African churches like to dress the way Jesus is depicted in pictures as dressing), to speak the language that he spoke (on the assumption perhaps that this was Latin), to heal as he healed, to teach as he taught, to die as he died (as some believers in the Philippines seem to be want to do), or even to keep his face as he kept it (religious types wear a beard). What does it mean to imitate Christ?

Missionaries are inclined to imitate Christ's words, regardless of the way those words are presented—hence tracts, radio broadcasts, even devotional books—none of which (we assume) Christ ever made use of. While such may not be wrong, Jesus' method of presentation of his words may still be worthy of study. This especially at a time when the contextual dependence of language meaning is increasingly recognised.[5]

A man telling his wife, "I love you," while brandishing a knife, is different from the one who does the same while holding a bunch of flowers. The former

5 For example, see Blass 1990, 260.

may mean that the husband's feelings about his wife's lover are sufficient for him to kill her because of his jealousy for her; this being quite different from the latter Valentine's gift. A wealthy businessman offering to contribute to the new church roof is clearly quite different from the same words expressed by a poor old widow. So was the context of the words uttered by Jesus also important?

Jesus walked amongst people, becoming materially dependent on them as he shared God's love with them (Luke 8:3). He illustrated God's love through parables and pointed to God's divine plan through miracles. His ultimate act of love was in his sacrifice of himself on behalf of the sins of others. Jesus' love was not primarily one of material giving. (The turning of water into wine and feeding of thousands I take as more exceptions than the rule.) When it came to material giving, this easily backfired (John 6:26–60). Those who followed Christ for the sake of material and social advancement were few and short-lived (Luke 18:23–25).

Although sharing of resources may be a part of a relationship of love, it alone is never sufficient to constitute love. This is for at least two major reasons. One, that wealth shared from a surplus is impersonal. Two, that receiving of alms puts the recipient into a subservient position relative to the donor, which he may put up with even if he doesn't appreciate it, and which implies that wealth may be shared in order to gain an upper hand and not necessarily out of love at all.

Jesus' words were uttered by him from a position of both material and political weakness. This means that they were also received either despite or even because of his weakness. This weakness, in human terms, came to be a part of his words. It was despite his weakness, or was it through his weakness, that he was what he was and did what he did? As giving someone a penny when you have ten pennies is different than giving them the only penny you have (Luke 21:2–3), so the meaning or at least the force of Jesus' words changes if uttered by the powerful.

3.2 The principle of poverty

The vows of the adherents of Catholic orders to poverty, chastity, and obedience remind us that the principle of poverty is not new in Christian circles.[6] Even such orders would appear to face difficulties in the current world—where what may be classed as "poverty" on one continent may be extravagant wealth on another.

The famous sending out of the seventy-two (Luke 10:4) has prompted much debate. Why did Jesus instruct his followers to take neither bag nor purse? Was this to be a lasting ordinance or a passing phase? The missionary Paul seems to have

6 As noted by Reimer (2004) in relation to orthodox Christianity.

followed this principle. He went around taking collections (Rom 15:27) and not giving handouts (except of course to the Jerusalem church for whom the collection was intended). Paul made collections from those whom he evangelised, apparently in order to quell ill feeling in his sending church.[7] (The tension between Paul and the Jewish church in Jerusalem, sometimes known as "the circumcision," is very evident in the pages of the New Testament. Unfortunately the New Testament is silent on whether the latter accepted the gift Paul carried to them, which would have demonstrated acquiescence to and a unity with the fast-growing, noncircumcising Gentile church. A few years later the Jerusalem church was, of course, destroyed.) The other apostles (apart from Paul, if one considers Paul as one of the twelve apostles) who remained in Jerusalem give the impression of having been poor. At least they were referred to as "the poor" (e.g., Rom 15:26).

Some simple rational reasoning soon reveals what might be the advantages of "poverty" for a missionary. A man poor in the eyes of the world who has an aura of contentment, is likely to arouse admiration. A poor man is not an immediate threat to those in or hungering for power as a wealthy man would be, thus enabling him to live peacefully with people in an otherwise competitive society. Not being a threat, a poor man can extend a listening/learning ear into a situation from which a powerful man would be cautiously excluded. Such listening/learning of a foreign people and culture is vital to gain an understanding that will enable evangelisation. A poor man is not going to be under pressure to utilise his resources to help in this, that, and the other situation, which would be demanding of his time and energy, so again is left free to be otherwise (spiritually) engaged. A poor man does not acquire a stream of visitors (as a rich man in a poor environment may), who have set out to tell stories that may or may not be true, aimed to convince him to part with his wealth.

Luke 16:13 tells us clearly that "No servant can serve two masters . . . You cannot serve both God and Money." It is clear that he who serves God will still, at least in a modern consumer economy, have need for money. The point is that he need not strive for it, maximise it, or orient himself to it. Let him orient himself to serving God, so that others come to provide for his material needs (this being of course a biblical principle; see, for example, Num 18:8–9).

7 "Because it was only by the volitionary participation of his churches that the collection would testify to the genuineness of their faith in Christ and thereby confront the Jerusalem Christians with the undeniable fact of the legitimacy of their membership in the body of Christ" (Nickle 1966, 127).

3.3 Valuing people as they are

Christ was born and raised in the community in which he later ministered and taught. He transformed people from being fishers of fish into fishers of men (Matt 4:19). This seemed to be a natural transition for them, once they had come to know God and his ways. It did not require the adoption of a foreign way of thinking, but a godly reorientation of their familiar way of life.

This is not what happens when Westerners get involved in "development" elsewhere in the world. In communities that have never produced a surplus, thinking economically is entirely foreign. (In many African societies, life's activities are based on guidelines and taboos passed down from ancestors, and not economic calculations.) Yet this is what is required for a project to be sustainable. A project is likely to involve considerable material and financial investment. Thus a material inducement is put out for someone to reject their people's way of life in favour of a foreign one.

To be able to hone someone's capability to function in a community, it would seem one needs to be a part of that community. Certainly this is true of language. Even the most accomplished linguist would have trouble training people to advance in a language with which he/she is unfamiliar. So also a culture or way of life that follows patterns set up by language and language use.[8] A Chinese person training British people will only be able to succeed insofar as he has first either adopted the British way of life (language), or has explained and taught the Chinese way of life (language). The former will require considerable prior effort on his part, and the latter considerable prior effort on the part of his students (on the basis that this Chinese man's words will not link in accurately at depth with the British culture without an appreciation of the Chinese culture from which they arise).

Development initiatives as also mission "from the West to the rest" these days tend to work on the latter principle. The rest of the world is expected to change and comprehend Western language and thought, so as to be able to apply its fruits to their lives. As it is impossible to erect the roof of a house before one has put up the walls, so the fineries of "development," such as the rules of economics and sustainability, are unfortunately not discernable until the rest of the culture has to a large extent been acquired. For a Chinese man to learn English ways while living in England may be easier than for the English to learn Chinese ways from

8 While the Sapir-Whorf hypothesis is rarely accepted in its entirety, "moderate Whorfianism" is often considered largely correct by academics. That is, that the particular nature of a language has a very influential determining affect on its understanding (Parr-Davies 2001).

one man staying in their country. So the difficulty faced by, say, African people to learn English ways sufficiently well while living in their own communities and continent. This degree of difficulty is such as to render this exercise effectively impossible. In reality, whenever an Englishman is trying to explain a particular capstone of his culture necessary for "development," he in effect has to explain the whole kit and caboodle of his way of life. "Success" is the transformation of an African person into a British person. A ridiculous project given its impossibility, bearing in mind that even should one person be so transformed, that leaves him with the same level of difficulty in transforming those who remain.

This model of development is the one being implemented around the world, or certainly in western Kenya. In some countries all children are taught and even are taught using European languages with such an aim in mind. The net result of this is great frustration and time wasting, and far from breeding independence, this is in effect a way of funneling a whole people into a climate akin to "worship" of the Western fatherland.

Christ accepts and values sinners. So Christians seeking "transformation" need to accept and value people as they are. Change that is advisory is dependent on the nature of the original state of a person. To advise on "change," one needs to know that state. True knowledge comes from experience. Hence development policies promoted by Christians around the world should be peculiar to each culture, understandable by that people, and arising from where they are; not from where they might be according to some idealistic, hypothetical model. The change agent is first required to change, and to change the most, before he can effectively bring others to helpful change.

4. THE STAND REQUIRED OF THE CHURCH

4.1 Third World church not a landing point for excess wealth

The existence of a worldwide church is an incredible opportunity for people from distant corners of the globe to share in fellowship. Such opportunity needs to be nurtured, and should not be abused. Its abuse arises when one party considers itself dominant over the others. That is when, instead of respectfully accepting the different ways in which diverse peoples worship God, one party out of the many aims to dominate the whole scene. This happens when a branch of the church, that from the West, gets so hung up on the notion of its own superiority as to become preoccupied in its relationship with the rest of the church around the world in issues at best peripherally Christian, and at worst grossly secular.

I might not take the above as being wrong in itself, if it was engaged in through such a means as to leave other parties free to choose whether or not to participate, and the degree of their participation. That free choice, whether or not to be involved in the worldwide Westernising process, is at the moment not there. Except, that is, for the very strong.

The Scriptures warn us frequently about the entanglements of wealth (for example, see 1 Tim 6:9). Western Christians try, to various degrees, to take a stand against the materialism around them, hard as that might be.[9] They rarely consider the necessity of assisting the rest of the world church in taking a similar stand.

The force of wealth is rarely sufficiently comprehended. Because an offer of finance is hard to resist, it easily becomes an imposition. Should church leader A want to refuse an offer of finance by foreigner B to fund project C, he had better look out. Not all in his church will be as spiritually minded as he, and should it be discovered that he has turned down food to help the hungry, jobs to help the unemployed, or clothing for the poorly dressed, his neck could be on the line.[10] Picture a situation where we have church A and church D. Donors tend to have a certain determination in what they do (they also have to succeed in finding a recipient in order to propagate their trade), so imagine their having been refused by church A, then going to church D. How will members of church A respond on discovering that the new buildings, clothing, food, jobs and prestige being enjoyed by church D would have been theirs if it had not been refused by their pastor?

I hope it is becoming clear that aid, projects, and assistance to the church in parts of the Third World such as Africa are almost invariably an imposition, to the extent that even the least thought-out of development innovations, when backed by sufficient funds, will be welcomed with open arms. Then the fighting for a share of the cake ensues. Corrupt practices are inevitable given the rootlessness of incoming funds. (Funds that "drop out of the sky" like this are "up for grabs" as they have not been earned and their ownership is ambiguous.) Such impositions cause fights, split churches, distract people from more meaningful occupations than fighting for money, and damage the reputation of the church in the eyes of the world. Those Western Christians who see churches around the world as landing points for their particular vision of compassion and development are creating major damage in the process. The degree of this damage has only begun to be alluded to above.

---

9 There is, at least in British Christianity, a movement against consumerism, perhaps typified by books such as *Rich Christians in an Age of Hunger* by Ronald Sider (1978).

10 Whatever else a "project" in a Third World situation brings, it almost certainly includes spin-off financial benefits for those closely associated with it. If not, then it is a no-good project!

4.2 Not to devalue what is not Western

Organisations promoting development and seeking to offer aid, work under particular pressures and have particular agendas to fulfill. Money that has come in must go out. Their rationale and *raison d'être* is rooted, not in poor non-Western communities, but fairly and squarely in the West. They depend on their donors, and it is their donors whom they must please to ensure their growth and sustainability.

Their donors, even if they be Christians, clearly live within a world that is influenced by a certain culture. While many of their values may be guided and even rooted in the Scriptures, the latter is a means of transforming a way of life and not a way of life in itself. (The Bible must clearly be read by people in their language. It is therefore invariably interpreted through their culture. The Christian way of life will therefore vary from culture to culture.) Donors will seek to guide the use of their funds along lines with which they are familiar and in ways that make sense to them in their own worldview. Anything contrary to their (Western) view of life is likely to be given short shrift.

This means that Western funding, unless very carefully watched, applies constant pressure toward a Westernisation of the rest of the world. What is not Western is devalued, and what is Western is promoted. Such is likely to meet minimal real opposition from the non-West where funding is being applied because:

1. You don't bite the hand that feeds you.
2. Westerners seem to be very clever—so they must know what they are doing.
3. Even if the project is way off target, there will still be plenty of people eating from it.
4. Corruption has taken over, and the thing may already be totally distorted.
5. If they are so stupid as to do this, then why tell them to stop?
6. And so on.

This results in the ridiculous situation whereby what is foreign and misunderstood flourishes and prospers, and what is indigenous, known, and valued, flounders. That Christians are contributing to this state of affairs is sad.

I can repeat that at which I have already hinted—a Western person having a Westernising influence is almost inevitable. As one cannot help someone to improve their language skills without first learning the language, so one cannot help someone adapt their culture without first learning the culture.

True development of a people is facilitated to the degree that someone takes the time to first learn their ways.

4.3 Not to link God's word with finance

Current wisdom in "development," shared largely by Western Christians in collusion with their non-Christian counterparts, has other ramifications; two of which I will mention here, being promotion of the prosperity gospel and racism.

The prosperity gospel is a subtle but powerful and potentially extremely damaging aberration of God's truth that is currently spreading like wildfire around the globe. While its particular domain may be Pentecostalism, it branches far and wide into mission and indigenously founded churches. It is a peculiar hybrid that arises and continues to be nurtured through Western contact with the "poor" world.

The essence of prosperity gospel is simple. The Bible speaks of having faith as a means to secure God's blessing (1 John 5:4). Western Christians arrive in the non-Western world claiming to acknowledge God's omniscience and power, while carrying numerous absolutely incredible devices and inventions—from clothes to calculators, shoes to mobile phones, money to hairspray. It is a short route to the conclusion that these must be the amazing things that God brings. Christians' "God talk" and emphasis on prayer show clearly that such come through prayer. In no time then prayer and even the whole of worship and Christian life is oriented to the acquisition of such. Role models exist to exemplify the possibility of success, being those local Christians who have succeeded in getting a link with donors, but give the credit for this to God.

This way of thinking soon comes to dominate the whole of Christian life. Hence suits are worn, English is used, Western devotional books are preferred, glasses are coveted (whether someone's eyes are bad or not), and the "cargo" is awaited (Balcomb 1996). The same value system is read back into the Scriptures. Moses, Elijah, Paul, and even Jesus are assumed to have done the same thing, and thus latched on to what is also known as "the white man's wealth."

Perhaps it is time this was called a "lie" or a "heresy." Yet it is not one always propagated by intent. It just happens—wherever a Westerner opens his mouth backed by Western money, as those from the non-Western world attempt to understand him from their cultural perspective.

The fight against racism reflects the Western value that all people are essentially equal.[11] (This value is clearly deeply rooted in Christianity.) Efforts made especially by Christians in the West to counter racism are admirable, but pitiful given the degree of worldwide inequality. I am frequently struck by the attention given by British churches to asylum seekers, who have temporary residence in the UK while their cases are looked into. They may be showered with wealth and attention, efforts being made to avoid their expulsion as if it is through landing on British soil that they have become human, while the millions of their "miserable colleagues" left at "home" can be relatively ignored. Such shows of wealth perpetuate racist notions.

For Western efforts at countering racism by raising the wealth of foreign residents to local standards to be consistent, then the reverse would also need to apply. That is, that Westerners who are foreigners outside of the West should reduce their wealth in order to generate equality. Such not happening means that the rest of the world is a constant source of racist thinking—in which white skin is associated with wealth.

5. WHAT IS NOT REALISED ABOUT THE CHURCH IN DEVELOPMENT

5.1 The un-Christian character of development

The adamancy of the Western church in its promotion of "development" seems to be convincing the rest of the world that the latter must be inherently Christian. This is an incredible supposition on the basis that, especially for Protestants, the Bible is claimed to be the foundation for the Christian life. There is a difference between using the Bible to guide a presupposed orientation to "development" and deriving "developmental thinking" from the Bible.

I would hazard to suggest that it is only a certain interpretation of the Scriptures that conveys what is known as "development." Nowhere in the New or Old Testaments do we find evidence for either the advance of science or technology, or the setting up of the kind of institutions associated with "development" today—such as hospitals, formal educational facilities, budgeting for business management, etc. Considering such as a part of Christian mission or ministry is in effect syncretism.

11 Clearly not shared by everyone around the world; notably India and its caste system.

I imagine that it is through prosperity coming to be measured by the abundance of "things" in the West, that the expression of love through the giving of gifts has become prominent, that has in turn brought a lower and lower valuation of the life of those who are materially poor. Yet the giving of gifts is only one means of sharing love and compassion, and one that may be far from ideal. Certainly (as argued above) it can hardly be taken as "biblical." It ignores expressions of love through sharing time; learning from one another; encouragement; heart-sharing; attending key familial events such as weddings, funerals, celebrations, and anniversaries; praying; singing together; and so on and so on.

5.2 *Wealth that results in submissive contrition*

The power of wealth in forcing its way into places is frequently insufficiently considered. I have alluded to this in section 3.1 above. It is a rare and strong pastor who can refuse the offer of a "development project" to him or his church. This applies almost regardless of the advisability of the project's actual aims. It may be a project to enable chickens to lay blue eggs with green spots, or to tie-dye clothes, or to vaccinate trees, or to (re)invent wheels—as long as it comes with money to support it, that is okay. "Better the project (money) come here than go somewhere else."

This means in effect that the whole decision-making process as regards the advisability of projects easily remains with the donor(s). Recipients can anyway hardly be expected to assist in such a process, as their outlook and objectives are not those envisioned by a donor. The long-term, calculated vision of a Westerner is unlikely to be shared by a recipient, who has more immediate needs and perhaps an immediate shortage of food in mind.[12]

5.3 *"Projects" are followed by confusion and havoc*

Havoc frequently ensues following the receipt of donor money or a donor project. This is covered up whenever possible—through fear that a donor's realising the impact of his development initiative may discourage him from giving further help. Sometimes cracks cannot be covered over, and examples are legion in which longtime friendships and church associations are blown to smithereens by the lust for material gain engendered through development initiatives. The fighting in Buru Buru Church of God in Nairobi, Kenya, resulting in violence that was

12 I am here skipping numerous linguistic and cultural considerations in my oversimplistic presumption that donor and recipient actually understand one another.

fully reported in the Kenyan media, is just one example (for a report on this, see Anon 2003). I would not like to share many examples, suspecting that such would make me unpopular amongst the church leaders who are hoping for a continued supply of development/aid.

I suspect that major churches, such as the Anglican or Catholic, have made some progress in ensuring that development aid that enters their non-Western parishes does so in such a way as to minimise havoc. This can be done by the careful formulation of guidelines that are vigorously kept so as to dampen the impact of aid and projects. Having a nonlocal in charge helps in this process, as jealousy will be less biting to him than to a fellow countryman who is raised from "rags to riches" just because he can sweet-talk foreigners. Careful, experienced donors also learn to try and avoid having a divisive influence—although they usually have to learn by first making mistakes. In these days of easy global communications there are more and more self-appointed amateur development experts around who do their damage, get their fingers burnt, then disappear.

A relatively good grasp of English and its usage on the part of Africans seems to be a barrier to understanding what is happening on the part of Western visitors to Africa, or at least western Kenya with which I am familiar. Many do not realise that knowledge and ability in a certain area (for example, language) does not mean that what is known is being put into practice in expected ways. In other words, the wide spread of European languages (particularly English) dampens the perception of European people to very deep and very significant cultural differences that amongst other things affect "development." What a Westerner hears is familiar, only because the non-Westerner has spent many years learning what is foreign. Much local reality remains hidden.

5.4 Outside projects suppress local initiative

The question has to be asked how "success" in development is to be defined. If "we" succeed in "developing them," then is that success, or is it social engineering or the material domination of a people? It is in this area that the final and perhaps most difficult questions need asking, as to the true impact of "successful" development.

To people accustomed to seeking blessing and progress from "gods" (however defined), white people's preeminence in development activities easily renders them identifiable as if they are gods (even if out of sight, their influence is rightly assumed to be critical). This can result in blatant idolatry.[13]

13 It is striking how white people seem to come to fit the space left by western Kenyan people in their lives for God. "In whatever the Luo did . . . they depended on God for their success," says Ogutu (1975, 118). These days they depend increasingly on Westerners.

Perhaps the most profound insights into the impact of many development projects would arise from considering the counterfactual. There appears to be a widespread assumption that without aid and development initiatives, economies and societies outside the Western world would be stood-still in the Stone Age. This assumes no initiative and pitiful levels of intelligence on the part of non-Westerners. (If intelligence really is so pitiful, then what is the chance for the success of projects once handed over?)

One outcome arising from the habitual link between projects and foreign funding is a serious devaluing of academia and local knowledge. It is a devaluing of local knowledge, because its implicit message is that knowledge alone is never of any worth unless it is knowledge of how to use outside funds. The implicit message is that someone cannot help himself, but must be helped. A sad message indeed. In fact self-help, while probably a more arduous process than merely plucking from a donor tree, may be exactly what can help an initiative to succeed, as it ensures that it will be valued. Dependence on funds gives the advantage to the wealthy and not to the intelligent (these two may, but may not, be correlated). Finally it devalues learning, because it is all too often driven, not by a growing knowledge of effective implementation, but by ongoing pressure from relatively ignorant donors.

The stir created by, and dominating effect of, foreign-funded initiatives in Africa alone, is such as to buy up the best brains on the continent into serving foreign interests in incomprehensible and unnatural (to them) ways. Not in tune with local ways of life, such initiatives are constantly clashing with people's own judgments. The promotion of foreign languages severely hampers the development of indigenous languages, which are the ones people understand. It is perhaps the narrowmindedness of initiators of foreign-funded and originated projects that is actually responsible for the cataclysmic continuity of rampant poverty in Africa and elsewhere, through suppression of local initiative. Let the church not be found guilty of this.

6. CONCLUSION

A transformation in the approach used by the Western church to the non-Western world, as here considered in the case of western Kenya, is badly needed. This needs to be a revival of truly godly and holistic thinking, to replace the imitation of secularist methodologies that is today widespread and debilitating. These are areas in which the church needs to lead and not to follow. Transformation comes through the heart—an empowering from God's heart to man's. In development terminology, such enables progress through local initiatives in line with local lifestyles. Not through "development projects" initiated from outside.

REFERENCES

Anon. 2003. Riot police lock worshippers out. http://www.nationaudio.com/News/DailyNation/03072000/News/News47.html (accessed June 11, 2004: site now discontinued).

Balcomb, Anthony O. 1996. Modernity and the African experience. *Bulletin for Contextual Theology in South Africa and Africa* 3/2: 12–20. http://www.hs.unp.ac.za/theology/mod.htm (accessed April 29, 2004: site now discontinued).

Blass, Regina. 1990. *Relevance relations in discourse: A study with special relevance to Sissala*. Cambridge: Cambridge Univ. Press.

Gutt, Ernst-August. 2008. The so-what factor and the new audience. Paper presented at the Bible Translation Conference, February 5–6, in Horsleys Green, UK. http://homepage.ntlworld.com/ernst-august.gutt (accessed June 11, 2008).

Harries, Jim. 2007. Pragmatic theory applied to Christian mission in Africa: With special reference to Luo responses to "bad" in Gem, Kenya. PhD thesis, Univ. of Birmingham. http://etheses.bham.ac.uk/15 (accessed January 2, 2010).

Mojola, Aloo Osotsi. 2003. Holiness and purity in the book of Leviticus: A problem in Luyia dialects. Lecture and discussion at the Annual School of Theology of the African Institute for Christian Mission and Research (AICMAR), August 12–15, in Butere, Kenya.

Nickle, Keith F. 1966. *The collection: A study in Paul's strategy*. Naperville, IL: Alec R. Allenson.

Ogutu, Gilbert Edwin Meshack. 1975. An historical analysis of the Luo idea of God c. 1500–1900. MA thesis, Univ. of Nairobi.

Parr-Davies, Neil, 2001. The Sapir-Whorf Hypothesis: A Critique. http://www.aber.ac.uk/media/Students/njp0001.html (accessed April 15, 2011).

Reimer, Johannes. 2004. Mission as kenotic action: Understanding orthodox theology of mission. *Missionalia* 32/1: 68–83.

Sider, Ronald J. 1978. *Rich Christians in an age of hunger: A biblical study*. London: Hodder and Stoughton.

Yule, George. 1996. *The study of language*. 2nd ed. Cambridge: Cambridge Univ. Press.

CHAPTER 4

Pragmatic Linguistics Applied to Bible Translation, Projects, and Intercultural Relationships: An African Focus[1]

1. INTRODUCTION

Translation issues have all too often been considered the rightful domain of SIL (Summer Institute of Linguistics) and UBS (United Bible Societies)—the Bible translators. This chapter challenges this restrictive wisdom. The linguistic guidelines proposed in this chapter are important for those engaged in church planting, theological education, and all kinds of support and development projects. While few missionaries doubt the value of having Scriptures in people's own languages, more need to consider the importance of not only *having* them but also *using* them, and building on the foundation that they represent. Missionaries need, I argue in this essay, to pay urgent attention to linguistic and translation issues that bear heavily on their mission and ministry.

Mission methodologies can be so misguided as not to be effective, even in "Christianised" parts of the world. This chapter attempts to provide guidance on knowing how to avoid some of the difficult problems of intercultural mission contexts.[2]

---

1 This chapter was originally published as follows: Harries, Jim. 2009. Pragmatic linguistics applied to Bible translation, projects, and intercultural relationships: An African focus. *Cultural Encounters: A Journal for the Theology of Culture* 5/1: 75–95.

2 For the purposes of this chapter, "pragmatics" is defined as the "study of the relations between language and context that are basic to an account of language understanding" (Levinson 1983, 21). Note also that "Africa" in this essay refers to "sub-Saharan Africa."

2. RECONSIDERING DYNAMIC EQUIVALENCE METHODOLOGY

The "dynamic equivalence" methodology of biblical translation, taken as standard in popular books such as Fee and Stuart (1993, 36), is considered to originate in Nida's work,[3] and is strongly affirmed by well-known names like Charles Kraft (2001). Unfortunately it can be seriously misleading, especially in intercultural contexts. I base this critique on the case that word meaning arises from having impacts on contexts (e.g., cognitive, social, personal, and textual).[4]

On walking into your sitting room you find a word written on a piece of paper on the floor. This could be any word—*chocolate* or *Christian* or *holiness*, or an unpleasant word such as *dead*, or a neutral word such as *house*. What could these words mean to you as you pick up the piece of paper and begin to read? Nothing. Nothing, that is, unless or until you add a context to the words. Has someone *left you* some *chocolate*? Perhaps your *husband has become* a *Christian*; or maybe your daughter is telling you that *you need more holiness*; or your son has found that *the dog* is *dead*; or your mother's *house* has *been sold*. But someone's leaving of the chocolate, becoming of the husband, telling of your daughter, finding of your son, dying of the dog, or selling of your mother's house are not in the word. These are contexts outside the word on the paper, which you are utilising in order to derive some meaning for the word on the paper! Without them the individual words mean nothing at all.[5]

What about a phrase like, "The cat is on the mat"? Unlike an individual word, this seems to mean something. But is this meaning context-free? What is a cat? Does one learn about cats by studying the word *cat*, or by looking at a *context* such as hearing cats, hearing about cats, stroking cats, and so on? The meaning of the word *cat* arises from the context of a cat around someone, and not from the word itself. So what of "on the mat"? What is a mat, and what is to be on it? Having once been told, "The pen is on the table," then seeing a pen on the table, someone will assume that the cat being on the mat will resemble the pen being on the table. The word *mat* doesn't tell you what a mat is. The context in which

---

3 For example, see Nida 1964.

4 For comparable critiques of dynamic equivalence methodology, see Thomas 1990.

5 The handwriting, the colour of ink, and the kind of paper on which the word is written are all parts of the "context" of the word.

the word has been used in the past does. So then phrases, sentences, paragraphs, etc., are as "full of contexts" as are words.[6]

People have different contexts and upbringings. Thus they differ in what they apply to a word to derive its meaning. This in turn means that different people will infer different meanings from the same words. In the course of translation by a process of dynamic equivalence, translators derive meaning from a word/sentence/text as understood in their particular context, then try to translate *that* meaning into the target language. Dynamic equivalence methodologies attempt to translate meanings (thoughts expressed in a source text) and not words, yet we have found that the meanings are peculiar to contexts. How can translators know that the context that they happen to use to translate is correct, or the one that the reader of the translation ought to get? To the extent that the context determines the meaning, which is a large extent, this decision is arbitrary.[7] What translators using dynamic equivalence methodology end up doing then is translating not words, but contexts.

When the Bible is translated into English by an Australian person, we get an Australian-English-context translation of the Bible. Such a Bible may be appropriate for use in an Australian (cultural) context, but may not be accurate for a non-Australian context. That is, Bible translations are accurate in the context in which they have been produced. A more helpful translation of the Bible into a non-Australian context may be a "literal" translation, which converts the *original* language as closely as possible word for word, to preserve original word order for interaction with this non-Australian context. That is, the context dependence of translation means that it may be better for people from a non-Australian milieu to use what is other than either the Australian-translated Bible or a version of the Bible translated from it.

I have indicated the serious weakness of the dynamic equivalence interpretation methodology *in cross-cultural context*. Thus, Bibles that are translated according to the principles of dynamic equivalence (such as the NIV) and in fact also free translations such as the Good News Translation or the Living Bible (because they use the same principle but follow a less systematic process) are strictly only appropriate for the culture in which they have been prepared.

---

6 It is often said that the Bible is correctly understood only when every part is read in the context of the whole. While this is correct, it is still the extrabiblical context that lays the groundwork for understanding all the words concerned. That is, individual parts of the Bible, such as lions, people, houses, God, crying, and so on, are first understood by people from *outside* of the Bible before they are found *in* the Bible.

7 If this decision is guided by the Holy Spirit, then this is not "translation" but "inspiration." The possibility of inspiration presumably does not do away with the need for careful translation.

This principle is rarely considered in the intercultural context. Bibles in other (especially African) languages, it appears, are increasingly being translated from dynamic equivalence translations such as the NIV rather than from biblical languages or more literal translations like the KJV. (This is the impression that I get from the African language Bibles that I am familiar with, and not a conclusion based on widespread research.) The most recent Luo language (the language of a western Kenyan people) Bible is certainly a case in point: "This IBS translation of the New Testament is for Dholuo [an alternate name for the Luo language], which is primarily used in Kenya. This translation uses an informal language style and applies a meaning-based translation philosophy. It is translated from the English NIV and was completed in October 2000" (Bible 2000). This results in the confusing situation in which translations of Bibles into non-Western cultures incorporate content arising from the expression of Western people's culture, and Western people's ignorance of non-Western people's culture.[8]

The same of course applies even more strongly to Bible *expositions* and *teachings* from the West. Moving such teachings outside of their home context will result both in the emergence of communication "gaps," or "baggage." Preachers and Bible teachers who move to foreign cultures but teach according to the context of their home culture often teach, not the Bible, but their own cultures.

This can be illustrated using the following examples. People who are used to seeing cows in a field will not comment on seeing cows in a field because to them this is normal. Those accustomed to seeing sheep in a field may well exclaim, "There are cows in the field." Hearers will not learn that there are cows in the field (they already know it, as the animals are before their eyes). Rather, they will learn that the speaker normally does not see cows in fields. The listener is not learning about their own context but about that of the speaker. Similarly, when someone says, "Pastors shouldn't inherit their dead brothers' wives," he will be revealing to listeners that this is a custom of the speaker's people. Telling someone that it is "wrong to be two hours late for a meeting" informs the listener that late-coming is an issue. Saying "Jesus loves even the Bemba people" reveals a problem in relationship with the Bemba people. Stating that "Christians shouldn't participate in Valentine's Day" could be *informing* someone that there is a thing called Valentine's Day, and so on.

Teaching the Bible to someone from another context will inform the listener about the culture of the speaker. Some African colleagues have told me that when

8 Such content is not a road map which may be helpful to someone to understand the West, but comments on passing scenery of a culturally specific nature, and thus is of no value to non-Western hearers/readers.

Westerners teach the Bible in Africa, they can distinguish foreign cultural elements from true biblical instruction. My own observation at many points, however, is that they fail to do this. Instead in Africa, English can become a "holy" language, prosperity gospel spreads, and misunderstandings, which may individually be small, accrue. Hence, missionaries ought not to teach the Bible until they have learned the context of the people they are reaching. Good Bible teaching must be intracultural. Necessary for learning cultural context is the learning of language. So also, the impact of Christian books from one cultural context, read in another, may be vastly different in meaning from what was originally intended. Theologies, to be in tune with local culture, should grow locally. As Sanneh puts it, "one can demand or even require a vernacular direction for the faith in the interests of orthodoxy" (1989, 174).

Some may ask, if acquiring meaning from words is all about context, and if we read the Bible through our context, where is God? The answer of course is—in the context. God is not paper and ink. He is a God who is living and dynamic, moving and working. God is an essential part of the context, who must be there in order for us to correctly understand his word. And I do not think that this is saying anything new.

3. ALTERNATIVE TRANSLATION METHODOLOGIES AND THEIR IMPACT ON DOCTRINE AND BELIEF

This chapter considers "modern" approaches to translation outlined by Aloo Osotsi Mojola and Ernst Wendland (2003), in reference to interpretation of the Bible, theology, culture, and in fact the whole of life. The existence of alternative translation methodologies shows that dynamic equivalence is only one of many options.[9]

Mojola and Wendland refer us to Christine Nord (1997) and functionalist approaches to translation. A reader "chooses the items they regard as interesting, useful or adequate to the desired purposes," says Nord (1997, 25–26). The *skopos* rule of Nord is to "translate/interpret/speak/write in a way that enables your text/translation to function in the situation in which it is used and with the people who want to use it and precisely in the way they want it to function" (Mojola and Wendland 2003, 13–14). So one way of translating Scripture is according to its perceived *function*. If Scripture is translated for use in the West according to the

9 In this chapter, I assume that making a sharp distinction between interpretation and translation is unhelpful because every interpretation is a kind of translation, and every translation requires interpretation.

intended function in the West, this is problematic when the same Scripture is to be used in another context where there ought to be a different function. To take a simplistic example, scriptural interpretation that emphasises the need for faith to a disbelieving secular society may have the unfortunate effect of aggravating magical beliefs in a holistic society rooted in a "magical worldview." (A North American preacher telling his audience that he "depends totally on God" will be understood by his fellow countrymen as meaning, "in addition to my pension, paid-off mortgage, two cars in the garage," etc., but could easily be understood by African people as implying that they need not plant any crops that year.) Again, as I have emphasised above, this applies to scriptural interpretation in the broad sense—including preaching, systematic theologies, devotional books, and so on.

An alternative approach to translation is to ensure that a description of an original applies to a description of the translated text. For example, if an original text is described as a "beautiful piece of poetry," its translation must be a "beautiful piece of poetry." If the original is "advice on how to find a wife," then the translation must be "advice on how to find a wife." Other similarities in content between these texts are considered to be of secondary importance. A "beautiful piece of poetry" may refer to flowers and sunshine, while the one that "translates" it may talk of romance. According to the descriptive approach, this will be a correct "translation." A text on "how to find a wife" will be very different in an American dating culture from a Hindu, Indian, arranged-marriage culture, and so on.

Missionaries and theologians need to consider carefully just when a descriptive approach is appropriate. Most scriptural translations have not followed this methodology. Words (meanings or impacts) of poetry and not rhyme or cadence are translated into contemporary Bible versions; the book of Proverbs, for example, can be totally nonpoetic in contemporary translations. The descriptive approach should certainly be considered if one is asked to translate a book on "how to plant a successful church" from American English to African English or another African language. Rather than words, sentences, or even paragraphs being recognisably similar to those of the original, what is important is that what is advocated in the text works in the African context, even if the content in terms of actual words comes to be different from the original. The same applies to preachers and teachers. Should missionaries tell their "foreign" audience how "they do it at home," or what works in the new host culture? The latter is only possible once they are familiar with the culture.[10]

10 Should visiting preachers *not* go about this process of translation, they are in effect leaving it for the locals to do so.

The text-linguistic approach looks at turbulence or dynamism in texts, especially where it has an important role to play. An American advising his fellow pastor to take a second wife in order to resolve a family issue has a turbulence arising from its incongruity, yet translated literally into many African contexts (especially of some indigenous churches), such textual turbulence may totally disappear, and advice given can be assumed to be very serious. For the African pastor, an alternative suggestion would need to be made to give the text an equivalent turbulence.[11] The question of turbulence should be borne in mind by Bible translators and in Christian ministry. The lack of cultural knowledge may result in cross-cultural preachers or teachers unknowingly creating or removing "turbulence" in their preaching/teaching.

Relevance theory attempts to explain *how* the impact of words onto a person causes "meaning." "Verbal communication typically conveys much more than is linguistically encoded," say Dan Sperber and Deirdre Wilson (1997, 146). "Relevance," according to Sperber and Wilson, "makes information worth processing for the human being" (1997, 46) in texts capable of (often widely) different interpretation. Using the principle of *relevance*, the correct meaning has "the greatest possible contextual effect" and requires the "smallest possible processing effort" (1997, vii). That is, readers or listeners generally make some assumptions. One of these is that the speaker will take the listeners to be able to discern which of the possible meanings that could be ascribed to a speaker's words is the one intended. Someone communicating with them will assume that they as listeners will assume the correct understanding for them to be the one that demands the least processing effort while having the greatest contextual impact on them. For details on this complex but profound and widely acclaimed theory, see Sperber and Wilson's text.[12]

"Postcolonial" approaches to translation consider its power implications. Taking translation as always having to do with questions of authority and influence, this approach assumes preachers or Bible teachers operate out of some self-interest. Translation, according to these critics, can never be an uninterested affair.

Literalist translations have recently gained respect following the discovery of serious weaknesses in the dynamic equivalence model of interpretation (as above). Some literalist translators maintain that retaining equivalents to original

11 It is hard to find an example to fit without causing misunderstanding among the non-African target readership of this chapter.

12 This theory was taught for the first time to Bible translators in Kenya at the Bible Translation and Literary Conference Center in Ruiru, Kenya on August 31, 2006.

words in the original order is more important in translation than correct grammar. This can be illustrated by considering adjectives. In English, one instinctively says, "a big, red brick house," while the Kiswahili rendering would naturally be "house big red of bricks."[13] The English word ordering leaves the reader (or the hearer) in suspense over what is to be described, whereas the Kiswahili word order produces suspense over the nature of the described item. Translation of suspense may require grammar to be incorrect.

"Translation wields enormous power in constructing representations of foreign cultures" (Venuti 1998, 67). According to Lawrence Venuti, translators choose between making a text appear domestic and retaining its "foreignness." While a translation can never be 100 percent accurate because the impact of words differs from one language to another, a translator can choose to conceal or reveal heterogeneity/foreignness, for example, by maintaining foreign words in the target language. Insisting that every foreign word be translated by an indigenous one is domesticating a text. Many English theological terms used in non-English theological texts show an ongoing tension with the "English" worldview. Translating every word would result in the text being a less accurate representation of the English original. Domestication can obscure very real cultural differences from view, whereas incorporating foreign words (or transliterations) can reduce flow and increase reading difficulty. Translators have to choose which route to follow, and that choice will have ongoing interpretative ramifications.

I attempt to illustrate the impact of these translation approaches by considering alternative options with respect to the extremely well-known verse of John 3:16, when translated into an African language.

The choice of a name for God affects his apparent *foreignness*. Choosing to use "God" in an African language Bible or theological discussion will have people assume him to have a somewhat "European" character. Calling him *Jehovah* or *Theo* will have him appear to be foreign to Africans, with a less-known character than that of "God." God's being "foreign" makes him more distant to the people being reached, but makes it easier for a missionary to define his nature. If an African name such as *Nyasaye* (used in western Kenya) is used, the African people will build all that they will hear subsequently on elaborate and complex preunderstandings.[14] They may reject a foreign missionary's teaching on *Nyasaye*, on the basis that their people know him better than do the missionaries.

13 My translation.

14 New insights about *Nyasaye* will be added to their ancient beliefs.

The Dholuo (an African language from western Kenya) Bible (1976) uses *wuode ma miderma* in John 3:16, where the English phrase commonly used is "one and only son" (Greek: υἱόν τόν μονογενή) (Marshall 1993). I presume this is because *wuode ma kende* (a more literal translation) implies a problem in a culture in which large families are preferred and someone could be looked down upon for having only one son.[15] The term *miderma*, while meaning an only son or child,[16] seems these days to be used only for Jesus (personal observation). So, to remove the implication that having an only son implies weakness, the Luo use a term that really implies "unique" (*miderma*) rather than "only" (*kende*).

The turbulence of "eternal life" (John 3:16) in the West arises, at least in part, from its being a scientific puzzle; is eternity where time is not, and how can that be? A strongly-held traditional African belief in the ongoing existence of someone's spirit either in a netherworld or partial reincarnation does not produce any such turbulence.

To draw from the relevance approach, I will share an example from my recent experience in an African mining community, shortly after a flooding incident killed scores of miners.[17] That "shedding of blood," I was told on a number of occasions, had resulted in more optimism for the miners who remained. This is because evil spirits are said to be satisfied by death, and shed blood is considered to have the power to bring good fortune. There were stories at the same time of sacrifices of children having been made at the mine in an attempt to enhance its productivity. Killing of a son by a father is recognised in some African witchcraft circles as a means to improve wider family interests (Magezi 2006). All these thoughts would be very foreign to the mind of a typical Westerner. To have an equivalent impact to that of John 3:16 in the West, this link between Christ's death and child sacrifice would need to be countered (if possible). Alternative options in translation methodology clearly have profound impacts on Christological, Trinitarian, and other doctrinal positions.

15 Should the only son die, the father is in trouble as he will have no one to fulfill his burial rites and other important roles in the home.

16 Odaga 2003, and see also Capen 1998.

17 Mererani in Manyara Province of Tanzania in April 2008.

4. SOME SUGGESTIONS AS TO THE NATURE OF APPROPRIATE BIBLICAL INTERPRETATION

In the light of the above, recommendations can be made regarding the most appropriate principles of cross-cultural biblical interpretation:

(1) In order to achieve comparability in a shrinking, multicultural world, I suggest that translators make greater efforts at following the word order and sentence structure of original texts, even with the loss of grammatical flow in the target language. This is especially important in the case of translations, such as in English, if they could end up being used by people of many different native languages/cultures.

(2) Already alluded to above is the importance of translating from original biblical languages, and *not* English or some other language's paraphrases or dynamic equivalence versions.

(3) The use of a lot of computers in Bible translation in non-Western languages should be discouraged. Since computers are expensive, exotic machines in much of Africa, they tend to prevent ownership of a translated text and create distance between translators and target audiences. Computers should be consigned to nonfield stations, such as at a capital city, a central mission station, etc. Pens and paper are less attractive to thieves and rogues and less invocative of jealousy, as well as more familiar and easy to imitate, circulate, and comprehend.

(4) Translators with little cultural knowledge need to be ready to allow translations which they themselves do not understand. What is clear to indigenous readers may not be so to a foreign translator.

(5) Translators should bear in mind that (following the relevance theory) people will seek understanding through searching for easy-to-process options which have significant impacts. This will involve the application of reason, which for many people in the world will be nonscientific in nature.

(6) Translators should avoid favoring themselves and their own people or culture.

(7) Domestication may or may not be a help in translation. Retaining foreign phrases or clumsy grammar ensures that listeners/readers appreciate that they are receiving something exotic which requires careful interpretation.

5. TRANSLATING PEOPLE AND PROJECTS

Consideration of translation issues should not stop with the Bible. Many more texts are being transported to Africa these days, including educational systems, languages, technological manuals, media broadcasts, recipes, novels, Christian teachings, theologies, and even political ideologies. What is their impact on the African scene?

Because words that make up these materials are dependent for their interpretation on their context (see above), and the context in Africa is unlike that of Europe, text meanings are transformed. Jean and John Comaroff consider the term "modernity." Because this is firmly rooted among people originating in Europe, "all other modernity's are . . . mimics of a real thing whose full realization elsewhere is, at best, infinitely deferred . . . at worst, flatly impossible" (Comaroff and Comaroff 2004, 331). As a result, "the various modernity's of African colonies contrasted markedly with modernity at the metropole and with each other" (2004, 332). The apparent movement of modernity from Europe to Africa has made Africa's "violence and magic . . . scandalously visible," they add (2004, 333). In reference to "liberalisation," its "impact . . . on ordinary lives across the continent appears to be persuading more and more people that mysterious forces are at work in the accumulation of wealth and power" (2004, 340). Such changes in word meanings are strongly supported by Blunt's research on Kenya: "Africa's occult beliefs have kept pace with Africa's particular forms of modernity" (2004, 304). Anthony Balcomb writes that:

> The fruits of the developed world, however, were too powerfully alluring to be ignored. They offered a lifestyle too attractive to be denied. But the relationship between the "goods" offered in this lifestyle and the means by which these goods could be attained was continuously misunderstood. It was still believed by many that the goods of modernity could be accessed by pre-modern means. This had many manifestations. Two may be cited. One is the Cargo Cult syndrome and the other is witchcraft. (1996)

"The African ability to integrate diverse cultural elements without the contradictions raised by the more dualist thinking of the West," Balcomb goes on to tell us, "could also provide a hermeneutical key for understanding many of the cultural, political, and religious phenomena of modern Africa" (1996). According to Placide Tempels, the "Bantu [a large ethnic group that dominates the population of many African countries] speak, act, and live as if, for them, beings were forces" (1959, 51). Tempels advises us that to study the Bantu on their own terms, "we must . . . make a clean sweep of our own psychological concepts" (1959, 96). Then we will realise that "every act . . . which militates against vital force or against the increase of the hierarchy of the *'Muntu'* is bad" (1959, 121). In order to avoid the perpetual widening of the gap between black and white, says Tempels, "we must devote ourselves to the service of the life which is already theirs" (1959, 179).[18]

Tempels also tells us that "what they [the Bantu, i.e., the Africans] want more than anything else is not improvement of their economic or material circumstances, but recognition of and respect for their full value as men by the Whites" (1959, 178). This is where, I suggest, whites have failed the African people. Instead of taking "their" approach to life seriously, whites have ever since Tempels' day been attempting to force Africans to accept a "white" way of looking at the world. This pressure, combined with the African people's desire for "recognition and respect as men" has given them two options. That is, either to stand by the truth of "who they are" and be considered primitive, or overtly acknowledge the white man's ways and be respected, even though that entails living a lie.[19]

"Our terms can furnish only an approximation to concepts and principles foreign to us," said Tempels (1959, 39). That is, European languages do not have the capacity for accurately describing African religions, beliefs, and philosophies. Hence discussions about African culture, values, and ways of life engaged in using English can only ever be approximations to the "truth." The frequent negative reception of such approximations by native-English speakers has resulted in African scholars publicly denying who they are for the sake of the respect of the West. While African people cannot allow the modern world to pass them by without participating in it, they also cannot participate in it using Western languages without denying a part of who they are. Scholars who deny their heritage for the sake of international respectability return to address, engage

18 Tempels' insights are particularly valuable because, although writing some time ago, he had a long-term, deep exposure to African people.

19 That is, to use language in relation to "reality" in a different way to that widely accepted by Westerners.

with, and share in that "heritage" when they go home. Refusal to take "the other" seriously on the part of Western scholarship unfortunately has isolated it from what is happening on the ground in Africa. This is, it seems to me, a *very serious* situation, given the amount of power that the West holds over vast numbers of African people, their countries, and their economies.

Westerners concerned with Africa need to consider very carefully this dilemma. Failure to do so results in a horrific current track record of "projects" in Africa: "Many projects and investments, especially in the rural areas [of Zambia], are bound to fail," shares Hugo Hinfelaar, because of African witchcraft beliefs that are rarely understood by Westerners (2007). A cycle can be seen repeating itself: in order to be considered respect-worthy, Westerners have to assume African people to be the same as themselves. They therefore design projects and interventions on that basis—ignoring the actual nature of the African people. The failure of projects is concealed so as not to reveal the "difference" that is there in the African culture or way of life, again out of respect. This unfortunately means that the next person who comes along again sets about designing another project by repeating the same blunder. At the root of this is the failure on the part of the West to come to terms with the "difference."

Our discussion of translation has taught us a number of important lessons. Dominant linguistic models in use in the West err in assuming the ability to communicate meaning interculturally with the use of words (when in reality meaning arises when words interact with "contexts," in the very broad sense of the word). This is well illustrated by the ongoing, widespread use of the dynamic equivalence model of translation, despite its serious weaknesses. This in turn results in an ongoing self-deception regarding global realities on the part of the West. Such self-deception is *very dangerous* in the current globalised world, resulting in poor decisions being imposed on much of the world's population through the ignorance of powerful Western scholars, and in turn, activists and policy makers. Those representing the "misunderstood" cultures of the world, meanwhile, are silenced through the inability of English to articulate their concerns, and their (very understandable) need to be respected in the international arena.

6. WESTERN LANGUAGES IN AFRICA

While international languages have their place in enabling international communication, their use in closely controlling other linguistic communities is like a cruel bludgeon forcing nonnative speakers (especially those of very distant cultures) to accept their own backwardness and forfeit their voice in their own community. In much of sub-Saharan Africa, country after country has seen no alternative but to adopt European languages to govern their own people.

The accountability of the West for this language dilemma can perhaps be traced through the peculiar formation of African "nation states"; ex-colonial and other global powers have to date failed to release the African people for self-rule through their ongoing support of the elitist structures that they originally set up.

It is not new for strong nations to conquer weaker ones. What is new, however, is for foreign powers to maintain a strong hold over empires by keeping a grasp on purse strings in the absence of effective authority or human presence, long after having supposedly been ousted from political leadership. Such control via faceless bureaucracy from a "safe" distance (foreign capitals thousands of miles away), when considered in the light of the prior parts of this essay, has been and continues to be a recipe for calamity. A major step toward any solution to this dilemma here proposed—would be the conscious withdrawal (or freeing) from outside support for promoting Western languages in education and governance of (in the cases here considered) African peoples.

Some aspects of foreign control have been enabled by modern technology. Cruel rulers in previous eras had to have a presence in order to exert control. Presence implies familiarity with local languages and contexts; "visibility" to local people; mutual, well-informed cultural and linguistic exchange; and feedback to the "centre" of power. The spread of language and customs through *people* via social and intellectual interaction is a far cry from today's Internet-based society, or the ability of publishers to duplicate their efforts into the thousands and millions so that, for example, many African schoolchildren these days are required to learn (foreign) English in their schools, without ever speaking to a native-English speaker. The culture needed to interpret the language is not to be seen. The "independence" of African countries, being curtailed by economic dependence, forces them into the ongoing use of little-understood languages.

What does it mean to reside in a country dominated by a foreign language? In Kenya, where I have lived since 1993, native languages are relegated to third place behind English (official language) and Kiswahili (national language). (While I have mentioned Kiswahili, its deep roots in African soil and its being very much an oral language means that it has few of the problems of English.) This relegation of local languages to third place discourages people from thinking. Profound or original thoughts in the mother tongue (MT) have little or no influence on the (formal) circumstances of life that are dominated by English. Instead, local people are taught to leave the thinking to foreigners. "Thinking" that is left for the locals to do is about how to drain foreign resources in their direction, by means often tainted with "corruption." Very few Kenyan people can engage effectively by communicating "on the level" with the international community that is dominating their lives (for which they must have a mastery of English of an international standard). Those who do have this mastery have acquired it at great expense and through extensive exposure to Western people and languages (surely with a loss in familiarity with their own people's contexts and languages).

Domination by a foreign language kills local initiative. I will give theological training initiatives as an example. Having been teaching and closely involved in a locally based, local-language theological training program in Kenya for over fourteen years, I observe that we invariably operate under the shadow of powerful foreign competitors. English-language alternatives offer career opportunities with good salary options, prestige, international recognition, free accommodation, good food, formal curricula, a variety of teachers, and all benefits to be gained for those who will accept learning things that are of marginal relevance to their own cultures and own people. (Much of the relevance of Western theological curricula, not to be scoffed at in the "real" world, arises because internationally recognised languages and knowledge can attract international funding and support.) The local program, working in local languages with people who are closely involved in day-to-day church affairs, can barely gain respect or prestige as long as foreigners are (economically) imposing their misplaced wisdom as incentives to the more mobile and more able. One may suppose that people would value that which is of local pertinence over and above the foreign and "irrelevant"—an assumption that Ericka Albaugh found to be wrong in Cameroon (2007).

In fact, assisted by the "magical" basis to African life already mentioned above (and below), African people have instead appropriated the "prosperity gospel" as a means of understanding that God himself stands behind the "whites" (Harries 2006, here chapter 11). It seems clear that capable local people who could be making a place for the church in a diverse "civil society" in Africa have realised that this is not an option (a "civil society" is often not there) (Danfulani 2007). They are forced instead either to remain within the traditional African worldview, hence continuing in their adherence to funeral/death rituals which are prevalent in much of Africa, or to leave that world and engage in redirecting foreign funds and influence in their direction—much as, in fact, their forefathers did with "mystical" or "witchcraft" powers—often by "corrupt" means.

As alluded to above, the foreign has relevance and impact on local society because it is central to power issues connected with central government and capable of bringing relationships, recognition, and finance from the international community. Locally indecipherable codes that constitute "foreign-oriented debate" are powerful and begin to have a sense of their own. The above discussion (Section 4) has shown African people's orientation to witchcraft/magic, whose category is being expanded to accommodate "the foreign." That is, terms, phrases, sentences, and texts that make a certain sense to those with a Western mind are valued in Africa as magical idioms. Powerful they are, as Westerners are strongly accustomed to responding charitably to those who succeed in reflecting back "their" terms about the world and what is right and wrong.[20] This of course applies inside and outside of the church.

I am presenting a Westerner's perspective on the African scene. One could not expect African people themselves to make the observations above. They are barely visible from "within." Hence academia cannot allow itself to be multicultural in its inputs if it is to be broad or multicultural in its output. Informed insider views by Westerners on Africa are rare these days for many reasons (some discussed above), which keep Westerners on the margins of African society.

The failure of "education" in foreign languages to be self-perpetuating in Africa leaves the West leading the educational field from afar. Formal theological education facilities on the African continent are almost invariably Western-funded, and often Western-managed. This vast, complex operation absorbs enormous quantities of time and energy. A concentration of effort is required to push the required knowledge onto the African continent for appropriation by the African people (often funded by scholarships provided by the West). The difficulty of this process increases as levels of education rise. (It is more difficult to offer an MA by extension to an African site than a BA, and so on.) The theological educational effort is precluding alternative options for missionaries, particularly those of actually getting close to the people being reached, operating from understanding, receiving relevant feedback, and therefore getting theological education to a position of relevance where it can become self-propagating. The counterfactual to the current drive to encourage the adoption of Western education in Africa is not "zero." That is, removing the requirement for Western educational impact should *not* mean that nothing is put into its place and missionaries go home.

20 As a student can "succeed" by telling his teacher what he wants to hear, whether or not the student has understood what is being taught.

An improved mutual understanding between West and non-West could bring fruits that are nowadays "unknown."

Western people appear not to realise that teaching someone your language is orienting them to your culture. Teaching African people English is creating and then perpetuating their dependence on native-English-speaking countries. Unfortunately, such high valuation of the "foreign" is an excellent way of encouraging people to devalue themselves. Many reasons contribute to the difficulty a nonnative will have in competing with a native speaker (other reasons are given above and below in this chapter). When the president of an African country presents a speech in English, who is he really talking to?[21] And something is wrong when a small foreign child can correct a president of an African country in his own official language.

I pay such attention to political factors to assist missionaries in appreciating how using a Western language in Africa can be supporting oppressive foreign policy decrees emanating from their home countries. This situation in much of Anglophone Africa forcing incompetence on its citizens is surely an infringement of God's will for his people that Christians should not voluntarily support.

Of course, African people stand to gain a lot through learning from "the West." People should travel and interact and learn any number of languages. But assisting someone to develop their own language and culture is like "teaching someone to fish," whereas forcing foreign wisdom onto them in foreign tongues is "giving them a fish." This has been proven over and over around the world; the powerful nations of the world today do not operate on borrowed languages.

Other issues closely related to this debate have been discussed in chapter 14 "Language in Education, Mission and Development in Africa: Appeals for Local Tongues and Local Contexts" (Harries 2007), which could helpfully be read at this stage as chapter 14 in this compendium. Working in a foreign language not linked at depth with the culture causes confusion—particularly if the language itself is still used by its originators (and therefore cannot successfully be "appropriated"). Meanwhile, those foreign originators become overconfident and assume the "foreign" to be "familiar" to them.

21 Perhaps he is talking to donors/potential donors instead of his citizens.

7. BEING INFORMED IN MISSION CONTEXTS

Missiological literature containing examples of how churches grow more quickly without Western missionaries (my personal observation that this is a favorite theme) has not prevented continued advocating of tired-out mission methodologies. The implicit problems associated with much of Western missionary activity struck me at my village home in western Kenya. I realised that the person who could most seriously undermine my ministry would be a fellow Western missionary. My missionary brothers and sisters in Christ who are not very careful in how they use their finances and language—buying people and opening them up (via modern technology) to the vices of the Western world—can be a hazard to those who are seeking to preach Christ *without* the bountiful servings of Western culture.

Missions to unreached peoples, including adherents of Islam, communism, and other religions could have much to learn. The "underground" church avoids the traps mentioned above. Mission activity among unreached people (on my observation) often does not. An example (filling the gaps myself with some details concealed): A Christian mission operating in a strongly Muslim context sets up a project to teach young women profitable means of dying clothes using imported Western technology. This "project" lured Muslim girls, who were then plied with gospel teaching. It seemed not to be understood that offering such economic freedom to Muslim girls would threaten doting Islamic families concerned for their reputation and careful to protect the chastity of their daughters. Muslims value women's domestic roles (Waines 1995, 95). Christianity was coming together with immorality. Could self-respecting fathers allow their daughter to be so allured to an immoral life? Suggesting to the Christians that what they were doing was inappropriate would of course have been interpreted as being an anti-Christian reaction. The only alternative left to the Muslim community was to try to eject this so-called mission group. It is sad when a mission is ejected for being an inducement to immorality.

Instigators of mission initiatives should ask themselves whether what they are doing would be acceptable to a Christian community in the same/related cultural context or ethnic group. Mission personnel should be trained by local Christians to avoid creating inappropriate activities. Foreign missionaries wanting to reach nonbelievers would be well advised first to work with local Christian churches, especially African indigenous churches (AICs) that are closely in tune with deep African culture. I do such work with indigenous churches, but no Islamic-outreach group has ever deigned to ask me for advice or sought an opportunity for mutual assistance. They choose instead, it seems, to plant American or Western churches in African/Muslim contexts, even where all neighboring Christian communities are expressing their faith in more African ways. Too few take the time to discover what an African church is actually like.

Outsiders need to be clearly informed before making key decisions affecting numerous people in highly significant ways. Being well-informed requires knowledge of local languages that can only be acquired through missionary vulnerability. Such vulnerability typically arises when a missionary embraces "poverty" in their ministry.[22]

8. REASONS FOR THE POPULARITY OF INAPPROPRIATE MISSIONS METHODOLOGIES

Why are some of the proposals not in line with mainline missiological practice? First, many people involved in aid, development, or financial provision as well as mission seem not to have realised to what extent such is a trap. In many Western nations, people can make choices in terms of occupation and livelihood. Offering a person a salary that is sufficient to live on in return for a service is not manipulative or coercive because someone turning down one offer can find comparable alternatives. That is, people are remunerated according to some reasonable "free-market" standard for that locality. A difficulty arises if an "employer" comes from a foreign context in which remuneration rates are much higher than in the country being targeted. To pay someone local rates can seem ridiculous by comparison with rates of pay in his home country. The employer may come under pressure from his home country to pay more. Unfortunately, as soon as rewards for services come to be higher than those set by local market forces, a distortion enters into the organisation, which results in corruption and lies. Corruption because people will be ready to pay bribes (in cash or other forms) in order to get the position concerned. Lies because they will find it advantageous not to be truthful (often under family and extended family pressure) to an employer (an ignorant foreigner who appears to have endless sources of money) rather than face being laid off. Once accustomed to a higher salary level, giving up one's position can be calamitous for the person concerned, as well as dependents in the extended family, thus making someone very reluctant to resign from a position or very bitter if they are given the shove. People who are "trapped" in this way cannot be expected to offer advice, no matter how pertinent, given that it threatens the status quo that maintains them.

22 This is discussed in detail by Domingues (2007).

Offering aid to a community is putting oneself into a "trap." Saying "I have $20,000 that I want to give you if you want it" is asking for trouble. The only way to give a community leader (however chosen) the freedom to refuse your offer without potentially getting themselves into a lot of trouble if they refuse is to make it while sworn to secrecy. (That is assuming that you can be trusted enough to keep the secret.) Should members of the community concerned hear that their leader turned down a generous offer of aid, especially if the money has now instead gone to a neighboring community, the leader concerned will have a serious problem that will certainly cost him popularity and may result in his losing his position altogether, unless the leader manages to convince the people that the potential donor is a liar with some heinous hidden agenda—not a response most donors are looking for.[23]

The computer that dominates the West today brings problems through its attuning of the human mind to its mechanical logic. Young people, especially those who are brought up in interaction with computers, are affected by it. They are inclined to apply reasoning they have learned on the computer to Third World problems. Ancient "wisdom" is thrown out of the window. The logical mind needed to solve computer problems is *not* always the best when it comes to resolving many complex Third World issues.

Western-oriented elites are usually the only people to whom foreigners have access, either because of their geographical location (in the West, in expensive areas of town or as owners of vehicles) and/or because they are the only ones who have a sufficient grasp of Western languages and cultures so as to be able to have sensible conversations with Westerners. When foreign missionaries say they are "speaking to the locals," all too often they are referring to this kind of person. This fact can lead to misrepresentation of the public opinion, which ends up creating more misunderstanding between cultures.

Linguistically, someone brought up in one community *can never* understand those of another to the extent of a native-born person. An elite person as described above rarely understands the West with the profundity or the depth of a fellow Westerner. Many African elites fill the gaps in their understanding of the West using their comprehension of "magic" (i.e., aspects of their culture that are outside of Western worldviews and experience). Such a person is often already in a "trap" such as the ones mentioned above—their ongoing supply of funds being dependent on them speaking and behaving in certain ways to please their wealthy

23 Imagine that your boss offers you a raise within earshot of your spouse. What kind of conversation will you have at home later that day if you decide to turn it down?

donors regardless of their actual heart orientation. The same elites often stand to gain the most from aid and donor policies for many reasons; not the least of which is that they often own the businesses that handle foreign funds and sell to donors. The elites can support religious positions to justify their stand in relation to donors—such as the "prosperity gospel." They can be yes-men. A prerequisite for a foreigner to know what the people really want and certainly then to know what will actually help them, is at the very least to learn a local language and interact with a wider populace from a position of economic (and other) vulnerability. That there are *very few* Western Christians doing this today is a disgrace to the church.

Closely related to this and already referred to above is the poor understanding of the translation process by many would-be donors and development experts. Given the close association between "meaning" and "context" of the use of words, already mentioned above, it should be clear that Westerners cannot understand non-Western people through the use of language alone. The widespread use of the English language today makes native English people, in particular those who are monolingual, especially vulnerable to deception (intentional or otherwise).

So then, why don't Westerners take the trouble to learn the ways of life of the African people? I suggest the following reasons: Firstly, it is difficult. Secondly, quite frankly, they are scared. Moving into another person's culture has many difficulties, usually compounded the greater the gap being bridged. The increasing material and financial dependence of "normal" lifestyles in the West is creating an ever-widening gap between the Western and the non-Western world. The reputation of Africa as a missionary graveyard, as infested with malaria, fierce wild animals and snakes, frequent bloodshed and war, hunger, famine, and extreme poverty deters many Westerners from desiring close fellowship with African communities. Hence the myth that one can "help" distant peoples while living in one's comfortable home, sitting at one's computer console, using one's own language, and through studying theoretical issues in local universities with just occasional, dramatic, adventurous excursions into foreign climes, is extremely popular.

9. CONCLUSION

This chapter assumes the meaning of words to arise from the *context* of their use. This underrealised truth forms the basis for a critique of the dynamic equivalence theory of translation, particularly in intercultural perspective; foreign texts are found to communicate a foreign culture, over and above their intended content.

A brief examination of alternatives illustrates that dynamic equivalence is far from the only option available to translators. Other options include translation based on function, description, turbulence, relevance, power interests, domestication or its avoidance, and so on. A short list of specific recommendations is given to Bible translators.

The questions raised on translation are pertinent to all areas of intercultural communication. Serious weaknesses in prior translation practices in projects, policies, and diverse kinds of international and intercultural exchanges are considered. Careful examination of the economic and power implications of missionary actions, drawing on the author's own practical experience, leads to the suggestion that it is immoral to force dependency on unworkable language policies onto African people. Because this practice aggravates problems, the church needs to distance itself from it. The importance of this is emphasised for real mission contexts. Because communication with locals is hindered by the religious stand-off of frontier mission situations, misunderstandings are particularly likely to arise in mission to unreached people. The peculiar economic dynamics arising from intercultural mission relationships between the non-West and the West are shown as being largely responsible for perpetuation of the negative and unhelpful practices mentioned above. Western missionary vulnerability and linguistic acumen are advocated as the means for overcoming them.

The limitations in popular wisdom regarding language and translation found in this chapter suggest the need for an urgent turnaround in twenty-first-century missionary practices. Contrary to popular wisdom and perhaps outward appearance, discovery of a key to the resolution of sub-Saharan African problems will require operating from within the African cultural milieu and languages concerned. Just as God became man in a specific culture at a specific time and manifested himself within the confines of that culture, so "solutions" must be "incarnated" from within the structures and language of a people for them to be truly Christian, whether in terms of translations or wider societal concerns. To seek a solution from the throes of Western academia in European languages is to postpone the call for African people to come to terms with their own ways of life and position in the world. Such postponement, if it continues to detract attention from key issues to its own misguided solutions, could spell catastrophe for African societies in the years ahead.

REFERENCES

Albaugh, Ericka. 2007. Language choice in education: A politics of persuasion. *Journal of Modern African Studies* 45/1: 1–32.

Balcomb, Anthony O. 1996. Modernity and the African experience. *Bulletin for Contextual Theology in South Africa and Africa* 3/2: 12–20. http://www.hs.unp.ac.za/theology/mod.htm (accessed April 29, 2004: site now discontinued).

Bible. 1976. *Muma Maler mar Nyasaye: Moting'o Muma Machon kod Muma Manyien* [Bible in the Luo language]. Nairobi: Bible Society of Kenya.

Bible. 2000. *Muma Manyien* [Bible in the Luo language]. Colorado Springs: Biblica. http://www.biblica.com/bibles/luo (accessed April 15, 2011).

Blunt, Robert. 2004. Satan is an imitator: Kenya's recent cosmology of corruption. In *Producing African futures: Ritual and reproduction in a new liberal age*, ed. Brad Weiss, 294–328. Leiden, Netherlands: Brill.

Capen, Carole A. 1998. *Bilingual Dholuo-English dictionary*. Tucson, AZ: Carole A. Capen.

Comaroff, Jean, and John L. Comaroff. 2004. Notes on Afro-modernity and the neo world order: An afterword. In *Producing African futures: Ritual and reproduction in a new liberal age*, ed. Brad Weiss, 329–47. Leiden, Netherlands: Brill.

Danfulani, Umar Habila Dadem. 2007. Anger as a metaphor for witchcraft: The relation between magic, witchcraft and divination among the Mupun of Nigeria. In *Imagining Evil: Witchcraft beliefs and accusations in contemporary Africa*, ed. Gerrie ter Haar, 143–82. Trenton, NJ: Africa World.

Domingues, Fernando. 2007. Poverty and mission. Service of Documentation and Study of Global Mission. http://www.sedos.org/site/index.php?option=com_docman&task=cat_view&gid=97&Itemid=37 (accessed February 27, 2008).

Fee, Gordon D., and Douglas Stuart. 1993. *How to read the Bible for all it's worth*. 2nd ed. Grand Rapids, MI: Zondervan.

Harries, Jim. 2006. Good-by-default and evil in Africa. *Missiology: An International Review* 34/2: 151–64.

———. 2007. Language in education, mission and development in Africa: Appeals for local tongues and local contexts. *Encounters Mission Ezine* 19 (August), http://www.redcliffe.org/uploads/documents/Language_in_Education_19.pdf (accessed November 1, 2007).

Hinfelaar, Hugo. 2007. Witch-hunting in Zambia and international illegal trade. In *Imagining evil: Witchcraft beliefs and accusations in contemporary Africa*, ed. Gerrie ter Haar, 229–46. Trenton, NJ: Africa World.

Kraft, Charles H. 2001. Can anthropological insight assist evangelical theology? In *Culture, communication, and Christianity: A selection of writings by Charles H. Kraft*, ed. Charles H. Kraft, 244–80. Pasadena, CA: William Carey Library.

Levinson, Stephen C. 1983. *Pragmatics*. Cambridge: Cambridge Univ. Press.

Magezi, Arthur. 2006. Dealing with issues of "superstitions." Lecture presented during Spiritual Emphasis Week at Kima International School of Theology, in Kima, Kenya.

Marshall, Alfred. 1993. *The interlinear NRSV-NIV parallel New Testament in Greek and English*. Grand Rapids, MI: Zondervan.

Mojola, Aloo Osotsi, and Ernst Wendland. 2003. Scripture translation in the era of translation studies. In *Bible translation frames of reference*, ed. Timothy Wilt, 1–25. Manchester: St. Jerome.

Nida, Eugene. 1964. *Toward a science of translating: With special reference to principles and procedures involved in Bible translating*. Leiden, Netherlands: Brill.

Nord, Christine. 1997. *Translating as a purposeful activity: Functionalist approaches explained*. Manchester: St. Jerome.

Odaga, Asenath Bole. 2003. *Dholuo–English dictionary*. Kisumu, Kenya: Lake.

Sanneh, Lamin. 1989. *Translating the message: The missionary impact on culture*. Maryknoll, NY: Orbis Books.

Sperber, Dan, and Deirdre Wilson. 1995. *Relevance: Communication and cognition*. 2nd ed. Oxford: Blackwell.

———. 1997. Remarks on relevance theory and the social sciences. *Multilingua* 16: 145–51.

Tempels, Placide. 1959. *Bantu philosophy*. Paris: Presence Africaine.

Thomas, Robert L. 1990. Dynamic equivalence: A method of translation or a system of hermeneutics? *The Master's Seminary Journal* 1/2: 149–69. http://www.tms.edu/tmsj/tmsj1g.pdf (accessed February 28, 2007).

Venuti, Lawrence. 1998. *The scandals of translation: Towards an ethics of difference*. London: Routledge.

Waines, David. 1995. *An introduction to Islam*. Cambridge: Cambridge Univ. Press.

CHAPTER 5

"Material Provision" or Preaching the Gospel: Reconsidering "Holistic" (Integral) Mission[1]

1. INTRODUCTION[2]

Differences in understanding of "holistic mission" between West and non-West, discovered by the application of pragmatic linguistic insights, are shown to be causing serious problems in its implementation. Solutions proposed including missionary "poverty" in ministry and use of local languages in addition to traditional anti-dependency measures, imply the need for revision in current Western missionary practice.

2. TRANSITION TO HOLISTIC MISSION

We "cannot properly help a person . . . while disregarding his or her . . . material or bodily needs" and "merely" preaching the gospel is a "misunderstanding of God's purpose," says René Padilla (2005, 15), as part of an occasional paper of the 2004 Forum for World Evangelization, hosted by the Lausanne Committee for World Evangelization at Pattaya, Thailand. Padilla cites the well-known British theologian John Stott in his support. However, Glenn Schwartz rings warning bells by pointing out that current mission activities create unhealthy dependency. He is "working hard to encourage church leaders, particularly in Africa and

---

1 This chapter was originally published as follows: Harries, Jim. 2008. "Material provision" or preaching the gospel: Reconsidering "holistic" (integral) mission. *Evangelical Review of Theology* 32/1: 257–70.

2 The views expressed in this chapter are those of the author, and do not necessarily reflect those of the WEA Theological Commission, which has raised some concerns with the author.

America, to stand on their own two feet and to discover the joy of breaking out of the stranglehold of dependency" (2006). These two approaches are quite different from each other, and it must be asked if these authors have realised that their strategies are inadvertently at loggerheads? Is there any resolution to these differences, and what is the way forward in mission?

Christopher Little explains how the parting of the ways in the evangelical Christian church occurred following disagreement between those who advocated the "horizontal" (relationships with men) as against the "vertical" (relationship with God) roles of the church (2006).

According to Little, the evangelical wing of the church turned to follow a more horizontal direction in the early 1970s—represented especially by a "change of mind" at the Lausanne convention in 1974 (Little 2006, 79). For Little, this represents an abandoning of the legitimate role of the church in the world as, after all, "the deepest impoverished state a person can suffer is alienation from God and therefore the greatest demonstration of his compassion is the remedy for this plight" (2006, 85).

Underlying this switch in emphasis, I suggest, is the current state of ideology in Western nations. Western Christians are influenced by an academia that has for centuries denied the role of God in human lives. Christians living in the West should be acutely aware that they see the world through tinted spectacles, with blinkers barring from view significant aspects of the nature of people and the nature of God as understood in the majority world.

Appeals for cultural sensitivity by Western nations relating to the non-West seem increasingly to fall on deaf ears. Reasons for this include: first, increasing emphasis on *short-term* mission, meaning shrinking opportunities for learning cultures and languages; second, the end of the Cold War and the ever-rising confidence of the West in its own capabilities has reduced the need for cultural sensitivity; and third, the rise of the Internet and global communication in general enables geographically isolated communities to continue to relate closely to their societies of origin, thus reducing the need to identify with a foreign (non-Western) people even if a Westerner is living among them.

Even if more experienced people were to advise new missionaries to learn the language and take a more accommodating and understanding approach to the culture they are meeting, new workers often ignore this. They are not looking at a clean-slate scenario of "untouched people," but a legacy of repeated expressions of a lack of cultural knowledge by their predecessors. Some African people, having given up hope of being understood by Westerners, are becoming less willing to be open, if only to minimise damage in sensitive areas (which is many areas) of church and community life (Harries 2007, here chapter 14).

The West's perception of international concerns is narrowing as a result of its operating from an ever-shrinking presuppositional base.[3] Mission emphasis today is frequently operated on the basis of a short-term involvement providing technical assistance. Those who consider these issues to be neutral to broader theological or ecclesial issues in Africa are unfortunately misguided for at least two reasons. First, African religion is rooted in a search for power, including financial power, so projects with outside funding become part of how Christianity (or other "religion") is understood in Africa. They are not seen as "extras" to the church, because there is no extra space beyond the category of "religion" that can be occupied by "secularism," as is the case in the West. (This is a part of what it means to be "holistic.") Second, relatively poor, locally funded, African church budgets are often dwarfed by ambitious schemes funded and administered from abroad.

Central to this chapter is the understanding that word meanings, including the meaning of the term "holistic" itself, arise from the context of their use. In parts of the world where the dominant worldview is secular, it means that the gospel is to be presented in hand with finance and technology to improve people's lives. In parts of the world where the worldview is "magical," it means that the gospel is accompanied with "magical" powers to improve people's lives. I acknowledge that the term "magic" is very difficult to define or translate. Numerous anthropological accounts of African people point to their dependence on ancestral spirits, witchcraft, vital forces, mystical powers, and so on, that I here refer to as "magic" (Harries 2000, here chapter 12). One people's science becomes another's magic.[4]

3. BIBLICAL BACKGROUND

We need to include reference to the biblical background because God's word is not presented hand in hand with projects, finance, aid, or technology—a fact which Western advocates of holistic mission seem to ignore. Instead, in the Old Testament, God is shown revealing his plan of salvation in a variety of ways.

3 One reason the "presuppositional base" is shrinking, I propose, is because inputs from outside of the West are increasingly being presented in Western languages, so obviating the need for Westerners to consider the loss of detail incurred in the course of translation.

4 It should be clear that asking an African person, "Do you believe in magic?" is not a valid test for this thesis, both because people will understand the term "magic" in different ways, and as they will respond in respect to particular agendas.

Then in the Gospels, we see Jesus presented as a teacher of God's profound truths, and in particular as a miracle worker and one who had a heart of love greater than any other man before or after him. This love was demonstrated in the ways that he interacted with those around him, culminating in his shameful (from a human point of view) death.

Never having risen to political fame or having vast quantities of earthly wealth, Jesus nevertheless acquired great renown because, as Christians have believed up until today, he is God incarnate. His followers continued his ministry after being filled with godly power, resulting in the existence of bodies of believers around the world up to today, known as the *ecclesia* or church. Up to now those in the church, colloquially known as "Christians," continue to follow the example of Jesus and proclaim his teachings around the globe. Some years after the life and ministry of Christ and his disciples, Christian writings were gathered together with what had become the Jewish canon of Scriptures to form the Bible as it is today. That Bible remains the written text that guides and inspires Christians. The words contained in it are considered uniquely inspired by God himself to provide counsel in all areas of life. Ever since, and even before the canon was closed, Christians have been challenged to know just how to interpret the Bible. This has become a particularly critical issue since the Reformation in sixteenth-century Europe resulted in the formation of the Protestant church, whose numbers include the World Evangelical Alliance and churches affiliated to it.

Even modern translations of the Bible do not mention many things that have become a normal part of day-to-day life by many in the English speaking world—especially technological things arising from science and from more recent thinking about society and the nature of humanity. There is no overt mention of electricity, of vehicles, of rockets or telescopes, even of strategies, programmes, or projects in the modern sense. The Bible does not advocate hospital medicine or primary and secondary schooling; formal universities are not discussed or referred to; pensions are not even alluded to; and neither is formal insurance in case of theft, damage, or death. The Scriptures rarely even mention countries outside the eastern Mediterranean basin and seem not to anticipate that one day there will be nuclear power, space travel, or X-rays as a means of examining one's teeth. Terms (and concepts) such as bureaucracy, socialism, capitalism, development, AIDS, and sustainability are not found in the Bible.

Every generation of Christians looks to the Bible for answers to questions as to how they ought to live. They attempt to understand the Scriptures through the guidance of God the Holy Spirit. They want to do the will of God. I am here trying to point out that knowing the will of God is no straightforward, mechanical task. God has not left us with closely defined instructions in a legal document. In the current, globalising world, questions on what to do and how to do it are more pressing than ever—as certain people in the globe find themselves with the technological means and powers to influence the lives of others on a hitherto unknown scale. How are they to know the will of God in this circumstance?

The practice of Jesus himself could support diverse positions in this regard. How did he respond to people whom he met? Does Jesus' healing many sick people justify Western medical projects as part of Christian mission today? Does Jesus' feeding 5,000 set an example for us to follow, or in the light of the response of those whom he fed (John 6), is it teaching us *not* to feed people, as Jesus' temptations strongly imply (Luke 4:1–13)? The words that people find on studying the Bible have to come out of their own cultures (see Harries 2009, here chapter 3). It has often been suggested that people read out of the Bible what they want to, although that is not entirely true. I arrive at the positions that I do from the context of what I believe to be a life of commitment and sacrifice in God's service, guided by his word and led by his Spirit (Harries 2006, here chapter 13).

4. POWER IN THE CHURCH

Personal observation (in Kenya, Tanzania, and Zambia) has taught me that donors offering finance and material to the Third World (African) church thereby acquire power to influence the church concerned. I have considered this in more detail elsewhere (Harries n.d.(a)). An offer of aid is like a trap that recipients cannot usually avoid. This is particularly true in contexts of "poverty" in which the extended family is powerful, and in which needs for finance are increasingly being advocated (such as education, health, the need to have things, and so on), as is happening as the "poor" world is being incorporated in the globalising process. That is to say—because a leader's refusal to accept assistance that has been offered will undermine their authority, he or she can be forced to accept an offer of help in order to maintain popularity, even if knowing that the overall impact of the assistance will not be to the people's advantage. Thus a receiver, at least in Africa, generally cannot avoid putting themselves into a position of dependence, even if they are aware that this is "unhealthy" (Maranz 2001).

5. DIFFERENT UNDERSTANDINGS OF "HOLISTIC"

A basic, important, but little-considered matter in the discussion of holistic mission is the implicature (what is implied by the use) of the term "holistic" itself. Whereas it may be clear to Westerners that the material side of holistic mission is achieved through rational means, others (certainly in Africa) are busy bringing it about through what can loosely (given the weaknesses of English in this area of discussion) be called "magic." Many African people have traditionally understood that they prosper if they can please their ancestors. The same reasoning can now be applied to the acquisition of wealth and prosperity in the modern world. So Balcomb tells us that for African people "the goods . . . could be accessed by pre-modern means" (1996). People debating the advantages of holistic mission are understanding the term "holistic" in profoundly and importantly different ways.

Examples of the "magical" approach abound in Africa. The classic is perhaps the African funeral and death rites, which are increasingly being incorporated into churches in some parts of the continent (including western Kenya, which is my home). Some African people will use massive amounts of time and resources in funerals and burial programmes. Additional ceremonies often occur again months and years after burial. An important orientation of all these activities is ensuring that the ghost of the departed not be troublesome; that is, that he or she not interfere with people's *acquisition of important basic needs*. The same orientation is reflected in a preoccupation in African churches with cleansing; that is, a rallying of spiritual forces aimed at the removal or deactivation of troublesome ghosts or spirits of the dead (driving out evil spirits). The difference between Africa and the West is not in the desire to meet needs, but in *how they are to be met* (see also Maranz 2001, 135).

African people who deeply and implicitly believe in magic cannot (from a Westerner's point of view) get their act together to run projects on the basis of Western rationality. Westerners who assume their rational route to be correct get frustrated, demotivated, and even give up when they realise that those being "targeted" are the very people damaging the structures that they so carefully set up, because they are interpreting them from the perspective of their own cultures. How felt needs are to be met—through Western rationality or through combating untoward spiritual forces—is an important question.

Designers of formal holistic mission strategies are typically Westerners. (If they are non-Westerners, then they will be imitating Western blueprints.) Non-Westerners are consumers of such "mission." Holistic mission designed by the non-West will be a combining of the gospel with "magic" (as defined in Harries 2000, here chapter 12) and not Western rationality.

The West assumes that physical needs should be met through donated contributions. This is clearly not the pattern given by the Scriptures. The classic instances in which Jesus fed thousands as recorded in the Scriptures are given as "miracles" (Greek *semeion*—"signs"). That is, Jesus did not raise funds and purchase bread in order to feed 5,000, but instead he multiplied a few loaves so as to suffice to satisfy thousands of people.[5] Similarly, Jesus did not heal people through the use of bio-medicines, but by praying for them and on the basis of their faith.[6] Jesus was a healer and "miracle worker," and not a project coordinator, highly trained scientist, or fundraiser. It is non-Western societies and not the rationally oriented West who are in this respect more closely in line with the Scriptures.

The difference between these is important. "Spiritual healing" (for want of a better term) and miracle working are not dependent on foreign links and a distant economy. They do not create dependency. Their operation is not restricted to a particular people of a particular culture and a particular economic and social class. Spiritual gifts of healing and miracle making may be given to anyone who genuinely believes in Christ.

Those who understand holistic mission as being the utilisation of Western reason from the platform of the global economy to be communicated together with biblical teaching are not following a biblical model. The economic rationality that underlies today's globalisation was not there at the time of Jesus. It is surely wrong to assume that because Jesus fed people by miracles (on very few occasions) and healed people (rather more often), Western Christians now have a mandate to create material dependence of the rest of the globe on them by imitating his actions using alternative, rational means. An extrarational justification and foundation for rationality is a questionable mixing of categories.[7] Modern technology and foreign-funded projects are not neutral mediums of action, but have numerous implications for the society to which they are being applied. These have been outlined in brief above. Making peoples and societies dependent on technologies that they cannot from within their own worldview understand, control, or perpetuate is, in creating a high level of vulnerability to foreigners, immoral.

---

5 John 6:5–13

6 For example, see Mark 2:5.

7 That is, justifying the spread of dependency-creating, "rational" technologies by Christ's command to minister to people spiritually.

6. HOLISTIC MISSION GONE WRONG

Whether or not he was himself anticipating this, Padilla's words, once validated by people like John Stott at the Lausanne congress, have been interpreted by others as ecclesial license for relief and development work. Padilla categorically states that "holistic mission is mission oriented toward the satisfaction of basic human needs, including the need of God, but also the need of food, love, housing, clothes, physical and mental health and a sense of human dignity" (2005, n.p). Hence "the atmosphere generated by the (1974) Lausanne Congress has been described as 'euphoric,' particularly for relief and development workers who 'could now appeal to the evangelical constituency as family, without the fear of either being rebuked for preaching the "social gospel" or being charged of compromising on evangelism (Padilla 2005)'" (Samuel and Sugden 2003, ix).

Did Padilla realise that his legitimising of the understanding that provision of mutual assistance should be a part of gospel preaching in the Third World would result in a class-segregated church leadership? That is, that proclaiming the importance of the church's role in meeting physical needs can illegitimise the evangelistic efforts of those not privileged to have access to a material surplus (or technological know-how)? Given that the church is now multicultural and multinational, that is a slap in the face to two-thirds or more of the world's Christians. Because it is the West that has the economic power to provide for the "basic human needs" mentioned, this suggests that a church not linked to benevolent Western donors will not be preaching the true gospel. Should such a Western domination of the world church be encouraged?

The ancient message deeply rooted in Scripture and church tradition encouraging persistence in Christian faith and service even in a context of poverty, suffering, and trials—never mind persecution—is nowadays all too often replaced by materialist, consumer-driven Christianity. That is saying in effect that non-Western Christians are given official (foreign), ecclesial approval to move to churches that have the most generous donors.

Surely choosing a church according to the possibility of socioeconomic advance through donor contributions is ignoring biblical mandate? Christ called his disciples to *leave* their worldly society in order to be his followers.[8] First Kings 17 tells how God sent a *famine* (and not food aid) in response to the sin of Ahab. The Apostle Paul endured much affliction in the course of his preaching. With the

8 John 15:19.

possible exception of the collection for Jerusalem, he initiated no "compassionate ministries" in the modern sense. I believe that the collection for Jerusalem was not assistance for the materially-deprived, but the making of an ecclesial/prophetic statement (Georgi 1992). Why then are modern-day prophets insisting on being prophets of profit?

Padilla tells us that:

> All too often, the stumbling block and the foolishness that prevent non-Christians to turn to Christ is not really the stumbling block and the foolishness of the gospel centered in "Christ crucified" (1 Cor 1:23), but the self-righteous attitude and the indifference to basic human needs on the part of Christians. The first condition for the church to break down the barriers with its neighborhood is to engage with it, without ulterior motives, in the search for solutions to felt needs. Such an engagement requires a humble recognition that the reality that counts for the large majority of people is not the reality of the Kingdom of God but the reality of daily-life problems that make them feel powerless, helpless, and terribly vulnerable (2005, 19–20).

Have the financial donor/dependency implications of the way this can be heard by a Western audience been sufficiently thought through? It seems to say that "those with money *must* give it to those without it." Have Christians always sought to resolve other people's "problems" in this way? The foolishness of the gospel and offence of the Cross[9] include that someone should give up worldly prestige or advantage on entering the kingdom of God. God's kingdom is like a treasure hidden in a field,[10] promising a deep, heartfelt peace and eternal reward to those ravaged by the storms of life. The insistence that the cross be accompanied by material reward is an offence to the gospel. The quote above bypasses the possibility, implicitly believed by millions of people around the world, that felt needs are met *through* the gospel itself. It is their faith in God that helps people to overcome the "powerlessness and helplessness" described by Padilla. It is through trusting in God that demons of poverty, disease, and helplessness are driven away. What do we say to people who believe this? Remember that Christ himself was heavily engaged in removing demons.

9 Galatians 5:11.
10 Matthew 13:44.

It is widely understood that a genuine Christian life will raise someone's economic standing. That is, someone will be better off as a result of becoming a Christian, without the church being actively involved in "social action." Many reasons often given for this include:

(1) Stable, monogamous Christian marriages rooted in true love and mutual respect between husband and wife.

(2) Avoiding excesses of alcohol and drugs.

(3) In the classic Protestant sense—expressing one's Christian commitment through diligence in one's worldly calling.

(4) Mutual support from a wide Christian family.

(5) Overcoming fear of ancestral spirits and thereby avoiding expensive and time-consuming funeral rituals otherwise necessitated.

(6) Undercutting the fear of witchcraft that dominates many societies and binds them to relations of mistrust, hatred, and suspicion.

(7) A unified and purposeful view of life that arises from belief in the power of a single, concerned and influential God.

These are extremely powerful factors contributing to improvements and changes in people's circumstances. Associating the gospel strongly with Westernisation, which holistic mission seems to imply, may by orienting people primarily to a search for material wealth, denying them access to the above. "Striving" in life comes to be for money and relationship with donors, instead of for productivity, personal holiness, morality, etc.

"The message of salvation implies also a message of judgment upon every form of alienation, oppression and discrimination, and we should not be afraid to denounce evil and injustice wherever they exist," shares Stott (1975, 24).[11] But is it always easy to identify and discern "evil" and injustice? Once identified, how is it to be tackled? Depending as it does on the desirability of ultimate ends, identifying evil is a theological process. The Bible is replete with examples of redemptive

11 As noted by Padilla (2005, 12).

suffering. Is it better for someone to live with pleasure and joy for seventy years and then go to hell, or is it better to struggle and suffer for sixty years and then spend eternity in heaven? Definitions of evil that ignore such questions make implicit theological assumptions. On what basis are these assumptions made if not faith? Surely this points to the foundational importance of faith and theology; that is, "preaching" to bring about social change.

What should be done to someone whose actions we find to be evil? Are they to be punished? Is change to be forced? Or is the primary role of a Christian to point out where they are wrong? The former is tempting but interculturally often paternalistic and arousing of (justified?) opposition, even if this is underground. The latter, while a demanding and complex task, is part of the essence of traditional missionary work, classically carried out by means of teaching and preaching that "holistic mission" proponents seem to be so unhappy with. Should the church join Western governments in using their economic, educational, social, or even military might to forcefully extinguish evil whenever it is "spotted," or is there a valid alternative of "appealing" to people through preaching?

Even if we choose to leave aside the ultimate questions regarding evil discussed above, complexities still abound. Is it wrong to steal, if theft is the only way to avoid death through starvation? Is wife beating to be condemned out of hand if it happens in a community in which the alternative is prostitution that results in AIDS? Is dictatorship to be outlawed if it is the only way to maintain peace between warring factions? Family disputes are notoriously difficult for outsiders to handle. Who will identify the "evil" in the actions of husband and wife to one another, or that occur within a foreign community? Ethicists have for centuries argued the relative advantages of deontological (norm-based) as against teleological (end-based) understandings of good and bad (Geisler 1971, 13). Do we now have the solution? Is it good to allow your child to enjoy eating chocolates from morning to night if he/she wants to, if the long-term effect is an early death through a heart attack caused by obesity? Is it good to assist African populations to mushroom if there is no visible way for them to sustain their increased population density, such that people end up engaging in mass homicides such as occurred in Rwanda in the 1990s? When are actions evil, and when does "aid" become "interference" in other people's lives? There are other similar examples that could be given.

Short-term mission is these days much on the increase. So is the differential in wealth between the poor and the rich parts of the world. So is the degree to which the "poor" world imitates and depends on the rich. Short-term workers from the West are greatly materially advantaged by comparison to most African people whom they come to meet. Is it helpful for such short-termers, in addition, to be told that they have divine authority to condemn the evil that they find? That is, that which appears to them to be evil, given their (frequently very limited) life experience and contextual training? An ecclesial stamp of approval on what can easily be a narrow, bigoted perspective is not, it seems to me, doing anyone any favours. It is much better to concentrate on "'merely' preaching the gospel" (see above) than to blunder forcefully, blindly, and destructively into other people's affairs.

To say that "the church fulfills her vocation as 'light of the world' not merely by preaching the Gospel, but by letting her light shine through 'good deeds'" (Matt 5:16; Padilla 2005, 21) is absolutely correct. I doubt whether any preachers would disagree. If some disagree, then let us pray for them to change.[12] The importance of the life and work of preachers to the effectiveness of their message has long been known. Differences between the current age in the West and New Testament times are that in the West: first, that preached words are themselves no longer considered effective either in drawing blessing or driving away bad spirits; and second, that love is all too often these days interpreted as being expressed financially in monetary generosity and gift giving, and not in empathising, spending time with people, listening, or understanding (except with rational or quantitative ends in mind).

Christians born and raised in the West are facing a dilemma; secular norms threaten to undermine their faith. Already, historically Christian nations present a secular face to the world. "Secularism" is an example of a great nontranslatability. It does not make sense in the "religious" majority of the world. I dare say that it does not make sense to God either, or to those who hold it in tension with some kind of "private religion." This confusing state of affairs should cease to be the front which the West presents to the world.

The key to comprehending a people has always and everywhere (except perhaps in the West in the last few centuries or decades?) been to understand what they believe about God(s). The key to bringing lasting, heart-rooted change to a community is to enlighten people on more of the great truths of who God is and what he is like. If the West is to have a helpful message for the world, then it should share what it knows about God, and not its confusion about "secularism." For "social action," in the broad sense of the word, to be a part of the work of the church is normal. But promoters of "integral gospel"

12 As suggested by the Apostle Paul in Philippians 1:15–18.

are unwittingly playing into the hands of people whose agenda can do more harm than good by promoting unhealthy dependency because what they do is rooted in secularism (see Harries 2010).

The problems of holistic mission are in its implementation. In reality people's problems are complex, so finding solutions is complex. It is in giving license to Western people to force their solutions onto African (and other Third World) communities using Western money and technology that holistic mission has not been helpful.

7. THE ANTIDEPENDENCY MOVEMENT

The growth in "holistic mission" in encouraging wealth transfers from the West to the "poor world" has aggravated dependency concerns. Schwartz is in my view correct to say that "dependency on outside funding" is "one of the most difficult problems facing the Christian movement at the beginning of the 21st century" (2000). He is absolutely correct to say that modern missions methodologies result in "the Gospel itself [being] distorted" and that people's interest in the gospel for the sake of material possessions means that "something goes terribly wrong in the spread of the Gospel" (2000). Schwartz has "stood in the gap," filling that difficult and apparently contradictory position of being the American who is telling people to give (or, in the case of Third World churches, *receive*) less.

Robert Reese calls dependency "a perversion of the Gospel" (2005, 64). He points out that "under the title of partnership local churches or associations have been able to circumvent established missionary policy based on field experience" (2005, 9), thus agreeing with other authors such as Van Rheenan that partnership has simply "frequently become a disguised form of paternalism" (Van Rheenan 2001, 3) and Helander and Niwagila's saying that in Tanzania "fixation in the roles of 'rich giver' and 'poor receiver' has taken place" (Helander and Niwagila 1996, 74). "There cannot be a partnership in a setting up of dependency and patronage," say Helander and Niwagila (1996, 85). "The sharing of material resources is perhaps one of the most difficult matters in the history of partnership" (1996, 125).

Promotion of dependency may be inadvertent: "American missionaries in Zimbabwe almost automatically seem to be preaching a prosperity gospel even if this is not their intention . . . In such a situation, missionaries need a strategy just to avoid adding to dependency . . . yet Africans are embracing them with zeal" (Reese 2005, 37). Such inadvertency occurs because African people make an implicit link between the gospel and the wealth of foreign visitors, as if the wealth has arisen directly *as a result of* the gospel. Western preachers may say things that are true in their own context, but far from true in the African context. For example, someone from America saying that they "trust completely in God" is assumed to mean this as "in addition to their pension and medical insurance." Such not being picked up by African listeners results in the prosperity gospel. Much could be added—many Christians visiting from the West claim to be "spreading the gospel" while being mostly engaged in dispersing wealth. "Bringing the gospel" can be like a cover for handing out money and material.

The solutions that Schwartz advocates to resolve dependency issues include: first, recognising that nondependent churches are healthier; second, addressing the issue with serious determination; third, teaching local people of their obligation to give to their church; fourth, encouraging spiritual renewal; and fifth, ensuring there is local ownership (2000). Reese talks of the need for mission programmes that do not create dependency, good training for missionaries, and mission euthanasia (foreign mission to be so effective as no longer to be needed) (2005, 77–80). He advocates steps that Zimbabwean churches and the American churches relating with them ought to take to resolve dependency issues (2005, 76).

I stand with the above in the solutions they advocate for resolving dependency. I add additional ones below.

8. ADDITIONAL MEANS FOR OVERCOMING DEPENDENCY

I would like to make two suggestions in addition to those above as aids to resolving the *dependency issue.* I do so in order to encourage "missionary work." I believe that the unity of the church will be aided by having more and not less people travelling between its branches and to the unreached. But I see such work as needing to have a different character than is common today. Western missionaries all too often use their control of the purse strings to "take charge" of or dictate (even if unwittingly—see above) to churches. I propose that Western missionaries not subsidise their ministries. In much of Africa, Western missionary superiority is almost guaranteed because official languages used are European. I propose that missionaries insist on ministering using local tongues.

8.1 Missionary poverty

Westerners are these days reluctant to take leadership in Africa through fear of accusations of paternalism. This is very different from in the West itself, where different races of people are actively being integrated into society. At the root of this difference is the wealth of foreigners on the African scene that (combined with their failure to learn local languages—see below) keeps them aloof from and so ignorant of local people's ways. This ignorance, plus the "don't bite the hand that feeds you" mentality inhibits what could otherwise be helpful cross-cultural interchange. The church, as a foundationally egalitarian body, should be leading the field in resolving this perpetuation of interracial barriers (Harries n.d.(b), here chapter 10).

I do not mean by this that Western missionaries should be too poor to keep themselves and therefore go hungry. Yes, it is good to have a "simple lifestyle," but most important is for missionaries *not to use their Western wealth to further their ministry*. This is in line with the biblical model of missionaries making their living by receiving from those whom they serve (1 Cor 9:11). The absence of foreign funding will force Western missionaries to operate according to the contours of African culture. Not being preoccupied in promoting their own culture will result in opportunities of all sorts for missionaries to learn from locals. This is not to say that missionaries should stop people from benefiting from what the West has to offer. They don't need to stop them at all. Only, their own energies should not be spent in promoting "Westernisation" (which is what "development" often amounts to) but in interacting with people using locally available means.

8.2 Use of local languages

Operating one's Christian ministry in the local language has numerous effects and benefits that are these days rarely considered. It results in "enforced humility" as the missionary begins as "learner." Using someone's language is boosting *their* self-worth and a sign of respect for *them*. Using a European language tends to confine a missionary to the upper classes, but using a local language enables ministry across the economic spectrum. Knowing and working in the local language will ensure a "fit" between ministry and the local context. Knowing and working in the local language will be building a foundation that local people will understand and can imitate. It is a way of avoiding serious blunders in communication.

Setting a foundation for people in other than their own language will, especially in this day of global communication and if the language is rooted in a very different culture, make them dependent on the owners of that language. This is currently happening over much of Africa and, in so rendering people incompetent in their own communities, prevents what could have been helpful, progressive thinking and activities from occurring.

9. CONCLUSION

Implementation of "holistic mission" strategies across Africa (and presumably elsewhere) has inadvertently resulted in serious problems, especially an unhealthy dependency of African churches and communities on the West, and a serious impeding of local African initiatives and ecclesial or social/economic development. In addition to antidependency measures promoted by Schwartz, this author advocates two mission strategies to be followed by at least some Western missionaries to remedy this situation—ministering in indigenous languages and not using outside resources to subsidise their ministry. These two strategies, together known as "vulnerable mission," will enable a clear, contextual communication of the gospel and an empowering of non-Western Christian communities.

REFERENCES

Balcomb, Anthony O. 1996. Modernity and the African experience. Bulletin for Contextual Theology in South Africa and Africa 3/2: 12–20. http://www.hs.unp.ac.za/theology/ mod.htm (accessed April 29, 2004: site now discontinued).

Georgi, Dieter, 1992. *Remembering the poor: The history of Paul's collection for Jerusalem*. Nashville: Abingdon Press.

Geisler, Norman L. 1971. *Ethics: Alternatives and issues*. Grand Rapids, MI: Zondervan.

Harries, Jim. 2000. The magical worldview in the African church: What is going on? *Missiology: An International Review* 28/4: 487–502.

———. 2006. Biblical hermeneutics in relation to conventions of language use in Africa: Pragmatics applied to interpretation in cross-cultural context. *Evangelical Review of Theology* 30/1: 49–59.

———. 2007. Language in education, mission and development in Africa: Appeals for local tongues and local contexts. *Encounters Mission Ezine* 19 (August), http://www.redcliffe.org/uploads/documents/Language_in_Education_19.pdf (accessed February 4, 2008).

———. 2009. Pragmatic linguistics applied to Bible translation, projects and intercultural relationships: An African focus. *Cultural Encounters: A Journal for the Theology of Culture* 5/1: 75–95.

———. 2010. Is secularism a mystical religion? Questions of translation in relation to millennium goals and mission in Africa. The Lausanne Global Conversation. http://conversation.lausanne.org/en/conversations/detail/10610 (accessed August 10, 2010).

———. n.d. (a), Power and ignorance on the mission field or the hazards of feeding crowds. http://www.jim-mission.org.uk/articles/power-and-ignorance.pdf (accessed April 15, 2011).

———. n.d.(b). Issues of race in relating to Africa: Linguistic and cultural insights that could avoid traps. http://www.jim-mission.org.uk/articles/issues-of-race-in-relating-to-africa.html (accessed April 15, 2011).

Helander, Eila, and Wilson B. Niwagila. 1996. *The partnership and power: A quest for reconstruction in mission*. Usa River, Tanzania: Makumira Publications 7.

Little, Christopher. 2006. What makes mission Christian? *Evangelical Missions Quarterly* 42/1: 78–87.

Maranz, David. 2001. *African friends and money matters: Observations from Africa*. Dallas: SIL International.

Padilla, René C. 2005. Holistic mission. In *Lausanne Occasional Paper* 33. Paper presented at the 2004 Forum for World Evangelization, September 29 to October 5, in Pattaya, Thailand. http://www.lausanne.org/documents/2004forum/LOP33_IG4.pdf (accessed April 15, 2011).

Reese, Robert Boyd. 2005. Dependency and its impact on churches related to the Baptist Convention of Zimbabwe and the Zimbabwe Christian Fellowship. PhD thesis, Mid-America Baptist Theological Seminary.

Samuel, Vinay, and Chris Sugden, eds. 2003. *The church in response to human need*. Grand Rapids, MI: Eerdmans.

Schwartz, Glenn J. 2000. Is there a cure for dependency among mission-established churches? World Mission Associates. http://wmausa.org/page.aspx?id=83812 (accessed February 17, 2007).

———. 2006. A voice for a new emphasis in missions. World Mission Associates. http://wmausa.org/Page.aspx?id=150494 (accessed February 17, 2007).

Stott, John. 1975. *Christian mission in the modern world*. Downers Grove, IL: InterVarsity.

Van Rheenen, Gailyn. 2001. Money and missions (revisited): Combating paternalism. *Monthly Missiological Reflection* 13 (January), http://www.scribd.com/doc/15176981/037-Rheenen-Money-and-Missions-Revisited (accessed April 15, 2011).

CHAPTER 6

Providence and Power Structures in Mission and Development Initiatives from the West to the Rest: A Critique of Current Practice[1]

1. INTRODUCTION

Healthy tensions in power relationships that are a normal part of Western businesses, schools, and churches help to render these institutions effective. But what of the institutions of "mission" and "development intervention" from the "West to the rest"? Rooted historically in the biblical command to go to all nations with the gospel (as found in Matt 28:19, Acts 1:8, and elsewhere), the latter can be said to be founded on a providential basis. Such a providential foundation for operations unfortunately leaves recipients with little effective authority for counterbalancing or critiquing the way in which they are carried out. While advocated in the Bible for the spreading of the gospel of Jesus Christ, the much wider application of such providentially based principles between the West and the rest today may not be wise.

This author suggests that power relations that include effective mechanisms for feedback from recipients to donors are vital in order to achieve successful aid/development programmes. Until these are put into place, the current system of doing development by foreigners is on dodgy ground. (The motivation found in Western societies today for engaging in development activities in distant

---

1 This chapter was originally published as follows: Harries, Jim. 2008. Providence and power structures in mission and development initiatives from the West to the rest: A critique of current practice. *Evangelical Review of Theology* 32/2: 156–65.

parts of the "poor" world is here assumed originally to be Christian. As in the activity of sharing the gospel, the continuation of development interventions is not dependent on their success, but arises from a perceived spiritual/heartfelt imperative.)

2. FOUNDATIONAL ASSUMPTIONS

In the arguments made in this essay I assume a linguistic incompatibility between the West and the non-West. The fact that one language (such as English) is used in international debate does not mean that people from vastly different cultural backgrounds, such as African as against European, can engage in intelligent dialogue, because the implicatures underlying African people's uses of words are as different from the European ones as are the cultures.

I also question the commonly assumed nature of "dialogue." Considering discourse as dialogue ignores the role played by "third parties." These could be ancestral spirits, witches, or gods eavesdropping on conversations, or the concern that those in a "dialogue" have as to how their words will be reported to others. That dialogues are actually "polylogues" with unknown participants is, I suggest, often insufficiently considered. "Speakers must take all their recipients into account to some degree [and this] . . . can lead to apparently contradictory utterances," shares Kerbrat-Orecchioni (2004, 7).

Given these factors, Western people relying on Africans to tell them about the impact of their interventionist strategies is as bad as African people's relying on Europeans to guide their country's development. For development to be effective, I suggest in this essay (as also elsewhere), it needs to come from the "inside."

I use the terms "missionary" and "development worker" largely interchangeably in this essay because of an apparent merging of roles in recent years. Rational and materially based means toward the promotion of material human well-being have usurped much of mission's traditional evangelistic and proselytising role. That is, more and more "missionaries" and mission agencies are these days involved in and concerned for "development activities," broadly defined, rather than primarily in gospel transmission. This is sometimes known as integral mission or holistic mission.

Many of today's charitable institutions, such as Oxfam, the UN, the World Bank, ODA, etc., operate on an apparently secular foundation. This is surprising to some African people, who understand God as being the source of good and the motivation for people to be compassionate in this world.[2] "How can some Western people be denying the relevance and action of God in their lives, yet continue to be motivated to be charitable?" they ask. One likely reason (to me the most plausible) is related to "the ghost of dead religious beliefs" (Weber 1930, 182). That is, the West continues to be driven by its Christian heritage even in cases (such as today's "secular" European community) when Christianity is officially repudiated.

We can take an example of how this has arisen from anthropological accounts of non-Western peoples, particularly those practicing primal religions ("animism"). Many researchers tell us that primal religionists are chiefly concerned for the well-being of fellow clan members or blood relatives. My own research into the history of the Luo people of western Kenya indicates the same. So for example, the theft of cattle is not traditionally considered by the Luo a crime if it is from those people outside of one's kinship network or clan (Mboya 1983, 12). It is biblical and Christian teaching, I suggest, that has given many Western peoples a global view of the world and a heartfelt desire for the well-being of otherwise unknown human beings with whom they have no blood relationship.

It is important to remember that the biblical command for love to nonrelatives, exemplified by well-known (in evangelical circles) passages such as John 3:16 and Matthew 28:19, originated in premodern society. Therefore the good news that it was commanding should be shared with people from all lands was primarily of a providential nature. That is, it was good news of what God has done and can do, and not good news of what man can do without God's help. I suggest that today's secular Western society has retained the moral imperative of being concerned for all of mankind around the globe, while rejecting its original divine workings.

This accepting of a principle while denying its source and the details of its original association is what I am suggesting has put current mission and development practices onto an uncertain foundation. Does a moral imperative for Christians to spread the Christian gospel extend to the same imperative for the spreading of Western wealth, technology, and civilisation? If it does, we can still ask whether the same methodology is necessarily appropriate for both, or whether the means for spreading the good news of material well-being ought to be different from those of spreading the gospel of Jesus.

I suggest that they need to be different, and that this is for at least one important reason: While the gospel is held by faith and spread by the use of words without creating dependency on either foreign thought forms, rationality,

---

2 Personal observation based on many conversations about God and godliness with African people.

or technology, the same cannot be said for so-called development. A basic fault with recent practice in the area of so-called development intervention is that it is inappropriately modelled on a Christian foundation, while the broader features of Christian practice are ignored. Development, and that part of Christian mission that goes beyond the biblical foundation of "vulnerable mission" (in which the carrier of the message is not loaded with material and financial advantage), has still to find a model for intervention that can render it truly effective.

Such a model needs to be politically, and not merely providentially, astute. That is, we should not rely on God to intervene to ensure that development thinking and technology takes root, just because he inspires people to accept the gospel of Jesus Christ. In other words, the model needs to overcome the tendency of creating situations whereby it is in the interests of receiving communities to accept the material that is being advanced, without necessarily understanding or implementing those parts of the original plan that are a prerequisite for the long-term sustainability of the intervention concerned on rational grounds.

Consulting the literature, one finds numerous anecdotal accounts of failure in interventions into the Third World. That is, numerous incidents in which projects supposedly designed for some long-term, self-sustaining strategy, are used for short-term material gain.[3] This is sometimes called misappropriation of funds, corruption, "eating" (East African English), or even theft. The very frequency of this occurrence however suggests that this negative perspective on such practices is not shared by many of the recipients of outside funds. That is, the donors concerned have failed to set up a dynamic that sufficiently orients recipients to postponed consumption, but have left loopholes which made it in their political interests to abuse the system as designed. In other words, donors place too strong a reliance on providence.

3. THE RUNNING OF INSTITUTIONS IN THE WEST

Western institutions usually operate in the West with (at least) two kinds of political players—those in charge and those under them. The tension arising from the interaction between these two groups, if well handled, results in effective performance of the task at hand. For example, college principals do not expect automatic and total acquiescence on the part of students. Rather a good principal (US English—president) will optimise acquiescence. Too little is called

3 This is explained well by Maranz (2001).

indiscipline. Too much prescribes innovation, initiative, imagination, and with it contentment, satisfaction and, we could say, normal types of healthy social interaction. The same applies to the director of a company, president of a country, parents of children, consultant in a hospital, or even pastor of a church. While the details in types and limits of authority vary widely, it is always true that authority exercised within appropriate limits results in a healthy tension between leaders and followers, whereas excessive or insufficient authority will result in problems.

An effective institution will have mechanisms for dealing with authority that is exercised in excess of, or below, acceptable limits. These mechanisms include: strikes, complaint procedures, verbal persuasion, incentive and reward structures, regulatory bodies, reprimands, the press, and regulations such as on the freedom of speech, rights of appeal, and so on. At the very basic level these include: a common language and culture between leaders and followers, mutual appreciation of the objectives of the institution concerned, commitment to a common aim, patience and perseverance, an ability to persist in the face of adversity, and so on.

Having described these very familiar authority structures, I want to go on to consider Christian mission and Christian or secular development activities from "the West to the rest" in the same respect. That is, given that Western societies are very careful to pay close attention to mechanisms such as the above in their key institutions "at home," I want to consider how they are handled in respect to foreign mission(s). How do Western-originated institutions ensure an appropriate equilibrium in authority relationships in promoting mission and development?

Authority structures clearly vary between types of institution. Mission is inseparable from the church. The authority structures of churches can be very different from those of other institutions. Some would argue that church structures need to be the starting point in considering mission. Characteristics of church authority structures appear to include that a church is (these days) a voluntary organisation. Most of the people contributing to the work of a church are laity. People function in the church on the basis of love. The church provides a context for serving and obeying God, hence theology is a key part of it. The motivation of both clergy and laity is assumed to be other than financial or material, and has much to do with spirituality, eternity and, of course, God.

Few Christians would question that mission work should be integral to the church. For some, mission defines the church, and it is a missions-oriented church that is a "renewed" church. "Contemporary theology needs renewal by mission studies," says Walls (1991). The prevalence of the word "mission" indicates that it also has its own distinct identity; that is, "mission" is not a synonym for church.

The existence of this distinction means that there must be some kind of power relationship between church and mission.

It may be important to consider this relationship. On which side can the "authority" figures be found? Who follows whom? How do the various leaders enforce their authority? What mechanisms exist for ensuring that authority is exercised appropriately? What happens when contraventions occur that would result in indiscipline or in too great a control of the church by mission, or mission by the church?

I am going to focus my attention on foreign mission as carried out by the Western church. Mission from the West is often considered to be bedevilled by paternalism—including mission studies themselves, according to Walls (1991). What are appropriate authority roles for these mission-sending institutions, whether they be professional agencies, committees put in place by churches, the missionaries themselves, or any combination of the above? What mechanisms are in place to ensure that an appropriate equilibrium is maintained for good relationship and effective performance in the various tasks engaged in by the two sides—mission and target community? Who holds the authority, pulls the strings, and sets the pace, and who are the "followers"? With what other institution can the relationship between Western missions and the people they are reaching be compared?

The initiative in mission from the West has been and is in the West. Hence mission consists of the Western church's efforts at reaching the rest of the world with the gospel of Jesus Christ, or motivated by the gospel of Jesus Christ. (Non-Western churches are also engaged in their own mission efforts. These are not my concern in this essay.) The mission enterprise is in this respect unlike a college (the example considered above), but more like a business. This is because, whereas in schools teachers work to meet expressed needs of parents to provide education for their children under the direction of government, in business the initiative is taken by a businessman to meet the needs of people for other reasons.

A missionary will take the initiative to meet the needs of people. But a missionary will not intend to make a material profit from the people, and the needs that a missionary will seek to meet are not only material or temporal but also spiritual and eternal. As a businessman will often attempt to make people aware of needs so as subsequently to satisfy them, a missionary may endeavour to make people aware of needs (for salvation, a relationship with God, an infilling of the Spirit of God, etc.) of which the people may have been unaware, before enlightening them on how to fulfill those needs. The accountability of a businessman to his customers occurs via the market and people's satisfaction with the product they receive. Government activity assists the market process by providing watchdogs to counter the setting up of monopolies, standards regulations, and a facility for the customer to take legal action should a product not meet specifications. But what are the measures that make missionaries (development workers) accountable to the people they are reaching?

We have already mentioned that a gospel missionary's prime motivation in making a "product" available is "out of this world."[4] Because customers do not pay Western missionaries for their service, there are no market mechanisms in place to ensure quality either of the product or its delivery. When payment by customers is not required to ensure the continuation of the mission exercise, then the market cannot be relied upon to ensure product quality. The same applies to many aid or development workers today who are funded from the West.

In terms of the valuation of its product, mission more closely resembles schools than businesses. Hence mission is about making "disciples," a term that is close in meaning to "students" (*mathātōs* in the Greek New Testament). Schools are forced to use examinations and assignments to evaluate their output. What then of missions? People evaluating the performance of certain missionary activity, typically the donors supporting the activity concerned, are forced to use types of "examination." Because the missionary (or development worker) is operating in a culture and context with which the donors themselves are largely unfamiliar, qualitative measures are generally ineffective (for example, the donor does not know the language of the recipients), so quantitative alternatives must be employed. These include measures of the number of people converted, number of churches planted, attendance at events, and less specifically, time spent on the field, languages learned by the missionary, perceived measurable changes in people's ways of life resulting from conversion to Christianity or adoption of a particular practice such as cell churches, and so on.

On the part of development workers, the situation is similar, where donors will attempt to measure some quantitatively discernable improvement in "well-being" of the target population—such as a reduction in the incidence of disease, improvement in longevity, or increase in the quantity of food produced.

4 This is only partially true. A Christian missionary assumes the Bible and the church to be God-ordained and for it to be in the interests of a person to come to faith in Christ with all that this entails for the benefit of this world as well as the next. Yet promoting the gospel in the interest of this-worldly gain easily results in the prosperity gospel. And because the gospel is considered to be ultimate truth, a missionary will share it even in circumstances in which its worldly helpfulness is beyond human comprehension. This applies also, I have argued above, to the development worker.

Both these cases differ from the businessman's model, because the products that they offer do not require payment.

The reader may want to point out that payment can be required. For example, a development worker may demand money in exchange for fertiliser, a hospital for medicines, and a Christian missionary for hymnbooks. While this is true, it is not the mission or development part of what they are doing. The whole point of their activities could be described as being "subsidy." That is, missionaries can bring Bibles for sale without charging for their transport, hospitals make medicines available cheaply, and development workers delivering fertiliser saves a trip to the store. Whatever charge is made is not a part of the missionary or development work, but a residue of the market system in the context of which the missionary or development worker operates.

The differences between mission as it is done "from the West to the rest" and the operations of a church include the idea that, whereas members in the West typically make a net contribution to their church, members (i.e., people) reached by Western missions are often major net recipients of funds from the mission. Whereas the church offers services arising from the contributions of its members, Western missions (as also development agencies) offer services that require its members to receive.

Whereas the operations of Western churches, schools, and businesses are well known and relatively easy to study, the same cannot be said for the receiving end of intercultural mission or development work. The primary reasons for this include the fact that the recipients are culturally, linguistically, and geographically distant from the West. In addition, because they have been made dependent on a supply system that they do not understand or control, the only role that they may be left with is that of doing whatever is in their power to ensure its continuation.

Perhaps a few more examples will illustrate this lack of effective feedback mechanisms. Someone who goes out to a shop (or uses the Internet) to purchase a new watch will be likely to return it and complain if it is not working, because not to do so would be to allow the money they have spent to go to waste. But they are much less likely to take action if an unknown foreigner makes a donation of a watch, and then the watch ends up not working. They may even thank the foreigner for their gift in appreciation of their good intent and choose not to say that actually the watch never worked, so as not to discourage the foreigner's charitable orientation. This applies to many kinds of gifts and services.

Schools have different kinds of feedback mechanisms to this, but are careful to ensure that they do exist. Students themselves can take action in schools, as can parents through all kinds of complaint procedures such as making an appointment with the principal, choosing to move to another school, speaking to the chairman of the parent-teacher association, etc. Church members communicate with their clergyman through their elders, by speaking up at committees, through visiting the clergyman, or threatening to leave the church.

Mission and development projects seeking to reach people in the Third World generally have none of these mechanisms. That is, recipients of services such as education in the Third World do not have access to its (Western) initiators. Whereas church members in the West contribute tithes and offerings to their church, members of churches in the Third World are often net recipients from their churches because church finances are bolstered by foreign aid. As a result, church leaders are not answerable to their members. It is difficult to complain or take action about something to which one is not contributing, so malpractice in provision of services through aid tends to continue. Nationals appointed to supervise aid/development projects are closer to the communities of the recipients than those of the donors and so, especially because donors anyway have only limited understanding of what goes on in Third World communities, will side with the locals on questions of (mis)appropriation of funds. One doesn't complain if something received is poor quality when it is given without cost.

To try and avoid some of the above difficulties, donors may insist that a proportion of the contributions to a given project or initiative arise locally. They apparently do not realise that there are other donors operating on the same basis, and it is not difficult for local people to use one donor to make the contribution which the other donor requires to be of "local origin." Communities can quickly tire of donors who think that, through having made their contribution, they have acquired the authority to force local people to take certain actions. After all, it is hard to say no to a donor because of the financial spin-offs that arise from almost all projects, or because it is not wise "to look a gift horse in the mouth," or because head-on confrontation with someone who has clearly expressed what they want to do is widely considered to be disrespectful.[5]

I began this essay by explaining the importance of having healthy interactions between givers and receivers of services and authority. I have looked at three models in the West—church, school, and business. I have found that mission (and development) work fall somewhere between these. But I have also found that a major difference between mission and the other three is in the feedback

5 See http://www.jim-mission.org.uk/articles/index.html for more articles on related issues.

mechanisms that are possible. Schools, businesses, and churches in the West can have effective feedback mechanisms, as each provide a service that costs the consumer, and/or in the success of which the consumer is closely invested, and/or of which the consumer has a relatively close understanding. None of these apply to missionary efforts as practiced by the West to the rest today.

4. IMPLICATIONS FOR PROVIDENCE AND POLITICAL INVOLVEMENT

It would appear that in institutions such as churches, schools, and businesses in the West, Christians (as others) make much use of feedback and regulatory mechanisms to ensure smooth interaction between leaders and followers. But then, why do mission-based activities continue on the basis of "providence" (i.e., without effective feedback mechanisms)? Is this not a double standard? In my view, this is unjust. It could even be considered racist, as such practices only continue for certain non-Western "races." It is certainly risky—as it is operating blind. The impact of doing "mission" and "development" in this way is these days being seen in the form of much-publicised, widespread failure,[6] although the source of this failure is less commonly understood.

Known negative impacts are largely anecdotal. But there are *many* of them, and stories of the disasters created by aid and paternalistic mission are widely known (see above). I suggest that trusting providence in the implementation of (integral or holistic) mission and development initiatives is not good enough. There is a need for political accountability. That is, attention to the power implications of the roles of the parties involved. Only this will enable us to bring about the kinds of interactions that are normal in effective institutions within the West itself.

The New Testament enjoins believers in Jesus Christ to spread the good news to all people. In recent decades (centuries?) the good news of Jesus being confused with the "good news" of Western material prosperity has resulted in the assumption that this prosperity needs to be spread like the gospel as a matter of providence. But this ignores the very real difference between the two. Spreading the gospel (if well done), because it does not need material investment, results in healthy relationship, interdependence rather than dependence, and a boosting of existing local culture and institutions (Sanneh 1989, 3–6).

6 See, for example, Phillips 2005 and Leonard and Straus 2003.

On the other hand, spreading wealth that happens to be generated through an economic system of questionable biblical legitimacy (capitalism) quickly, and it seems unavoidably, generates dependence, corruption, division, idleness, and so on. (Some continue to argue that this is avoidable within the existing system. These people are determined to engage themselves in trying to avoid it while continuing with the development/mission process in the same way. But, given the lack of effective control mechanisms mentioned above, I suggest that these problems are an inherent part of the way mission/development is done these days, and not an unfortunate, occasional anomaly.) The way the West continues to spread wealth without consideration of the political (i.e., power) dynamics that arise as a result is an inappropriate leaning on "providence."

As a result, I suggest that the model of doing mission (and doing development) with extensive use of resources from the wealthy West needs to be reconsidered. What I have clearly identified in this essay is a lack of (or even the absence of) feedback mechanisms in current ways of operating. The causes for the absence of such mechanisms need serious attention in order to get responsible institutions onto a realistic foundation. The ways to do this include:

(1) The use of the language of the people being reached to be used in the design, implementation, and evaluation of a project.

(2) Having projects that are not dependent on foreign financial or material inputs, so as to avoid the imbalance in power and dependency that this generates.

(3) A reduced reliance on "providence" by the West in activities that they would never consider carrying out through "providence" in their own contexts.

An alternative to (3) would be to adjust institutions in the West to be more reliant on providence. That is, allowing a greater role for God in Western society will assist Westerners to understand how institutions operate on the basis of providence, and therefore be more able and informed to honestly operate in the same way in the non-West. That is, for Western societies (such as the European Union) to be more overtly theological in their operations.

5. CONCLUSION

This chapter has shown that the West is happy to allow the impact of aid through missionary or other engagement with the Third World to be worked out "providentially," even though equivalent actions by the West to their own people are carefully planned to include feedback mechanisms that ensure effective outcomes in other ways. This double standard—an expectation for God to work amongst foreign peoples that is not there in the West's own context—is unhelpful, if not immoral. It needs to be corrected by attention to the power balance. That is, correcting the current situation in which almost all formal power in integral mission and development efforts is in the hands of the donating West.

This correction requires a conscious self-depowerment on the part of the West and Westerners in these activities. Development and mission is these days guided primarily by Western languages, and powered by Western money. The way forward that I suggest is that it be guided by languages local to the point of implementation and be independent of Western funds. This is not to say that Westerners should not be involved in mission or development of the "poor" parts of the world, but that they should operate using local languages, without subsidising their key activities using resources of foreign (Western) origin.[7]

REFERENCES

Kerbrat-Orecchioni, Catherine. 2004. Introducing polylogue. *Journal of Pragmatics* 36/1: 1–24.

Leonard, David K., and Scott Straus. 2003. *Africa's stalled development: International causes and cures.* London: Lynne Rienner.

Maranz, David. 2001. *African friends and money matters: Observations from Africa.* Dallas: SIL International.

Mboya, Paul. 1983. *Luo kitgi gi timbegi.* Kisumu, Kenya: Anyange.

Phillips, Michael. 2005. Unanswered prayers in Swaziland: U.S. preacher sees his dream vanish. *Wall Street Journal*, December 19.

Sanneh, Lamin. 1989. *Translating the message: The missionary impact on culture.* Maryknoll, NY: Orbis Books.

Walls, Andrew. 1991. Structural problems in mission studies. *International Bulletin of Missionary Research* 15/4: 146–55 (electronic edition).

Weber, Max. 1930. *The Protestant ethic and the spirit of capitalism.* Trans. Talcott Parsons. New York: Charles Scribner's Sons.

7 For details of activities related to "vulnerable mission" as here espoused, see http://www.vulnerablemission.org.

CHAPTER 7

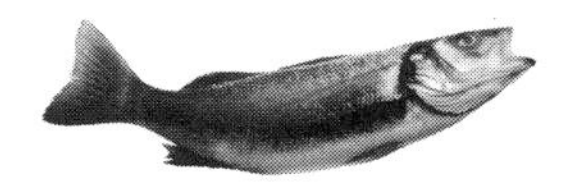

A Linguistic Case for the Necessity of Enculturation in Theological and Economic Teaching Based on the "Shape of Words": Including a Case Study Comparing Sub-Saharan Africa with the West[1]

1. INTRODUCTION

Our perception of reality arises from our understanding of the workings of the world around us. Part of that world is the languages that we use. Assumptions that we make about language affect the ways that we think about things. If our assumptions are inaccurate, then so will be our "reality."

Languages are commonly assumed to be equivalent. That is, it is commonly assumed that what can be said in one language can be said in another. While perhaps less an assumption of scholars, this is very much taken for granted in day-to-day life. If they were not equivalent, then translation could never be accurate. In essence, translation would be impossible. For translation to be inaccurate (or impossible) would be a great concern in today's multicultural, international world. The changes arising in the process of translation tend expediently to be ignored.

---

1 This chapter was originally published as follows: Harries, Jim. 2008. A linguistic case for the necessity of enculturation in theological and economic teaching based on the "shape of words": Including a case study comparing sub-Saharan Africa with the West. *Journal of Intercultural Communication* 18 (October), http://www.immi.se/intercultural/nr18/harries.htm.

In fact, a translated text cannot have the same impact as the original.[2] A translation, I suggest, is always an invention. This has major implications for communication. If translation is an invention and not a reproduction of an original, the difference between the two could be functionally, aesthetically, historically, or in other ways of critical importance. "The debate on translatability is now frankly and thoroughly a part of epistemology," says Steiner (1998, 279).

This would be expected to be the case especially in relation to science. Unlike "religion," science's claims to objectivity require precision. Scientific assumptions hold true only if a scientific worldview is in place. In the absence of such a worldview, science's claims will be interpreted religiously (or holistically). Science cannot be built on a religious superstructure, because then the necessary foundations are not in place to enable its use.

I attempt to illustrate this in a very simple but also very practical way in this essay, by taking words that are used in language as two-dimensional shapes. While doubtless a simplification of the full complexity of the nature of words and their role in communication, I suggest this provides a helpful demonstration of a complex reality.

I follow Sperber and Wilson in denying the code theory of language (1995, 13). To say that words have or carry meanings is, I suggest, fallacious and misleading. Spoken words are sounds of certain wavelength and magnitude that strike the ears and then mind of the hearer. The hearer must make sense of those sounds. Neither ink on paper (1995, 1) nor varying wavelengths of sounds themselves carry either life, intelligence, or "meaning." The meaning arises entirely from the reader or listener. Words have impacts on people's ears and minds, and those impacts by some means, perhaps akin to that described by Sperber and Wilson and referred to as relevance theory (1995) result in people's intelligent acquisition of knowledge or response to a situation.

I apply this study by considering it in relation to Christian mission and development assistance from the West to Africa. I will ask whether and how communication across cultural boundaries can occur. I hope that my readers will, on realising what goes on in the process of cross-cultural, interhuman communication, come to appreciate the importance of rooting the gospel and other "knowledge" into local contexts, and how difficult it is to try to run things in a foreign place (for example, sub-Saharan Africa) from contexts that are very different, such as Europe or America.

---

2 "The . . . claim . . . that the lexical items of languages stand in a one to one correspondence across languages . . . is very obviously false" (Kempson 1977, 97).

2. SHAPE THEORY OF LANGUAGE

Any word in any language can be said to have a range of impacts. Such a range can be illustrated spatially by a diagram of a word as follows:

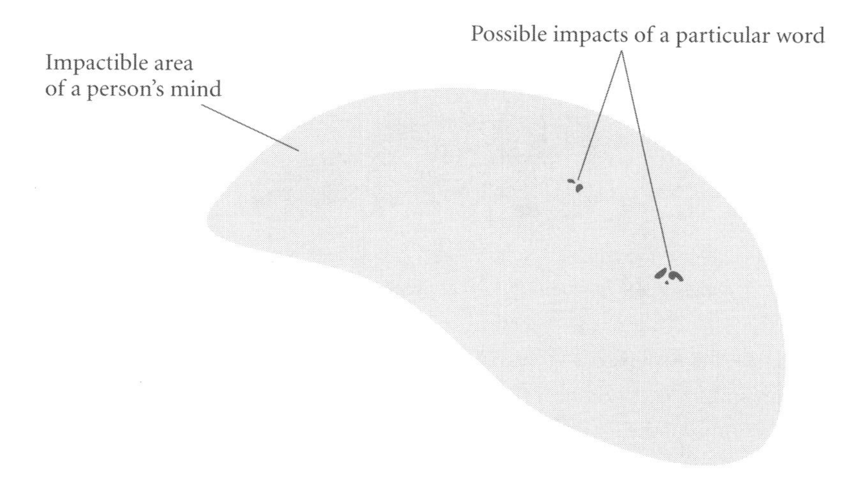

Fig. 1. Range of impacts of a word

Because alternative impacts of a word tend to be related, word "impacts" may be in clusters. For example, take the word "rule." This can be the rule of a sovereign, or the rule of law. These impacts resemble closely, so are in a cluster. But words can also have apparently unrelated impacts, so to rule is also to draw straight lines on a piece of paper. Hence Fig. 1 has two clusters of impacts. These could represent ruling in the political sense, and ruling in the sense of straight lines.

Each impact will have a certain, if unclear, influence on the other impacts.[3] That is, if we talk of the "rule" of a certain king, this will be associated, even if obscurely, with drawing lines on paper. (Such associations are often a source of humour.) So we can say that the good rule of a king straightens out people's lives, as a ruler straightens out people's line drawing. Hence different words are never absolute synonyms. A word that may seem to be a synonym of "rule," such as "govern," is not a synonym insofar as it does not have the association with straight lines that "rule" has.

3 This is known as polysemy, as against homonymy in which meanings of words are assumed to be unrelated (Kempson 1977, 80).

I suggest that a word can helpfully be represented by a diagram such as Fig. 2 below. In this case diverse impacts are collated to give a word a particular *shape* within the theoretical "total range of impacts" of any word. Any word in a particular language can be represented as having a particular and unique shape.

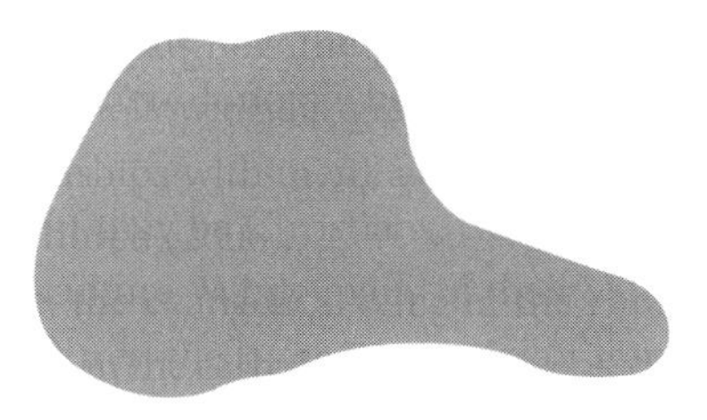

Fig. 2. Diagramatic representation of the shape of a word—including its lexemes

As the shape of words varies, so also does the shape of the impactible area of a person's mind. A word cannot have an impact if there is nothing for it to impact on in the mind of the listener. Often only a part of a word will "impact." A classic example often used to illustrate this is that of types of snow recognised by Inuits (Using English 2011.). Let's imagine that a certain snow is called "firidsnow."[4] The impact of this word is given below, on an Inuit as against a typical British person:

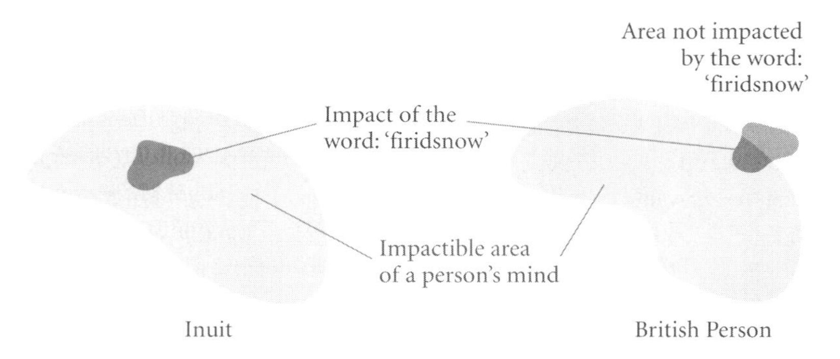

Fig. 3. The impact of the term "firidsnow" on an Inuit and on a British person

4 "Firidsnow" is a word that I have invented. Inuits have many words for many different kinds of snow, one of which I am assuming to be "firidsnow." An Inuit will immediately know what is described by this term, but an English-speaking Brit, who cannot distinguish types of snow, will not know how to distinguish "firidsnow" from "snow."

Because this British person has not had experience with different types of snow, part of the impact of the term "firidsnow" is lost (lighter shaded area for "firidsnow" of British person on right is the part that is lost, so the darker shaded area on the right is what remains), and thus the shape of the impact is different than it is for the Inuit (darker shaded area of "firidsnow" of Inuit person). In fact, the same word can never have exactly the same impact on people whose culture differs. The greater the cultural difference, the greater also the likely difference in the impact of a particular word on a person. Hence the shape of words can vary greatly, as received as against as transmitted, according to differences in impactable area, as illustrated in Fig. 4.

Fig. 4. Transmitted and received shape of "firidsnow" in Fig. 3 above

It is important to note also that words translated from one language to another will, at least to a large degree and sometimes totally, *take on the shape of the word in the language that is translated into*. The original "shape" of the word is lost and substituted for a different one. For example, if we translate "rule" as *utawala* (Kiswahili), the latter has its own shape that is unconnected with the drawing of straight lines (see Fig. 5).

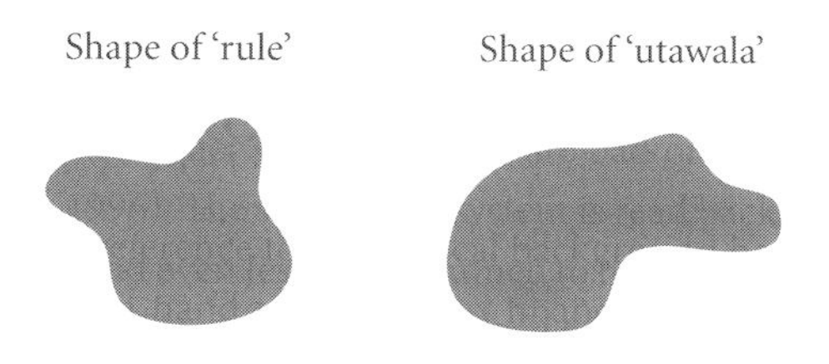

Fig. 5. The shape of "rule" as against the shape of "utawala"

Words that are taken to be synonyms can only be such in certain cases. Let us take the example of "door" and "gate." On some occasions a gate is also a door, or a door is also a gate. Fig. 6 illustrates the relationship between door and gate "shapes."

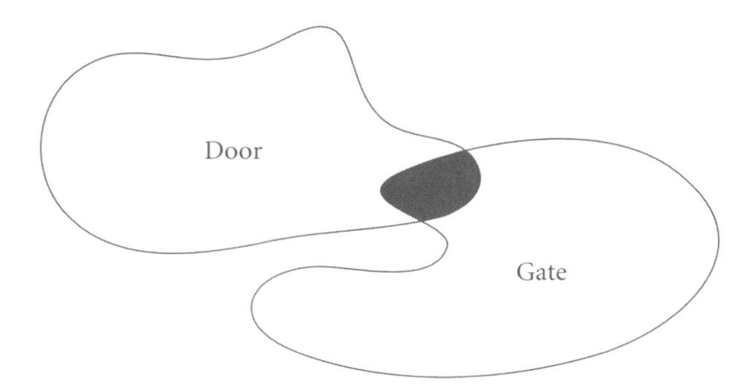

Fig. 6. Diagramatic representation of "shapes" of "door" and "gate"

It should be clear that this diagram is unique to English. No other language will have the same range of impacts of translations of "door" or of "gate" as in English. Clearly even English used in different places will not be identical. Hence no word in any other language will accurately translate the precise range of meanings of the terms "door" or "gate." The types of doors that are also gates are another set of impacts that is unique to, in this case, English.

Note that these words are synonyms only if used in the overlapped section, here shaded. While some doors are clearly not gates, and some gates are just as clearly not doors, there are also some doors that could be called gates, and gates that could be called doors.

Fig. 7 illustrates what happens when we add another word "hatch" to our diagram:

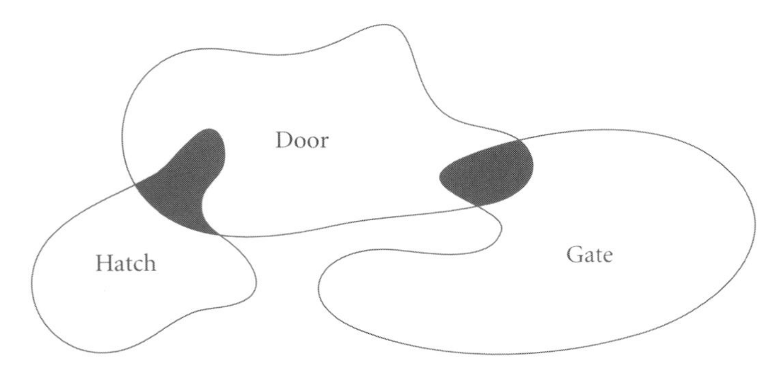

Fig. 7. Diagramatic representation of "door," "gate," and "hatch"

I here assume (I believe correctly) that although some hatches may be doors, and some doors may be gates (shaded areas above), a door that is a hatch cannot be a gate, and a door that is a gate cannot also be a hatch. If a "door" is mentioned in a text or discourse, then it is of course normally the context that will indicate the kind of door being referred to (a hatch-door, a gate-door, or a door that is neither a gate nor a hatch).

This nature of synonyms of course applies interlingually as well as intralingually, so whereas a word in Dholuo (the language of the Luo people of western Kenya), *dhoot*, can be used as the translation for "door," this translation will only be accurate in certain circumstances. *Dhoot*, literally being "mouth of the house," may not, for example, necessarily be a good translation for a door in an outside wall. The correspondence of "door" and *dhoot* will be only partial, as illustrated by Fig. 8.

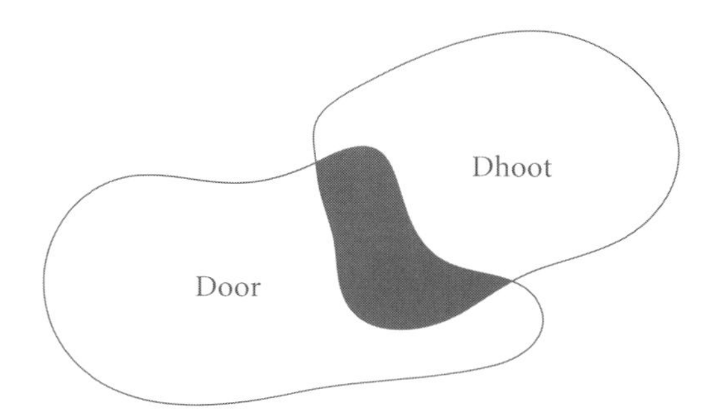

Fig. 8. The overlap in impact found between two of the same words in different languages

To tell someone that *dhoot* translates "door" is therefore going to be only partially accurate, or correct only in certain circumstances.

This is obviously a difficulty that translators frequently run into. One word in one language will not correspond exactly with a word in another language. This means that one word may need to be translated in different ways, even in the same text or discourse. For example, the English word "door" could be translated into Dholuo as *dhoot* in some circumstances, *dhorangach* in others, and *thuolo* in others. The question, "What *is* a door in language X?" (where X is not English) has no clear answer, because it will depend on the context (historical, literary, textual, social, academic, discourse, environmental, and so on).

The peculiarity of the shapes of words is added to by the ways in which words are used in relation to their companion words. For example, "the door is open" translates into Dholuo as *dhoot oyawore*, but as well as doors in Dholuo, the "world" (*piny*) also "opens" (*oyawore*). The same term *oyawore* can in Dholuo be used in place of "good morning"—as a greeting to be used early in the day. So then *oyawore* refers to the openness of a door and is used as a greeting at the start of a day, but "good morning" is very different in impact from "is open" in English. Words are interrelated in an exceedingly complex web.

Native language speakers are accustomed to using words in context of a web more complex than can be given in any written account of their language. Dictionaries are mere rough guides to language uses that must be learned in detail by observation and participation with native speakers. That is, a full lexicon of the words of a language would be infinitely large, yet the human mind copes and constantly adds to its personal lexicon, and to its understanding of the social lexicon of its community. Almost any experience will cause someone to add to their implicit lexicon.

It should be clear that lexicons are derived from the ways that words are used in contexts. These may be social, physical, spatial, discourse, and of course linguistic contexts. Lexicons are infinitely large because contexts are infinitely diverse—a full lexicon would need to describe how every word could be used in every possible context—in practice an impossibility.

What is often not sufficiently appreciated by scholars, I suggest, is that members of a community that share a language are enabled to communicate successfully with it only insofar as they share also the context (and/or assumed context) of its use. The words and impactible areas of communities with different contexts (physical, social, historical, linguistic, and other) will vary in shape (see above).

For a British person assuming it is winter, to say, "it is *cold* outside," means something different to another British person who says, "it is cold outside," while assuming that it is summertime. "She is my friend" in reference to a certain woman means something different said about her to her husband by a man, than by a lady about her to a child. Saying, "I own a computer," meant something different in 1970 to what it does today. To say, "I really must go," after being offered a cup of tea is different from "I really must go" after being asked if one can forego a visit to the bathroom for another ten minutes.

The importance of shape in forming a strong structure socially can be illustrated by comparison with a physical structure. Fig. 9 is a "wall" built with "bricks" that are the words of a particular language.

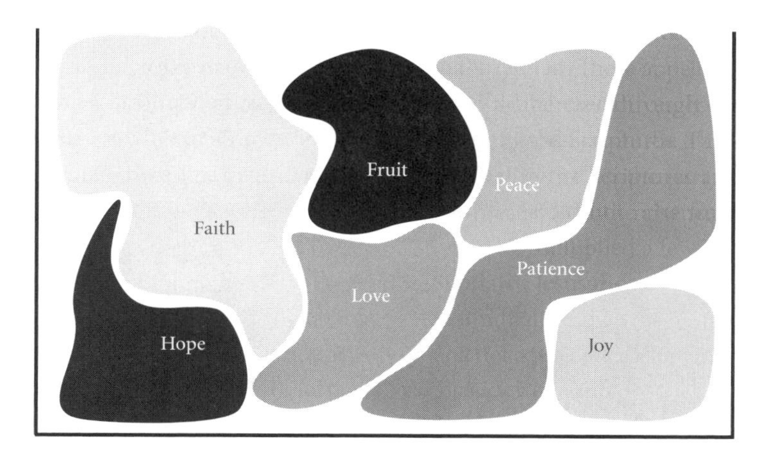

Fig. 9. A language wall: combinations of words that fit together to give appropriate teaching in a language

The words in Fig. 9 fit together well, so that the wall that they build is strong and regular in shape. But what happens if we attempt to use the same arrangement of words when translated to a different language? I have attempted to do this in Fig. 10. Note that the words are arranged (roughly) in the same positions as in Fig. 9, so "fruit" comes above "love" and to the left of "peace," and "faith" is on the far left and above "hope."

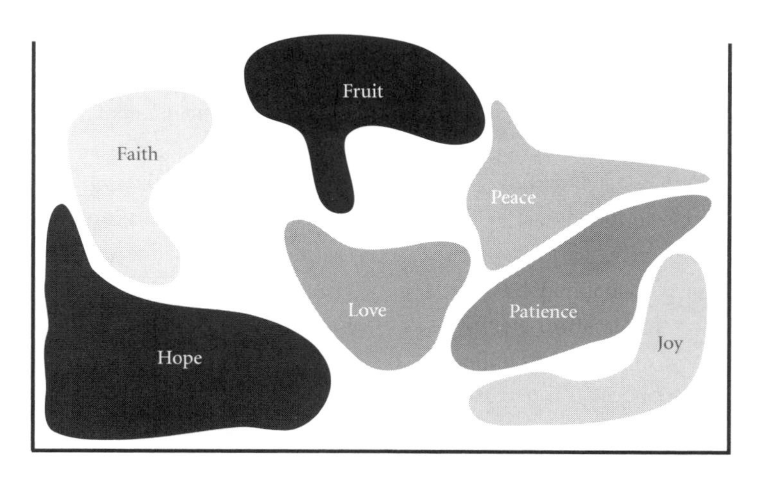

Fig. 10. Words of a different shape put together in the same arrangement as in Fig. 9

It should be clear that the wall in Fig. 10 will not be as strong as the wall in Fig. 9, if the "words" (bricks) are positioned in the same way relative to one another, because massive gaps remain between them. A much better arrangement may rather be found by refitting the differently shaped words in different sequences and arrangements. Or alternatively, other words need to be found to fill the gaps if the same arrangement is to be maintained. Fig. 11 gives an example of the latter.

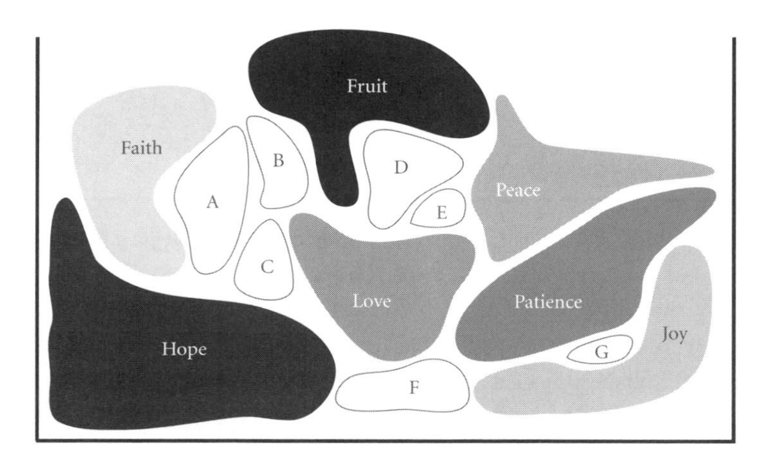

Fig. 11. The case of misfit due to missing words

The missing words A–G may be such as the English words "kindness," "impartiality," "congeniality," and "forgiveness," the content of which may in another language be included into other words.

An alternative would be to alter the sequence and arrangement of the "words" so as to enable them to fit together better.

Producing helpful sequences and arrangements of words and impacts is of course the essential task of education. (Classroom education is a process of rearranging preexisting knowledge so as to form new knowledge.[5]) Appropriate education is that which so arranges the contents of the mind so that given combinations of words have particular desired impacts. It should be clear that this will depend on a context. "Context" must be understood to mean all types of "context" (see above). The instruction needed to guide the placing of the "bricks" of language is the teaching that is appropriate for a given community. Insofar as

5 There is an epistemological difficulty in saying that students learn new things in a classroom through the use of words alone. How can mere sounds (of language) provide what is entirely new? They must instead be rearranging existing knowledge. Particular rearrangements of preexisting knowledge can be considered to be new knowledge. Some implications of these suggestions go beyond the scope of this paper, so I mention them only in passing.

this analogy is correct, then education that is appropriate for a community will depend both on the shape of its words, and the context of their use. In other words, the content of education for one community (if it could in some way be "translated") may not be appropriate for another.

The above brings problems especially where there is a "language of education." In much of sub-Saharan Africa, formal education is conducted in nonindigenous European languages. A child learning such languages in school will clearly learn by relating the new language to the language with which he or she is already familiar. The "shape" of a word will therefore be determined primarily not by its shape amongst the original users of that language (for example, English people in the case of English) but by the choice of indigenous words with which it is considered to be equivalent. For example, if "house" is assumed to be *ot* by a Dholuo speaker learning English, then he or she will assume English uses of "house" to be the same as Luo uses of *ot*. Even advanced learning of English will never entirely eradicate this association from their mind.

I will consider this situation by looking at an example of Christian life (relating to Christian mission work), and then an example of economic life (relating to a development project's impact on Africa).

2.1 The Christian life

I will take the word "love" by way of example. In Christianising people, should they be taught to have love that is the "right" shape, or that has the best fit? If there is a "correct" shape for love, then it may well not fit into a person's context. According to the rules of contextualisation, a person must learn to love in such a way as is appropriate for their context. So it is the fit that is important rather than the shape. Then should a Western missionary to Africa attempt to impart the kind of love that Western Christians have, or the kind of love that is most appropriate for African Christians? How can they know the shape of love that is appropriate for African Christians until they have immersed themselves into the African way of life?[6] Love cannot be communicated in a contextualised way in the absence of a knowledge of the culture concerned.

A prominent term that in my experience often takes the role we consider ought to be of love in African contexts is "respect." People act out of respect for others, rather than love for others. The space remaining for (or need for) "love" can therefore be said to be smaller.

6 The reader may think it is clear that "love" should fit the context. But this can clearly only happen once the context is known, and if "teaching" is based on that knowledge. This in practice is very rare in formal education in sub-Saharan Africa, because languages and texts used in formal education are not indigenous and are not of local origin.

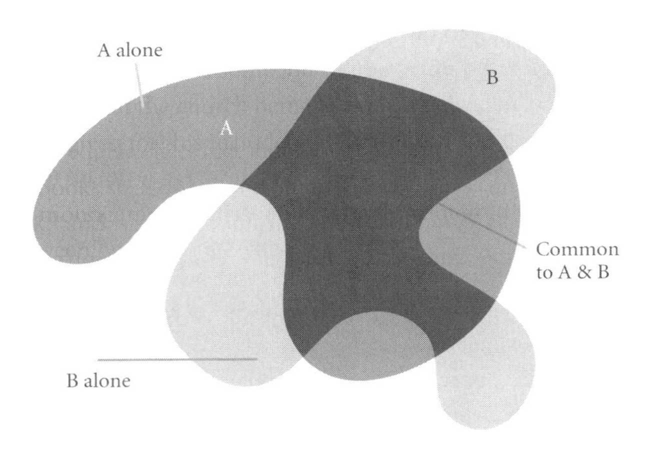

Fig. 12. Two shapes of love and their respective overlaps

Fig. 12 illustrates two "shapes" of love. Let us assume that A represents a Christianised people who are guiding people B into knowing the form of Christian love. According to this model, there are parts of the understanding of love of people B that are common to A and B (the darkest shading), other parts that are missing to B (medium shading) and need to be put into place, and other parts that are apparently non-Christian and need to be removed (lightest shading).

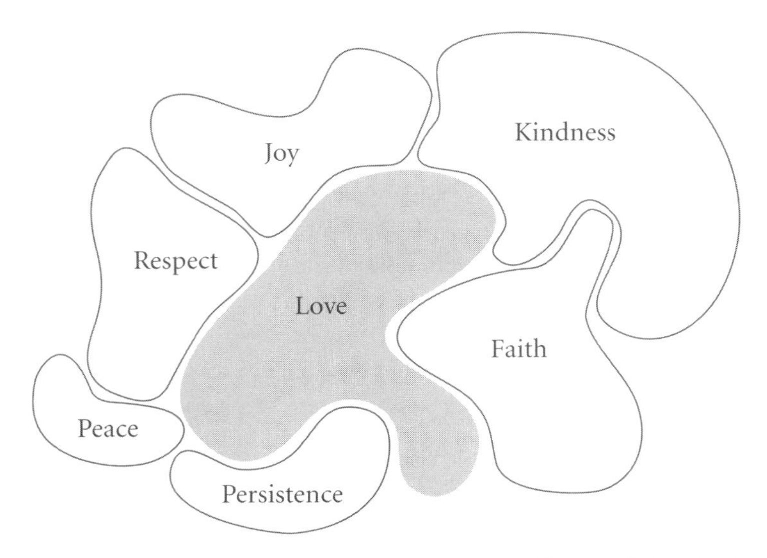

Fig. 13. The shape of the word "love" in relation to its fellow words (people A)

The predominant way in which education and mission by the West to Africa is done today, is by trying to change the shape of African words to fit an assumed European ideal. The ideal shape of a word is constructed in the context of the Western people and culture, and then is exported for appropriation by the non-Western (African) people. Hence African people are through formal education taught to understand and use words in a way that is appropriate *as if* they were in a Western context.

But is this the correct way in which to understand words cross-culturally? Let us take a different model and consider a word in relation to its fellow words, and of course broader context, in Fig. 13.

The shape of "love" is in this case clearly contextually appropriate. This simplified diagram illustrates it in the context of certain other related terms. (The full reality would of course be far more complex, but this diagram illustrates our point.) We see that "love" has very effectively filled the space left for it by surrounding words (and we assume the broader context of people's lives). But this has of course only happened because surrounding words have a particular size, position, and shape. Let's consider that the shape of "love" for people B is as follows:

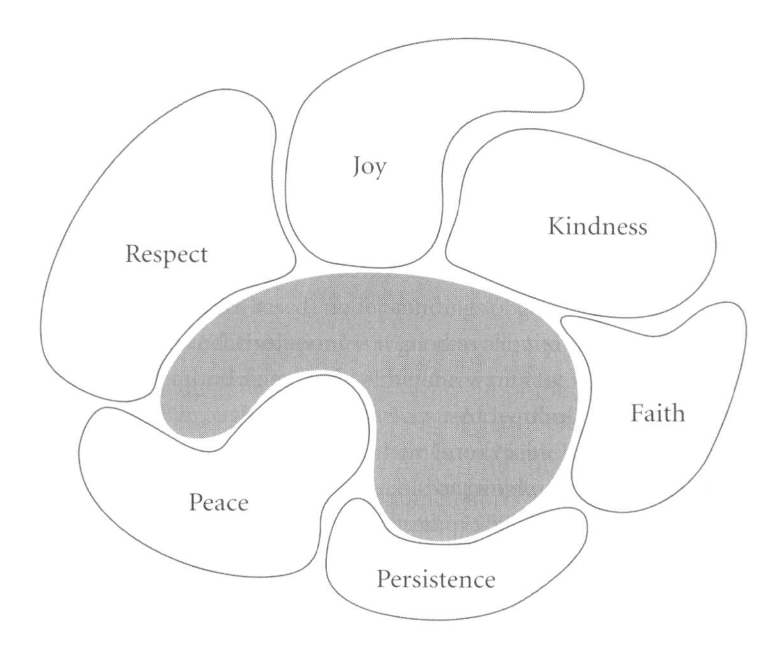

Fig. 14. The shape of the word "love" in relation to its fellow words (people B)

Sure enough, if we try to fit the "love" of people A (see Fig. 13) into the space left in the lives of people B, then there is a problem, as shown in Fig. 15.

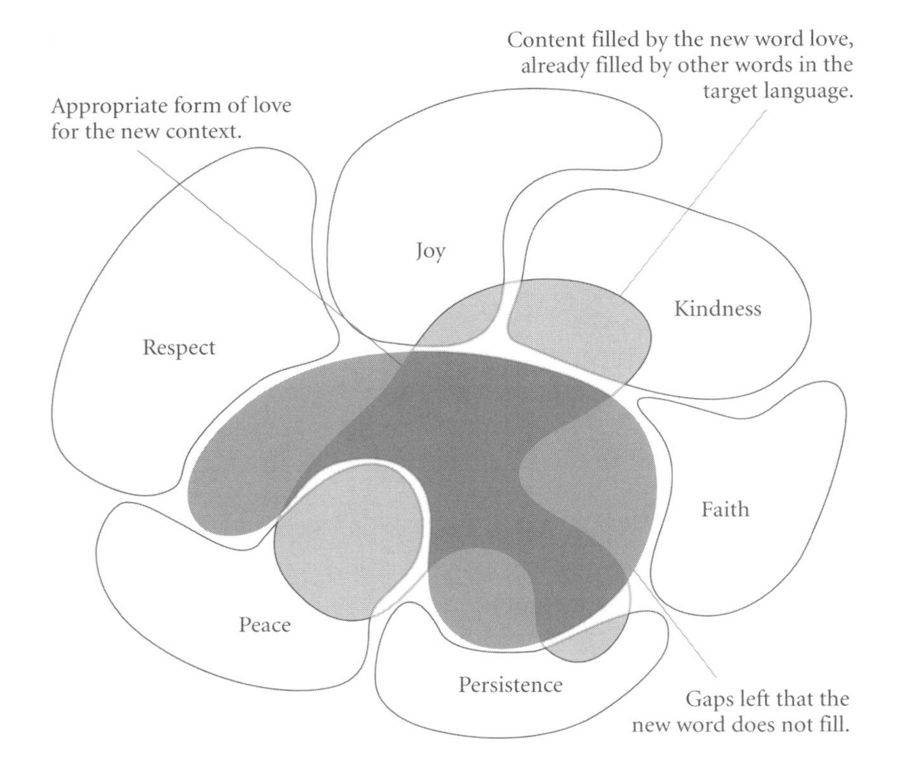

Fig. 15. A shape of "love" of one culture fitted into another

In Fig. 15, the area of the darkest shading represents appropriate teachings of love, whereas the medium shading represents gaps where love ought to be but, according to Western teaching, won't be. The lightest shaded part represents areas where love is taught in an area that is really the domain of another word! The amounts of the various overlaps of course depend on the size of the "love" shape that is inserted.

Despite their being a gross simplification of reality, the above figures do illustrate some important points. An example of a contextual difference that affects "love" as found between husband and wife is the context (societies) in which polygyny is a norm. (This is *not* to say that polygyny is a right Christian practice. But it is to recognise that such a long-held, deeply seated institution has an important effect on its contexts (social, linguistic, behavioural, etc.) and will not disappear overnight.) The need for a man to be intimate with two women makes him prone to lying, as both will want to be assured that they are "most loved." The legitimacy of polygyny forces a woman to accept sharing her husband. The risk of the second woman gaining an unfair share of the husband's attention can result in a woman's devotion to her husband being motivated by rivalry instead of love. The risk of suspicion on the side of one wife of what a man is doing if he spends a lot of time with the other wife—bringing envy, wrangling, and discord—puts the man under pressure to spend more time alone or with male company, and so on. The tradition of polygyny and risk of polygyny will affect a monogamous household in a polygamous society. It should be clear that the "shape" of love between men and women—as against respect, self-interest, competition, fear, and servitude—will be different in a society that allows polygyny as against a monogamous society. This needs to be reflected in Christian teaching on love in order for that teaching to be appropriate (i.e., contextualised).

2.2 Economic life

Where love is advocated by Christian missionaries, entrepreneurship is often advocated by economists. This includes (in the present era) encouraging the free market as against interventionary behaviour.

I will take the public transport system as my case study. This is frequently relatively minimal in Western nations where there is widespread private vehicle ownership. Buses form a much higher percentage of vehicles on the road in sub-Saharan Africa.

Preexistent values in Western countries determine the parameters for an acceptable public transport system. For example, it must be time oriented—thus precluding the system of waiting and then leaving only when a vehicle is full. Effective, functional bureaucracies make fairly certain that only licensed companies will operate in the West. Functional speed cameras help to ensure that speed limits are not broken. The confidence of the public and the absence of widespread witchcraft fears mean that people are ready to report on those who engage in misdemeanors. The small scale of corruption means that police will uphold the law, and so on.

The picture is very different in many African contexts. Many of the above may not apply. Owners of vehicles can pay drivers and conductors at such a rate that they will not make money unless they break speed limits and overload their vehicles. Profit-maximising behaviour in the absence of sufficient controls can result in a chaotic system benefiting fat cats, with an extremely high mortality rate due to poor vehicle maintenance, overloading, and speeding causing accidents. The shape of "free-market" public transport becomes very different to that in the West.

A parallel question arises as to that of the Christian life above; is it appropriate to alter the "shape" of public transport to make it "correct," when this will make it into a misfit with its context (i.e., it won't work)? In other words, is someone familiar with the public transport network in a Western country qualified to advise on changes that need to be made in an African country? The task of rectifying a public transport system is actually, I suggest, much more complex than this and requires a knowledge of contextual factors. Simply taking one contextual factor ("brick") and trying to change its shape from "as it is in Africa" to "as it is in Europe" is insufficient means for providing a remedy for a complex situation.

3. CONCLUSION

Western scholarship frequently assumes that discourses and texts translate between languages and cultures. Translation is here discovered to be invention of something new. This is particularly significant for scientific texts and those whose value depends on the existence of a certain rationality in the target language/culture. This is because language alone does not transform someone's worldview from a nonscientific to a scientific one. Words are found to have impacts on existing mental structures. They do not "carry" meanings. The existence and nature of the impacts of a language arise from the nature and impactability of the mind of the hearer as well as the word itself. The impact of a word is different for every person and context, and especially different between people of diverse cultures and contexts (such as European versus African).

Both words and impactable areas can be considered to have particular shapes. The nature of the impact of a word will depend on the shape of both, and the point of impact. Words are never true synonyms, as they vary in "shape." The impact of a word will depend on its alternative uses as well as the context of its use. All the above mean that lexicons are infinitely large.

As well as particular shapes, words in a language/culture also have arrangements and fits with other words. Such arrangements and fits are unique to a language. Imposing either a shape, fit, or arrangement of words from one language onto another is invariably problematic. Hence education from one language/culture cannot have a good fit in another. Examples given above illustrate in practice how teaching on Christian love and on economics in Africa must be foundationally different from what is appropriate teaching in native-English-speaking countries. Helpful education is, by implication, homegrown and in native tongues.

REFERENCES

Kempson, Ruth M. 1977. *Semantic theory*. Cambridge: Cambridge Univ. Press.

Sperber, Dan, and Deirdre Wilson. 1995. *Relevance: Communication and cognition*. 2nd ed. Oxford: Blackwell.

Steiner, George. 1998. *After Babel: Aspects of language and translation*. 3rd ed. Oxford: Oxford Univ. Press.

Using English, 2011. Language, Thought & Sapir-Whorf. http://www.usingenglish.com/speaking-out/language-thought-sapirwhorf.html (accessed April 15, 2011).

CHAPTER 8

Intercultural Dialogue: An Overrated Means of Acquiring Understanding Examined in the Context of Christian Mission to Africa[1]

1. INTRODUCTION

Dialogue is sometimes seen as the "cure-all" for communication failures in intercultural contexts. If only there were sufficient opportunity for careful dialogue, some appear to say, many of the world's issues would be solved. This chapter draws on pragmatic linguistics to question this assumption. The focus in this chapter is on "dialogue" between (sub-Saharan) African and Western people. I hope that the observations made here will result in missionaries and other intercultural workers having the desire to share in the lives of the people they are reaching as a prerequisite to serious attempts at dialogue with them. My motivation for writing arises from problematic understandings that arise from dialogues engaged in that bypass this step.

Dialogue is often understood from the term "dia-" as being a discussion that occurs between two individuals, such as the representatives of two different groups. It can also be used to refer to "discussion" more generically. I make the case in this chapter that there are always more than two participants in a "dialogue," and that acquiring understanding for practical purposes requires having a mutual culture as well as a mutual language.

---

1 This chapter was originally published as follows: Harries, Jim. 2008. Intercultural dialogue: An overrated means of acquiring understanding examined in the context of Christian mission to Africa. *Exchange: Journal of Missiological and Ecumenical Research* 37/2: 174–89.

2. THE LIMITATIONS OF DIALOGUE

Dialogue can be extremely effective in assisting two people to understand one another, if they already have a significant foundation for mutual comprehension. That is, if the dialogue is concerned with a part of a mutually recognised and acknowledged body of understanding that both then articulate in ways that are mutually comprehensible in anticipated ways. Thus it is good at resolving difficulties or improving comprehension between people of the same worldview, culture, background, or training.

For example, dialogue is a good and helpful means of discussing a book if it has been read by two different people of similar backgrounds. It is obviously not very helpful if, unknown to them, the people attempting to engage about a book have mistakenly read different books, except to get them to the position where they understand that they have made this error. It can be as unhelpful if the two people's approaches to a book are very different. For example, if one is concerned with checking the grammar, and another with enjoying the flow of the narrative.

Dialogue is good and helpful if the parties concerned have a mutual language to engage in. One monolingual person entering a dialogue using Russian while another speaks French is obviously going to be of very limited benefit to either. The potential for dialogue being helpful grows as the languages used come to be more closely related. A monolingual French-speaking person dialoguing with a Spaniard may achieve much more significant mutual understanding, because French and Spanish are more closely related than are French and Russian. A dialogue between people speaking a different dialect of the same language will have yet more potential for success, and of course the greatest potential for success arises if the same dialect of the same language from the same region is used in the discourse concerned.

Another example: two football players could helpfully dialogue on how best to improve a particular team. There will be less potential for good dialogue should they inadvertently be discussing different teams, and even less should they mistakenly be discussing different sports. For example, should one person be discussing soccer (known in England as "football") while another is assuming that the discussion is about American football. Dialogue is effective where the subject of the dialogue is mutually known.

A prior step of finding common ground is often required before helpful dialogue can be engaged. This may be considered a useful part of the dialogue, such as someone's discovering that an engine being discussed is a diesel and not a petrol engine appears to be typical of the kinds of helpful processes that dialogues evoke. Assuming, that is, that this person is familiar with a diesel engine. If not, then the dialogue becomes a time of instruction in which a colleague must explain what a diesel engine is and how it works before further progress can be made. The same applies to the example of sport above. In the above language example, either one party must learn Russian or the other French for the dialogue to continue. Dialogues may require periods of teaching and learning to bring participants together before they can be effective. To summarise, we have in this section found "dialogue" to be helpful in situations where there is mutual knowledge and experience. We will continue to see its limitations in intercultural communication in which this mutuality is, almost by the very definition of the term "intercultural," limited.

3. DIALOGUE REQUIRES A COMMON LANGUAGE

In the absence of a translator, dialogue requires a common language. (We will see below that, in fact, even with translation, dialogue still requires a common language, in the pragmatic sense.) One key question then is, which language? I will try to show below how the choice of language can profoundly affect the form of a dialogue.

I will take my example by comparing two quite familiar and closely related European languages—English and German—and indicate the importance of language choice by focusing on three commonly used words: "bread" (*Brot*), "bicycle" (*Fahrrad*), and "wife" (*Frau*). (Note that according to German grammar, nouns begin with capital letters.) I will look at these words in terms of their implicatures, and not primarily in terms of their meanings as may be found in a dictionary. I will consider the implications of using these words in one language rather than in another.

Brot in Germany is usually more colourful and varied than bread in Britain. Rye is frequently a component. *Brotchen* (small bread or bread rolls) are especially favoured for breakfast. German people will think nothing of having *Brot* as staple for two meals daily. Bread in Britain, on the other hand, is very often sliced, white, and mass produced to be sold prewrapped in plastic bags in supermarkets. It is invariably made of wheat and not rye, and generally eaten for just one meal daily, or less.

Germans are proud of the precision engineering going into their upright, stout, and sturdy *Fahrrad*, on which brakes are often applied by pedalling backwards. English bicycles are more likely to be lightweight for racing. Brakes are hand applied, and reliability is considered more important than engineering tradition for bicycles. Bicycle lights are battery powered, whereas *Fahrrad* lights are dynamo powered.

Frau translates the English "wife" ("my wife" = *meine Frau*), "woman" ("the woman" = *die Frau*), and "Mrs." ("Mrs. Smith" = *Frau Smith*). The word that is historically related to "wife" in English is the German word *Weib*, which is an offensive word to use. It is said that a German *Frau* is proud of the fact that she works hard to keep her house spotlessly clean and tidy. English women's houses are often comparatively unkempt.[2]

Assuming the above to be broadly true, and assuming (I believe correctly) that similar differences can be found throughout the vocabulary of these two languages, the choice of languages becomes consequential. Saying that we should have *Brot* for lunch (made of rye, multicoloured, with more emphasis on taste than on mass production) is in a sense very different from saying we should have bread for lunch. Saying that someone loves riding his bike (likes going fast down the hills) is also different from saying he likes to ride his *Fahrrad* (has a gratifying feeling of smartly propelling a sophisticated machine along the road). There are serious dangers in translating the equivalent word to "wife" (*Weib*) in German, because *Weib* is a very impolite term for a woman. Translating "Mr." and "Mrs." Smith into *Herr* and *Frau* Smith, literally translated back to English could be Lord and Woman (Lady?) Smith. Are such differences inconsequential?

The choice of language would seem to be consequential but, my reader may choose to point out, this is simply because a language is associated with a culture. Two English people choosing to say *Fahrrad* instead of "bike" or *Frau* instead of "Mrs." would surely attach English meanings and implicatures to those words. Especially if they have no knowledge of the differences between German and English cultures.

Such simple attaching of English meanings and implicatures to German words may become difficult, if on further exploring the German language, the English discover that *Frau* covers "Mrs.," "woman," and "wife," or that *Fahrrad* actually translates as "drive wheel." In other words, word-for-word correspondence may not work, even in the absence of cultural exposure to the other. The vexed question of linguistic determinism makes an appearance. Does the term *Fahrrad* mean that German cyclists will be more free to use unicycles and tricycles (which

---

2 While I believe the contents of this paragraph to be broadly true, I ask readers to accept any inaccuracies they find in these descriptions so as to allow me to use them for purposes of illustration in this article.

the English word "bicycle" theoretically excludes)? Is it culturally more difficult (or easier) for a woman to be single in German-speaking than in English-speaking countries, because the same word is used for "woman" as for "wife"? Whorf's name has been particularly strongly associated with the belief that "Linguistic patterns determine what the individual perceives in his world and how he thinks about it" (Steiner 1998, 92).[3] Scholars these days accept that there is some truth in this.

We would probably be right to say, contrary to Whorf's more extreme claims of linguistic determinism, that English people using the German language while living in England and engaging with the English culture, will adapt this language to the English context.[4] (This will be confusing to a German should he then find his language being "abused" in this way.) Then, except to the extent that the structure of a language itself dictates meaning, what is more critical in a dialogue is not the language used, but the culture to which that language is being fitted in the mind of the person using it. Whether English or German is used in a dialogue between an English and a German person, the important question is whether it is the English or the German culture that underlies the conversation. Bearing in mind of course that language in the absence of an assumed culture or context in its use is meaningless. For example, for the word "chair" (or any other word) to be meaningful, someone must have an idea in their mind as to what "chair" refers to, and that idea will be coloured (or determined) by the culture or context that the person has in mind. If both parties are clear in which cultural context they are using their language (English or German), then, assuming that their knowledge of that particular culture is mutual, they should understand one another relatively well.

This requirement for dialogue to occur in the framework of a mutually understood context (culture) in order to enable clear communication has unfortunately already disqualified many so-called intercultural exchanges. That is, whereas intercultural communication assumes that dialogue is possible across cultural boundaries, we have found that it is only truly possible insofar as a culture is common. Having a common language such as English is not sufficient, because the language following the contours of respective cultures will mean that it will be used and understood in very different ways by the two parties to the dialogue.

3 Much has been said over the years about the ways in which language can determine the nature of thought, and in turn the course of life. Benjamin Lee Whorf (ca. 1897–1941) continues to be renowned for having made the case that a language will determine the way in which people think. See Lee 1995.

4 Contrary to the extremes of the theory of language determinism which would force us to conclude that either the German language cannot be used in respect to the English culture, or that its use will, of itself, "Germanise" the English.

Strictly then, dialogue is only practical intraculturally. That is, familiarity with a people's culture is a prerequisite for clear dialogue with them.

The examples of English and German that I have chosen above for illustration are closely related languages and peoples. The intercultural gap is much wider in other cases, such as between European peoples and languages and African peoples and languages that form the main focus for this chapter.

The reader should appreciate that the kind of differences that I allude to above can soon get very serious in practical communication situations. The chosen examples can illustrate this. Calling a German woman a *Weib* is serious abuse. Sending someone to buy a bicycle and they get a tricycle can be serious. Expecting Germans to eat stodgy, tasteless, sliced white bread when they are used to freshly cooked, crusty, tasty rolls made of various grains, could be serious, and so on. This study of just three words has shown that entering into dialogue with Germans, while profoundly unfamiliar with their culture, can very quickly mark one out as an outsider and could have other negative consequences. How much more in the case of Europeans engaging with African people.

4. THE ROLE OF OVERHEARERS

We have in the above section assumed that the two people engaging in a dialogue are alone. But is there ever a situation where a dialogue is actually confined to two people? Geographically, and in terms of a limited time and a limited context, perhaps. So Bill can have a conversation with Jane while they are walking by themselves on their way to work. Even in the case of such a conversation, however, I suggest there are actually a multitude of "overhearers."

An overhearer is someone whom a speaker is not directly communicating with, but who will pick up all or a part of the message concerned, and of the context of the message concerned. Their having only a partial grasp of either message or context means that an overhearer will interpret differently to the listener being overtly targeted by the speaker. Because in pragmatics we learn that word (sentence and text) meanings arise only in interaction with a context (Leech 1983, 6), so as context or order or combination of words changes, so meaning changes, indicating that overhearers are at risk of misunderstanding.

Examples will illustrate the different kinds of overhearers that we need to consider, and the dilemmas that result. I will begin with the more obvious examples. Let's imagine that a man is with his wife in a crowded place when he meets his mistress whom he has repeatedly assured that he is unmarried.

Both the wife and the mistress are initially blissfully ignorant of the identity of the other person. The mistress talking to the man, while ignorant of the identity of the other bystander, thinks that she is engaging in dialogue. The man, while acutely aware that the situation is one of trialogue, is determined not to reveal this either to his wife or the mistress. The responses of the man, unless he is extremely gifted, are likely to appear incoherent to the mistress, given her assumption of dialogue. She is likely in due course to put two and two together, and to the embarrassment and consternation of her lover, realise the actual trialogue going on. One way of recognising a trialogue situation is when the behaviour of a partner in dialogue indicates the presence of another person.

A closely related example would be that of a pupil B, unaware that the teacher is in their classroom, whispering something to a fellow pupil C. Pupil B would be baffled by C's unresponsiveness, until B realised that the teacher was standing right behind him or her.

Third parties can be brought into conversations whether or not they are within earshot. If my boss tells me that I need to move to work in a different factory ten miles further from my home, I can tell him that my wife will not be happy with that. From here on, my boss has to contend with this third party in the conversation. He will be aware that my bringing her into the conversation in her physical absence enables me to put words into her mouth, but that such putting of my words into her mouth has boundaries related to the possibility of my boss calling her to join the conversation or speaking to her later. I am unlikely to say that my wife would rather commit suicide than have me work further away, if this was going to threaten my relationship with my wife should my boss report this revelation to her. Hence certain conventions limit the role of my wife in this conversation within flexible boundaries.

Having pointed out that I can add a third party who is largely unknown to the other participant of the dialogue in this way, one can ask whether this third party was not actually there already. A wise boss speaking to a married employee would surely be constantly aware of a partner's influence on his worker's behaviour, state of mind, motivation, performance, etc. He will be aware that his telling his employee unexpectedly that "you must work all night till tomorrow" will immediately take the employee's mind to the consequence of doing this on his wife and children. Added to the wife and children, there is his mother who has been nagging him to move his family nearer to her home, there is his good friend who has offered him a more pleasant job but with less pay, then there is even his late father who, while still alive, had always advised his son to be self-employed so as to avoid getting "aggro" (problems/hassles) from his boss. All these people are now playing a role in this "dialogue."

While all these people may be physically absent from this conversation, they may well be potentially present, and the boss needs to be aware of this. The man could report to his wife, "He said such and such," which could have her get upset and thus affect the decision of her husband. The children of this man may be friends with the boss' children at the same school, and an overrash decision on the boss' part could have his children come home disliking their father because their friends at school were upset over the implications for their father of the decision made by him. So there are any number of people potentially and actually involved in the "dialogue" going on between boss and employee.

My point here is that there are always absent participants in conversations. The same applies on the African mission scene. My African colleagues may or may not be aware of my "supporters'" whims. My assumptions regarding the view of my supporters from Europe may have me reject offhand a course of action that can appear very reasonable and helpful to the African people advising me. At the same time a course of action that could appear very reasonable to me may be rejected by my African colleagues because of some anticipated reaction to it by their extended family, clan, ancestor, and so on. As it may be hard for me to explain just why my distant supporters may prefer one course of action over another, so for the African person it can be hard to explain to a Western missionary just how negative the response of their family may be to what could seem to the missionary to be a very helpful course to follow. For example, Maranz tells us just how offensive it is in an African community to seek to hold someone accountable for donated funds (Maranz 2001, 38).

Allow me to add some more examples of how third parties enter into dialogues:

(1) A child visits the home of her friend when no adults are present, and then as they talk, the visiting child puts her feet and shoes onto the sofa she is sitting on. Her friend may suddenly become tense, knowing what her mother would say were she there.

(2) A German person wanting to engage in serious dialogue with an Englishman may be unaware that the Englishman had been told by a reputable authority, "Never trust a German."

(3) The very tenets of the Islamic Shia religion authorise its followers to deceive nonbelievers over what they actually believe.[5]

(4) There are some widows who continue to plan and orient their lives to please husbands that may be long dead.

(5) Unbeknown to you, a certain woman is very friendly and helpful to you even though you have met her for the very first time, because you remind her of her son.

In the latter example, the woman's behaviour to you may well be motivated by the death of her son. Her seeing you as somehow replacing her lost son, is an example of a way in which the dead continue to affect dialogues amongst the living. This kind of effect is particularly marked amongst certain people in the world, many African people included, to whom the dead are never truly dead and can be very active amongst the living community while they remain in living memory (Juntunen 2001). In these cases the dead not only speak through the legacy they left when they were alive, but can continue to listen in to conversations and to speak after they have died—particularly in dreams. In Africa these living dead are often known as having some evil intent.[6] Hence in the African context knowledge is concealed through fear that evil powers (spirits), assumed to be constantly eavesdropping (overhearing), could turn it against you (Harries 2007, 44). This has a major impact on dialogue with people of or affected by African cultures and has a massive effect on the possible boundaries of engagement. Imagine someone who is setting out to destroy or kill you being able to overhear all your conversations.

How then are we to consider "dialogues" in the light of the above? We have found that overhearers of many different kinds form part of the context that in turn determines the direction of dialogues. The presence of overhearers speaking into people's heads means that we could redefine dialogues as "polylogues." Kerbrat-Orecchioni tells us that polylogues are very flexible, unstable, and unpredictable (2004, 7). Then there is no such thing as a dialogue in the sense that two people freely discuss with one another. If we continue to call such discussions "dialogues," then we should be aware that participants in dialogues are attending to unseen overhearers and contributors to the conversation in question. For the purposes

5 The doctrine of *taqiya* allows a Shia Muslim "to lie and deceive and deny what they really believe, so long as they continue to adhere to the belief in their hearts" (Sookhdeo 2002, 66–67).

6 African spirits have in recent times increasingly become known as evil (Harries 2007, 58).

of this chapter, I prefer to say that there is no such thing as "dialogue" in the real sense, but I will continue to use the term "dialogue" to refer to people who are conversing with each other. (This could be by phone, face to face, over the Internet, through a handshake or wink, in writing letters, even in exchanging glances, and so on.)

Dialogue in the sense of being a mutually enlightening conversation between two people can work to the extent to which overhearers are mutually known. Unknowns, who are clearly there in intercultural dialogue by its very definition, easily render dialogue as ineffective as if participants were using different languages, because amongst the contextual factors that determine what can be said, how it is to be said, what it is to mean, and so on, are the overhearers.

Christians carry the message of one true and loving God. God's presence should be a demotion of other "overhearers" to a secondary status, thus giving Christians their confidence in contexts where others are fearful, especially of the activities of the dead and of witches, but also of fellow human beings. This is one basis for the strength and worldwide unity of the church.

5. POWER ISSUES

There are many ways of concealing one's power interests in a society or community. Many of these are very socially normal and acceptable. Such concealment can however result in difficulties when it comes to dialogue. As with the above considerations, power issues often become apparent in a wider context rather than in words used in a dialogue. They are also culturally defined and therefore culturally relative. All this means that they are easily missed in an intercultural exchange.

Courting procedures are a complex example of such power play. The agenda of "boy meets girl" is in a sense as clear as a bell, but in another sense often carefully occluded by culturally related insinuations. The failure to grasp these, and for these to work together within the wider social scene can be very problematic in intercultural boy-girl dialogue. Courtship procedures illustrate how apparently innocuous activities are actually oriented to a clearly self-interested goal. A dialogue between a boy and a girl does not have to overtly mention marriage and sexual relations for these to be a part of the picture. When a single girl comes looking for a job, for example, one can never be sure that she is not more intent on finding a husband. This is implicit in her singleness. A similar circumstance arises when considering other power issues.

Some examples of power interests in intercultural exchanges will illustrate their complexity. Is the Iraq war currently engaged in by America to do with oil or not? No carefully worded statements will totally erase this notion from people's minds, because the context (massive, wealth-producing oil fields in Iraq) speaks louder than any words ever could. The Christian-Muslim dialogue is beset with a similar issue. Will there ever be such dialogue in which Christians are not intent to convert Muslims to their faith, or Muslims Christians to theirs? Anyone aware of the context of such debates will know that such intent is there, even though it may never be overtly mentioned. If such a major issue can be there in the context but not the content of a debate, one must ask oneself just what else may be concealed rather than revealed in words used in exchanges. Businessmen interested in clinching a deal will try to convince. Their primary objective is not to set out the total picture in order to communicate truth, but to get to a position where they can make a profit. Here is another somewhat hidden (in any individual transaction) context—the profit motive. Those who remain ignorant of this motive are liable to be exploited.

It should be clear that a (or the) key to the understanding of many dialogues is found outside of the actual words used, in the context of their use. Power interests are often the ones being concealed. A failure to realise this and be aware of "real" interests such as the interest in profit by a businessman making a sale, can result in one being exploited or certainly appearing naïve. What then are the hidden power games played and issues involved in Christian mission from the wealthy West to the poor in Africa? Could it not be that wealthy people who are promoting their beliefs using their money are drawing the attention that they are due to the latter, even if this is never mentioned in actual dialogue? (Or even if this is overtly refuted in dialogue?) Numerous other concealed power concerns may also be at stake.

On careful consideration I suggest that actually to expect this not to be the case is unrealistic. Rather, it is to be expected that people, even if not actually businessmen as implied above, will be interested in promoting their own financial and material well-being. In contexts such as Africa, in which relative poverty abounds, this becomes a particularly important consideration, and even if not overtly mentioned may still underlie all negotiations (dialogue) with Westerners. As in business, where salesmen are not expected to tell customers that "my interest in you is for my own profit" (such is an accepted norm), so neither will African recipients of foreign mission moneys necessarily make the dominance of the financial interests known to donors. As in other dialogues, the real issues may be found in the context of dialogues and not in the words themselves.

Does this matter? Is it a problem to find that recipients of Western mission efforts are in it for the money? Yes, I suggest it is, at least because the Westerners involved are rendered ignorant in the process. Also because it is a foundationally un-Christian way of operating. The New Testament mentions this temptation and this danger: Christ was tempted to "buy" followers by turning stones into bread, but he refused in Matthew 4:3–4. In John 6:26 Jesus accuses people of following him for "bread," and indeed many left him (John 6:66) when they discovered that material provision was not his purpose. Christ avoided it by making "himself nothing, taking the very nature of a servant,[7] being made in human likeness" (Phil 2:7). Instead of utilising the power that he had, Christ "did not consider equality with God something to be grasped" (Phil 2:6), very unlike many missionary and "development" efforts from the West to Africa today, which are grasping for financial and other forms of power to assist them in fulfilling their task. This kind of orientation to money in mission is also a problem because it promotes the prosperity gospel, with all that this entails, and it results in grossly unhelpful dependency. Any initiatives in the church in Africa may have to be Western or Western backed (so Western approved) in order to achieve legitimacy, because God's word is only accepted as legitimate when it looks foreign and is accompanied by money. Finally and perhaps the alternative to the last point would be that it promotes operation through a process of corruption and/or lies that are hardly very appropriate for the Christian church.

The basic nature of intercultural dialogue is vastly different between the West and the non-West. Westerners enter into it voluntarily when and if they feel like it, and are generally free to opt in or out. For more and more people in Africa, it is their lifeline that dominates and dictates the rest of their existence. Opting out is not an option, unless they are ready to accept poverty. This is like a marriage in which the husband (the West) can choose to go from partner to partner, while the wife (Africa) must be seen to be faithful if she is not to lose the ongoing source of her material existence. The creation of such situations of international dependence of the life and existence of one on the whim of another is, I suggest, immoral.

Another consideration under this heading of power issues, is the way in which power and relationships are expressed in covert and guarded ways. Verbal

7 The Greek is *doulos*, a "slave" (Marshall 1993).

commitments entered into in Africa are nothing like as binding as those in the West, as Inge Egner discovered in the Ivory Coast (2002). An African friend promised to attend her function, even though he knew that at the time he would be at another distant town.) Time is often understood differently—10:00 a.m. meetings beginning at 11:30 a.m. or 12:00 noon are not unusual. Even should meetings begin "on time," it is accepted in Africa that many people will continue coming after they have begun. Talking about food as one eats, which I have found to be very common in the USA, is considered inappropriate in the parts of western Kenya with which I am familiar. Two men holding hands as they walk, understood as raising suspicion that they are gay in the West, is a perfectly normal way of behaving to express healthy friendship in the parts of Africa known to me. Terms like "having a girlfriend," that are acceptable and normal for young people in many Western Christian circles, imply illicit sexual relationship and therefore immorality in many African Christian contexts. Words, even if in the same language, have different meanings in one part of the world as against another. These differences are often not grasped in the course of dialogue alone, particularly when the dialogue is in written form or at a distance and so excluding the option of mutual cultural exposure. The differences begin to be grasped when interacting in someone's living context. Differences become apparent through observation in context and not in the course of dialogue alone.

6. DIFFERENT TYPES OF REASONING

Amongst particularly consequential differences between peoples that can be concealed rather than revealed in their dialogues, are types of reasoning. These are so central to much of life, and so implicit in people's behaviour and actions, as often to be excluded from view in discussions. That is, people are so convinced of the universality and correctness of their own reasoning systems as to make it difficult to perceive, never mind appreciate or value, someone else's. But, I suggest, differences between European and African ways of reasoning are very significant. In brief, African reasoning is ritualistic, heart based, or magical, whereas Western reason is much more strongly rooted in the laws of science (Harries 2000, here chapter 12 and Harries In press, here chapter 3.)

Such differences can for a long time remain in the context rather than the content of a dialogue—particularly if one international language is used in that dialogue. (The differences between the parties in the dialogue will be in the content and implicature invested in words, and not in the words themselves). A few examples will illustrate these differences.

Millennium Development Goals (MDGs) have captured people's attention by their claim to be able to alleviate poverty.[8] Few will contest such an admirable aim. Questions arise regarding the real possibility of implementation and not in the desirability of the end, although it is by confusing these two (assuming that a desire to solve a problem is sufficient in order to bring the resolution) that contributes to the success of the MDGs' attempts to acquire supporters. It is ironic that promoters of MDGs end up ignoring the root causes of the poverty that they attempt to resolve, through their failure to realise the contextually rooted implications of African language uses. While planning is guided by Western reason rooted in science, implementation is based on magical[9] reasoning rooted in ritual, prayer, and belief in blessings that counter the effects of demons. Instead of "teaching someone to fish" (surely connected to the worldview of Western peoples), the MDGs are busy giving out fish—demonstrating what can be done from a Western worldview perspective—while the latter remains out of reach of the people, whose magical outlook on life is ignored or even promoted by MDG activities. (Magical processes can be given credit for the prosperity that arises from MDG activities). Opportunities for all sorts of corrupt practices are in the meantime also provided, thus adding to already rampant levels of financial abuse.

I will list more examples of practical differences between these types of reasoning:

(1) Illness is in the West a malfunction of biological processes, whereas in much of Africa it is caused by untoward spirits, witches, breaking of taboos, curses, and so forth. "Medicines" in African languages are products that are effective against such maladies, such that Western medicine must from the African perspective be either limited in its effect in only dealing with symptoms, or must itself have antiwitchcraft powers. The latter understanding obviously has ongoing ramifications for the ways in which medicines are used.

(2) "We must raise funds" sounds like a collective activity, but when stated by a Westerner in much of Africa, it means "from the West."

8 There are eight goals that 192 United Nations member states have agreed to try to achieve by the year 2015 (UN n.d.).

9 I understand that this kind of use of the term "magical" may be offensive to some. I refer them to Harries 2000, here chapter 12.

(3) Is the solution for waterborne diseases to be found in prayer, repentance, an animal sacrifice, or in scientific treatment of the water supply?

(4) Is a woman's barrenness to be resolved by her being examined by a biologically trained physician, or by a curse being removed through a ritual that includes the slaughter of a goat?

(5) Is the need for a road a question of praying, begging, or using one's own efforts to repair or build?

In each of the above cases, the implications underlying contributions to a dialogue may be worlds apart between a Westerner and an African, even if the language used is the same.

Finally, we can have dialogues occurring over issues that are not usually available for discussion at all. The attempt to bring sexual activity into street-level conversations in Africa on the part of AIDS campaigners is one such. Whether or not they have had success, and whether that degree of success has actually resulted in constraining rather than aggravating extramarital sexual activity is an important question. It may be that potential recipients of aid will engage in "bedroom talk" in public only to please donors, and then maintain traditional taboos for the sake of social sanctity and acceptability once they are out of earshot. Many other issues that Westerners may like African people to talk about, even as simple as the welfare and prosperity of their own children, are taboo in different African cultures (Mbiti 1969, 198). These kinds of constraints put Western reason way out of African people's reach. Being fed by fruits that they cannot themselves produce can be at the very least frustrating, but also dependence creating, and in due course generative of corruption and disillusionment.

7. CONCLUSION

We have looked at intercultural dialogue, focusing particularly on that between Africa and the West. We have seen some very severe limitations, as dialogue uses words whose meanings and impacts arise from cultures that are by definition (insofar as we are considering intercultural exchange) different. Dialogue is fruitful if it occurs between people who already know and understand one another's cultures and contexts. Otherwise, it may create confusion, and harmful and potentially harmful misunderstandings. At best, intercultural dialogue is a form of learning about the other. As someone in the first year of an undergraduate programme at a university is not put in charge of a business or factory, so someone beginning to enter into intercultural dialogue should not give undue weight to what they hear.

Dialogue itself is most fruitful within a common context. For a Westerner to learn about an African (and vice versa) through dialogue, it should be over an extended period of years while both are sharing the context which is being explored. It is most helpfully engaged in using a local and not an international language, and is certainly hindered if one party responds in powerful (for example, financial) ways, especially while the dialogue is still in its early stages.

REFERENCES

Egner, Inge. 2002. The speech act of promising in an intercultural perspective. SIL International. http://www.sil.org/silewp/2002/001/silewp2002-001.pdf (accessed April 16, 2011).

Juntunen, Anitta. 2001. Professional and lay care in the Tanzanian village of Ilembula. Academic diss., Univ. of Oulu. http://herkules.oulu.fi/isbn9514264312 (accessed April 15, 2011).

Harries, Jim. 2000. The magical worldview in the African church: What is going on? *Missiology: An International Review* 28/4: 487–502.

———. 2007. Pragmatic theory applied to Christian mission in Africa: With special reference to Luo responses to "bad" in Gem, Kenya." PhD thesis, Univ. of Birmingham. http://etheses.bham.ac.uk/15 (accessed January 2, 2010).

———. In press. Heart-led development: An East African study. In *The modern world reader*. Pasadena, CA: Institute of International Studies.

Kerbrat-Orecchioni, Catherine. 2004. Introducing polylogue. *Journal of Pragmatics* 36/1: 1–24.

Lee, Penny. 1995. Benjamin Lee Whorf. In *Handbook of pragmatics*, ed. Jef Verschueren, Jan-Ola Ostman, and Jan Blommaert, 1–21. Amsterdam: John Benjamins.

Leech, Geoffrey H. 1983. *Principles of pragmatics*. London: Longman.

Maranz, David. 2001. *African friends and money matters: Observations from Africa*. Dallas: SIL International.

Marshall, Alfred. 1993. *The interlinear NRSV-NIV parallel New Testament in Greek and English*. Grand Rapids, MI: Zondervan.

Mbiti, John S. 1969. *African religions and philosophy*. London: Heinemann.

Sookhdeo, Patrick. 2002. *A Christian's pocket guide to Islam*. Ross-shire, Scotland: Christian Focus.

Steiner, George. 1998. *After Babel: Aspects of language and translation*. 3rd ed. Oxford: Oxford Univ. Press.

UN, n.d. MDGs. http://www.undp.org/poverty/devglossary/M/MDGs.html (accessed April 16, 2011).

CHAPTER 9

Mission to the South, Words to the North: Reflections on Communication in the Church by a Northerner in the South[1]

1. INTRODUCTION

This chapter considers Jenkins' well-known book *The Next Christendom* (2002). It asks whether a Northerner based in the North can sufficiently understand the Southern church to write as confidently as has Jenkins. Are indigenous Southerners, who are the stalwarts of the church, able to understand Jenkins? Would they agree with him? How can we tell? Does Jenkins describe a reality on the ground, or a peculiar perception of the North reflecting on itself? Is Jenkins, having captured the imagination of many Northern theologians and missiologists, "correct"?

Economic, social, and cultural domination by the North of the South helps to proscribe the possibility of clear, open communication between them. International debate is almost all in Northern languages. The process of translating the South's real issues into such familiar (to Northerners) linguistic contours results in a deceptive resemblance to Northern orientation, values, and culture. What the Northerner receives can as a result be homely and familiar regardless of the nature of the original languages or issues being translated (Venuti 1998, 5). The South would perhaps not even have interest in communicating with the

1 This chapter was originally published as follows: Harries, Jim. 2007. Mission to the South, words to the North: Reflections on communication in the church by a Northerner in the South. *Exchange: Journal of Missiological and Ecumenical Research* 36/3: 281–98.

North, if it wasn't for its enormous dependence on it. How can one know that mandated communication is truly heartfelt? Kenyan children these days have *no choice* but to learn Northern communication systems—as primary school education modelled on the North and in English has been made mandatory by law. (Universal, free primary education was recently introduced in Kenya.) Over the African continent millions of people are spending long periods in the prime of their childhood (at least eight years in Kenya) learning how to communicate in a Northern way.

Foreign domination and much use of foreign languages have made it difficult to find evidence for a deep intellectual attachment to Christianity in sub-Saharan Africa (SSA). Christian bookshops on the continent contain volumes and volumes of books written by Northerners in Northern languages from Northern Christian perspectives. (Secular bookshops are much the same being typically dominated in Anglophone Africa by English-language textbooks rooted in the North, written in a Northern way, or as arising out of a Northern worldview. These very books are then used in African schools.) Should one chance upon an African author, he has probably had to spend many years in the North (typically doing a PhD at a foreign university) in order to gain sufficient familiarity with Northern ways (and of course language) to be able to write in such a way as not to offend a Northern Christian publisher (or donor).

This practice has a negative impact on the growth of indigenous knowledge. It means in effect that the parts of African ways of life that are different from Northern ways of life are ignored by authors (and readers). Northern authors write from the perspectives of their own cultures. African readers cannot fully understand them because they are presupposing knowledge that most Africans do not have. They at the same time ignore profound complexities of life in Africa that happen to be unknown (or relatively unknown) in the North. This concern is worthy of expansion.

2. MODELS OF LANGUAGE AND CULTURE

Because it is the impact and not the abstract meanings of words that are important, and because a word's particular impact will depend on its culture of use, we can say that every word in one language (culture) has a different meaning to every word in another language (culture). If I say, "I have a house," in the Luo (a people of western Kenya) language (*an kod ot*), this means that I have a wife, as well as that I have built a structure (that may be made of mud) for this wife. "I have a house" in British English is taken as referring to a building, made of bricks, that I own. I can easily have a "house" in British English, even as a single man. These examples illustrate the importance for clear scholarship of talking of the "impact" of words on a context rather than their "meanings" (Sperber and Wilson 1995, 109).

Numerous examples illustrate this point. "I ate at the table" may be an alternative to eating while sitting in front of the TV in some cultures, but a sharp contrast to the norm of eating while sitting on the kitchen floor in others. It is very acceptable to have a "girlfriend" in some parts of the world, but the same term implies an illicit sexual relationship amongst another people. Going to work on a bicycle may suggest someone who is particularly courageous to face the cold weather in some places, but an improvement on the alternative (which is walking) somewhere else. Love may be expressed through keeping a respectful distance in one place, but through sitting closely to someone in another.

Because imported words do not carry all the meanings that they have in their culture of origin, the adoption of a foreign language does not do away with local ways of using words, although it may conceal them. So while my use of a British English phrase such as "he has been healed" implies a biomedical healing in England, that implicature is not carried over even if English is used, for example, in an African culture, where the same phrase could refer to having been healed from being bewitched (i.e., a spell).

Questions of witchcraft are especially pertinent. Southern Christians are engaged in assisting the Southern population in dealing with the spirits of ancestors and threats of witchcraft (Jenkins 2002, 123). Schoffeleers explains that Southern Christianity is an adaptation of the old *nganga* paradigm (1989, 163). (*Nganga* is often translated into English as "witch doctor." "Healer" would sometimes be a better translation.) Witchcraft is often considered as anathema as primitive, syncretistic superstition by the North. Preferring not to be despised by their wealthy neighbours, the Southern Christian interpretation of what goes on is often oral and in vernacular languages. When it is written and in English, much of the reality of the vernacular portrayal is lost. How is the North to respond to this?

The unavoidable reality is that in interacting with a people who "believe in" witchcraft, one is also interacting with witchcraft.[2] Anyone perceiving that their problems are caused by witchcraft searches for someone who can solve these problems as they understand them. A pastor functioning in a "witch-bound" society (Melland 1923) must be able to assist people engaged in this search.

2 For an understanding of "witchcraft," see Evans-Pritchard 1976.

Recognising a witch's capabilities is unfortunately empowering her (or him). Certainly the issue of finding an appropriate theology for dealing with witchcraft is unfamiliar to the North, thus there is a need for an understanding of African cultures in the thinking going into theological formulations.[3]

3. LANGUAGE PRAGMATICS

I suggest that the use of one language (English) internationally and cross-culturally is a root cause of many communication blunders. This is for *many* reasons, which I draw on heavily but can in this paper only outline in barest detail.[4]

(1) The critical eye of non-Northerners who can read the Northern language concerned prevents the Northerner from stating publicly that which is evidently true, because to do so would either:

(a) offend the non-Northerner, or
(b) cause the Northerner to consider the non-Northerner to have been offended according to the former's (sometimes false) perception of the nature of the non-Northerner.

(2) There is a limit to how foreign a thing can appear when the language used to describe it has to be familiar. The foreign, obscure, and incredible easily appears domestic and familiar when the only metaphors available to picture it are thoroughly commonplace (Venuti 1998, 67).

(3) The fact that people will interpret "in line with their experience of the way the world is" (Yule 1996, 141) cuts both ways. Wonderful truths, be they scientific, technological, social, or theological, are frankly grasped in a different way by those in the South than is anticipated by those in the North. Explanations by Southerners to Northerners do not reveal "what is," but an imagined middle world somewhere between reality on the ground in the South, reality in the North, and Northern mythology and fiction.

(4) Enormous context dependence of language unveiled in recent research in pragmatics and discourse analysis has shown that mutual understanding is

3 See also Douglas 1999.
4 See Harries 2007 and Harries 2005.

possible only insofar as one has a mutual context (Gutt 1991, 97). The more distant the context of communicators, the lower the level of understanding. It is hard to imagine a more distant context than between some Northern and Southern societies.

(5) While misunderstandings occur in very simple day-to-day activities, these linguistic difficulties apply the most profoundly and intricately to the complexities of spiritual life, meaning, value, and purpose, which are the bread and butter of the work of the theologian and missionary.

The attention already given in missiological circles to the issues briefly previewed above is, in my view, still inadequate. Hence my emphasis on it in this chapter. I hope that I am making my readers aware of the importance of language and cultural learning as prerequisite for understanding and engaging in cross-cultural mission, and thus by implication some weaknesses of scholarly work engaged in by those who have not passed through such learning.

4. THE CHURCH IN THE SOUTH

Jenkins has, I suggest, given insufficient attention to the interdependence of Northern and Southern churches. The South—and particularly Southern Christians, for the Northern Christian community—have become the focus of charitable giving. (It has been my frequent observation that materials aimed at the popular Christian market in the UK usually portray Africa, and Southern communities more widely, as places to which to donate funds.) The intellectual dependence of the Southern on the Northern church, that has already been mentioned, extends also into material and cultural spheres.

The character of the church in the South is in many ways that of an antiwitchcraft movement. I do not say this disparagingly, and do not claim to have objective evidence to support it, but do suggest (as have many others) that this is how the North could easily find the church in the South to be if it were to take sufficient time to examine her closely.[5] Once deprived of a view of Northern culture and ways of life to imitate, the Southern church would lose the alternative model that it has been copying since its inception. Sanneh tells us that "the Biblicism of extreme Protestantism . . . acted to shield indigenous cultures from Western religious and intellectual dominance [thus conferring] on the vernacular

5 For example, see Murray 1970.

an autonomous, consecrated status . . . more in tune with indigenous attitudes toward language than the attitudes of missionaries" (1989, 208). We could restate that as implying that a church that develops in Africa on the basis of a text written in its own language (a translated Scripture) will be much more inclined to operate on the basis of indigenous principles (for example, as pertaining to witchcraft) than a church (such as the Roman Catholic Church) that imports its live traditions along with the Scriptures (1989, 203). Hence African indigenous churches (AICs), that much more frequently arise from Protestantism than Catholicism, are usually overtly active in countering witchcraft.

I have little doubt as to the good *intentions* of the vast majority of mission efforts from the North to the South today. *I do doubt whether many practitioners in the North understand what is happening in the South.* It would be helpful to consider the church in the South as a mystery, to be approached with humility and wonder rather than a knowing, confident assumption of superior knowledge that results in an overquick assuming of the role of "teacher." Inappropriate cross-cultural mission policies all too often arise and are perpetuated if people do not realise that all kinds of Northern mission efforts can be valued for their side benefits (salaries, gifts, sponsors, access to the formal or international sector, etc.), and not for their content.

Vulnerable, insightful, humble mission is all too frequently forestalled by the failure to consider the linguistic issues mentioned above. Approaches such as that of "ask the people what they want first" are looking for trouble. For example, not wanting to offend the Northerner, whom the local knows is best at and feels happiest at sharing Northern culture and wealth, the latter are said to be wanted. You do not share your deep, heartfelt problems with a foreigner who has not made major efforts to understand you. The nature of the solution on offer dictates the nature of the "problem" referred to. A medical doctor asking me if I have a problem will cause me to remember the strange ache I had last week, whereas the local architect asking the same question will have me ask if he can improve the design of my kitchen. So then what is my "real" need?

In a day when the North dominates the world church, the Northerner who is determined to share the gospel from a position of vulnerability and familiarity with culture will face very real difficulties. Southern Church authorities are unlikely to place a Northerner into a position where he/she is vulnerable, preferring rather to take advantage of their powerful skills and contacts, especially as Northerners are usually much more effective in raising money from their "own people" than are Africans. (There are clearly exceptions to this, and some African people are very effective at winning the hearts of Northern donors.) The ideal place for them from the African point of view may well be in the finance office. Many Northerners anyway quickly tire of close interactions with grassroots African culture. Having financial and other clout, they can easily do damage arising from misunderstanding or jumping overquickly to conclusions if they get too close to sensitive local issues. Meanwhile Northerners fear that African lifestyles will bring them early demise or (biomedical) debilitation. Overall we can say that it takes considerable fortitude, including standing up to the pressure of both sending and receiving leaders, for a Northerner to succeed in being put into a vulnerable position on the mission field. It then takes even more fortitude to survive in such a position without all relationships being as of a "patron." (For more information on how to avoid being a "patron," see Harries n.d.(b), and for an explanation as to just how widespread the patron/client system is in Africa, see Maranz 2001.)

Ironically, the more that Northern mission strategies are influenced by English-speaking "Southerners," the lower can be the prospect by Northerners of understanding the South as it is, and working with the people from *within*. Relying on inputs from Southerners, who are themselves trying to understand something that is foreign and often perceive the gospel as closely linked with "prosperity," is unfortunately often adding misunderstanding to poor understanding. Not because the Southerner is unintelligent, but because he/she is being asked to communicate about something in a way that is foreign to their people and worldview. In addition, most highly educated church leaders from Africa have in the course of their education drunk deeply from, and become dependent on, the perpetuation of springs of Northern wealth. They are of necessity careful to protect those springs.

Theoretically, the exceptions to the above rule would include those "Southerners" who have major exposure to Northern cultures and are able to communicate clearly and accurately with the North by operating as "coordinate bilinguals."

> Psycholinguists have drawn a distinction between a coordinate bilingual and a compound bilingual. A coordinate bilingual is said to operate in two (or more) languages somewhat independently of each other. In essence a coordinate bilingual "controls" two cultures and two "worldviews" corresponding to the two languages in their repertoire. Switching from one language to another means crossing cultural and cognitive boundaries to a different mental universe (Mazrui 1993, 353).

5. NORTHERN CHURCH "HELPS" SOUTHERN CHURCH

The supposed reorientation of mission from paternalism to partnership has been much critiqued. Van Rheenan concludes that partnership has "frequently become a disguised form of paternalism" (2001, n.p.). Yet it continues to be the stated aim across the board. Asking "Am I/we being paternalistic?" is no panacea to this issue. The intermingling of paternalism with dependency, sometimes known as patronage, makes for a powerful force. Patronage is a widely accepted system of social relations in SSA. We must ask: Who will prefer partnership with hunger to patronage with a full stomach?

Maranz does an excellent job of bringing the patronage system in Africa to the attention of scholars in his 2001 text *African Friends and Money Matters*. This text, which rings strongly true both to Europeans who have lived in SSA and African people themselves (my personal observation), explains clearly in a noncondemnatory way how friendship in Africa is inherently integrated into dependency relationships. Maranz suggests, and I concur, that it is almost impossible to develop a friendship within African circles in the absence of a relationship of material dependency (Maranz 2001, 25). The best intentions of a Northern church aiming for "partnership" are not even understood in the South, where having patrons and then pleasing patrons is presupposed as a normal part of relationship.

Yet doing mission with money is a recipe that in the long term spells disaster. This has many aspects: paternalism is perpetuated; racism (in which whites become god-like) is constantly reconfirmed; the ignorance of the Northern missionary ("Don't bite the hand that feeds you") is boundless; and Northern superiority continues with no end in sight (Harries n.d.(b)). Local initiative is sidelined, belittled, and even ridiculed and demonised. The widespread interest in Northern theological education in SSA should not deceive us as to its "real" value to the African people. How can Northern theological education as we know it link in with a holistic, "magical" worldview and Christological paradigms based on the *nganga*? In short, often it doesn't, for many reasons.[6] In the indigenous view, words are valued for their power and not primarily for their *meaning*. In other words, the popularity of Northern theological education in SSA is less an indication of its meaningfulness for Africa, and more of the wealth and power of the church that stands behind it.

6 See also Harries 2006, here chapter 13.

Being easy to understand (as it's *a Northern* thing) and easy to do (it's in *a Northern* language and rooted in *a Northern* worldview), the North is quick to jump to using its economic might in pushing its theological terminology into the far-flung corners of the South. All too often their prepackaged solutions are considered to be applicable to any context around the world, regardless of local conditions, cultures, languages, politics, beliefs, or patron-client traditions. (Global University uses its curriculum for "training the found [disciples]—everywhere" (2006, 9).) It does not seem to be realised that this contradicts some of the very foundations of Protestantism. A major point of the sixteenth-century Reformers, that was to result in the birth of Protestantism, was that people should read and interpret the Bible in their own language and in respect to their own cultures. Then why are missionaries these days forcing foreign theology in foreign languages onto African people? Such theology can be like a wet squib damping local theological initiative. Relevant local language programmes that are able to reach the people are seen to be the "lowest of the low" by those searching for career ladders and prosperity. The foreign, wealthy, and irrelevant thus oppresses the apt and indigenous.

"How can this be?" my readers may protest. Two mechanisms, I suggest, make this not only likely but actual. One could be termed "dependency syndrome." It is amazing how reluctant African people can be to say "no" to the white man, given his financial bounty. Very often the answer is "yes," "yes," and "yes," until a crisis point. Many have learned the profound reality that if you follow the Northern way, you can continue to get bountiful funding. But any suggestion by you that the Northerners have not understood or are misleading people, and you can soon be back on the "poverty heap" with the rest.

To this can be added the deeply ingrained faith by Africans in what we can term "magic." Sub-Saharan African versions of rationality do not search for cause and effect in the same way that Northern ones do. They are more likely to be convinced by that which has power, even if its internal logic is inconsistent.[7] Northern theology is evidently powerful for reasons already mentioned above—its links with powerful Northern churches. That in itself makes it formally acceptable in many African circles.

Those who would argue that it is "better to do something than nothing" need to consider the counterfactual. A course of action achieving a given objective is far from proving that course of action to be the best. There may well be better options to having a foreign-subsidised network of English-language theological

7 See also Tanner 2004.

institutions that teach Northern theology scattered around the South. What appears to be "help" may in the long run be denying the African church its chance to put deep roots into local soil. How much more effective would education be if presented in a language that people understand and in a way that enables the theologian to benefit from life exposure to local cultures and dialogue with people on a par, rather than being a stand-aloof purveyor of superior mysteries? (In fact, once he or she relinquishes the use of European languages, the possibilities for learning on the part of a Northern theologian increase greatly, especially if he/she comes to work in someone's true mother tongue that touches deep heart issues.)

Various factors, including particularly the failure to comprehend the contextual dependence of language and understanding, cast a question mark on the real value of much of the "help" provided by the Northern to the Southern church.

6. SOUTH SEEKS OWN SOLUTIONS

Is the South seeking its own solutions? How do we understand this as happening? Language meaning being contextually dependent presumably means that Jenkins' understanding of this is from a Northern perspective (as Jenkins is a Northerner and writing to Northerners) (Jenkins 2002). That is, Jenkins will by default be assuming Southerners to "think as he thinks" and therefore to be seeking solutions in much the same way that he would. (Or in more detail as mentioned above, that Jenkins will be operating from an "invented in-between world.") "Neither the liberal nor the conservative dreams will be fulfilled," we are told.[8] But could there be another dream being fulfilled that is not recognised by the North? What could this be?

Is it possible that the truth about the church in the South may defy the North's wildest dreams? In reality, I suggest, along with Steiner (1998, 486), that the North is in some respects very narrow in its thinking. A consideration of the extravagant inventions emerging from Hollywood well illustrate this point. While not a connoisseur of film production by any means, I can nevertheless quickly recognise the style of American movies. In other words, the American ideology and identity underlying Hollywood heroes (perhaps seen the most clearly by non-Americans) graphically illustrate the limitations of human imagination and acknowledgement of what is "possible," in social/human terms. The solutions that the African church is likely to "seek for itself" may easily, speaking from a Euro/American-worldview perspective, be "out of this world"!

8 Frans Wijsen, "Nijmegen Missiology Conference Oct. 2005/Jenkins," email sent by Wijsen on February 3, 2005.

Oversimplistic language comprehension can be responsible for the failure of Northern people to realise this (see above). English, into which communications from Africa have to be translated, does not have the means to cover the width and breadth of African beliefs and practices. Much that is common experience in sub-Saharan Africa falls *outside* of the range of life experiences shared by Northerners. This, and especially the overt Northern devaluing of "superstition," renders much of African ways of life invisible to the North. Intent (i.e., ignoring African ways because they are full of superstition) is not even needed for a Northerner to be grossly deceived as to what is happening on the ground in this continent.

In reality, and speaking to the North and not to Africans (for linguistic reasons mentioned above, I cannot pretend to address both at once accurately), life in much of SSA is dominated by witchcraft beliefs, mystical forces, and the rule of the dead. These beliefs and such powers do not disappear in an instant on the encroachment of either the modern (whatever that is) or Christianity. "Confrontation with the spirit world is a central element in African thinking. Western theology, on the other hand, regards demons as superstitious trash," said Kapolyo, "although Jesus Christ himself drove out demons" (2006, 2). As the decision making of Northern Christians is (from an African perspective) dominated by science and rationality, so the reasoning of African Christians is and will continue to be dominated by what could loosely in the North be termed "superstition."

The Southern church, as the Southern community as a whole, in seeking its "own solutions," will apply spells, blessings, incantations, exorcisms, antiwitchcraft strategies, divination, and so on, in seeking for the solution of its problems. Blunt illustrates this in showing how strongly Kenyan society is oriented to deliverance from satanic powers (2004). The history of the church indicates to me that these are not "nonsense." It is often recognised that the Bible speaks more clearly to worldviews rooted in magic than it does to the modern, rational, and so-called sophisticated. If this is the avenue that God chooses to use in maturing the Southern church, then Northerners need urgently to improve their own learning strategies. (That is, to be vulnerable to, and ready to listen to local people by operating from within their own languages and cultures so as to acquire the ability to comprehend what God is trying to do amongst them.)

I refer those horrified by these suggestions back to section 4. Yes, help *is* needed where what itches is currently hardly scratched. But use of a foreign, "rational" language bypasses the key issues. Theological education *is* needed, and the North *could* help to provide it, but then this help *must* be presented in local languages, and in response to "local" worldviews. Reasons for this include that the use of foreign languages will always leave the foreigner in a dominant position. It will not (given the vast cultural gap between North and South) be able to accurately express Southern truths or address Southern contexts. It will severely hinder the opportunities for Northerners to learn from Southern contexts, so that as well as dominant they will be ignorant. It will leave all Southerners' attempts at devising theology wide open to critique by Northerners who will understand the Southerners' writing (or speaking) better than its authors. (See also chapter 1 for further reasons for the need of the use of African vernacular languages in theological education in Africa.)

This is not to say that every single African dialect must have its own theological college and library. Rather, that the above problems are much reduced between one African language and another as they arise from comparable cultures. The difference in lifestyles between neighbouring African people groups is generally minute by comparison with the gap between Northern and African peoples. Regional African languages, while not perfectly suited, are eligible for use.

This situation could change if European languages were allowed to become African. Should communication with European originators of the foreign languages used in Africa suddenly cease, then the very languages will become Africanised. This is not currently happening, because (at least in East Africa) Northern languages are valued exactly because of the links that they enable with the North, and are assessed using foreign standards.

7. EXPLOSION OF NORTHERN CHRISTIANITY

That which explodes can be being destroyed or multiplied. Jenkins, living in the North, sees the weakness of Northern Christianity (2002, 162), whereas I, living in the South, see the weakness of the Southern church. Perhaps this difference in perspective is important. Do any one of these perspectives have a greater claim to ultimate truth?

The linguistic contours in common use in the North are deluding us (Steiner 1998, 22). For "secularism" not to be included in the list of "world religions" is one such. Much can be said of the term "religion," which through translation into African languages and back into English would most often become "life." "Religions" are in the North referred to as "faiths," implying that (unlike ideologies such as secularism and modernism) they are held "by faith alone;" that is, without evidence. What can scholars of religion and missions do about this circumstance?

Perhaps they can start by correcting their writings to debunk those misleading fallacies, and cease to give secular religion privileged status in discussion.

Secularism's privileged status as "not a religion" undoubtedly aids and has aided its spread, as it thereby bypasses different religions' means for protecting their boundaries. (The God of the Bible is jealous of sharing his rule with other gods[9], but secularism has no "gods"!) Claims by secularists to being nonreligious in nature are not true historically, as secularism has arisen in historically Christian places. It arises through the choice of a particular philosophy in preference to another. In Africa it creeps in under the cover of Christianity, all too often leaving African people bewildered as to just where it has come from; it is spread by the very people who claim to believe in nothing but the Bible, which does not seem to even mention many of its tenets! (This puzzle leads some people in Africa to believe that a supplement to the Bible or a secret religion is being kept hidden from them [Turner 1979, 271].

The syncretism of Northern Christianity is grossly evident from the South. Many mission activities, from Northern medicine to numerous projects, are hybrids with secular culture. (They are not found in the Scriptures.) A particular syncretism has given Northerners an aversion to "religiosity." Why are British people embarrassed to pray before a meal in a public restaurant? Why do so many families (apparently) not sing together? Why do our people have so little respect for "men of God"? How can an intelligent people pay so little attention to ultimate questions of the meaning of life and what happens after death? Why are people so easily deceived into believing that having wealth is so much more important than being at peace with their Creator?

This has resulted in a strange paradox in mission to Africa. Secularists deny that their faith has anything to do with Christianity, while Northern Christians largely ignore the fact that many of their actions arise from secular beliefs. Many of the pieces of the puzzle needed to recreate Northern life in Africa thus being hidden from view leaves thinking African peoples all too often floundering. (And then reverting to so-called prosperity theology.) To resolve this situation, I suggest that secularists should cease to conceal their innate Christian nature, and Northern Christians should either "desecularise" themselves or acknowledge the secular beliefs that influence them. While it may be extremely difficult or impossible for Northern Christians to live and work as if they were not influenced by secularism, the tenets of secularism being foreign to African (Southern)

9 Deuteronomy 5:7–10.

languages and cultures make this an urgent requirement for the sake of clear communication. (Perhaps teaching of Greek classics and philosophers would be an aid toward Northern honesty in self-presentation to Africans. The writings of the ancient Greeks, addressing cultures that resemble some African ones, make them into a potential "bridge.")

Secularist religion clearly has important weaknesses (such as that it offers no hope for eternity). Its grandiose claims being a deception, I presume that it will pass and return people to its living roots—vital Christianity. An increasing proportion of the population becoming aware of the deception of secularism may result in a boom in Christianity in the North. Those who see Islam as a greater threat than secularism to Christianity in the North are probably correct. By comparison with the long history of strained relations between Christianity and Islam, the threat of communism has been merely a small blip, and so probably will be the fate of secularism.

8. FURTHER COMMENTS ON JENKINS

Jenkins has scratched where missiologists have itched. His research may have been thorough, but his being heavily grounded in Northern-worldview perceptions has given his writing significant weaknesses.

Jenkins' own acknowledgements as to the weaknesses of the quantitative approach that he uses, appears to be an attempt to preempt his critics. (For example, see Jenkins' intentional critique of "clever men" as if to set himself up as straw man, but then to remain standing (2002, 211)!) His frequent, distant extrapolations of current trends and his heavy reliance on numbers, indicates methodological weakness and a lack of theoretical depth and profundity.

Jenkins considers that it is they're being "ordinary" that results in there being less interest in mission churches than in AICs by researchers in the South (2002, 58). I suggest that the difference between these groups is not fundamentally in nature ("ordinariness"), but in degree of openness. That is, AICs do openly what mission churches hide in their attempt to imitate and please the North. Jenkins considers that people in the South are adapting Christianity to their cultures (2002, 51 and 133). I find this to be a common but erroneous understanding amongst missiologists. Southern Christians perceive themselves as adapting their culture to the gospel, but that gospel being as understood in their own language (Kuhn 2001, 89).

While Jenkins does not reveal his own stand, his considering Christianity's appeal as "surprising" (2002, 39) suggests that he writes as a secularist. While Jenkins' heralding of missionary work as a great success story (2002) is long overdue, he makes insufficient effort to consider the strengths and weaknesses of different mission policies. He reveals his own secular foundations by promoting mission by money (2002, 213), even though later contradicting this position in sharing that Christianity fares the best in a situation of relative poverty (2002, 218).

Jenkins' lack of awareness of the importance of linguistic considerations in his research, while perhaps not uncommon, takes him off course. His having accepted Northern (English) language categorisations (classically in the use of the term "religion"), while claiming to write on many non-Northern cultures, is perpetuating some of the very paternalism he seems to want to dispense with.

9. CONCLUSION

I find myself in disagreement with Jenkins' pessimism on the North and optimism on the South. Recognising secularism for what it is—a new religious movement (NEREMO) that has broken away from mainstream Christianity—will help us to avoid its deceptions. Recognising that the North does not "know" what it thinks it knows about the church in the South, once having perceived the deceptiveness of language use, will help us to realise where the church in the South is in its need for relationship with the North. An open recognition of Northern Christianity's syncretism with secularism could easily be followed by a renewal of Christianity. Mission to the South can then benefit from renewed spirituality and consist of a seeking to share the gospel of Jesus with people as they are, instead of the recent preoccupation with short-term efforts at secularisation in the name of Christianisation, and presupposing that "Southern" Christians (and non-Christians) are really much the same as "Northerners." Pragmatics, specifically the consideration of language in terms of its impact rather than its meaning, is used to question the legitimacy of Jenkins' knowledge of the Southern church. Northern domination of Southern Christianity (and the South in general) is seen as a threat to the Southern church. Colonial, and particularly postcolonial, North/South relations aggravate corruption in the South and promote a shallow imitation of Northern ways, which forms a thin veneer over lives that are deeply rooted in magical/witchcraft worldviews. The widespread, negative evaluation of Northern Christianity is here identified with a linguistic idiosyncrasy arising from the preeminence of secularism in the North. "Southern English" makes different sense of the term "religion." Christianity is a way of life. Secularism is also a way of life, and it was its being omitted from Jenkins' look at the world religious scene that has given it a misleading singular status.

REFERENCES

Blunt, Robert. 2004. Satan is an imitator: Kenya's recent cosmology of corruption. In *Producing African futures: Ritual and reproduction in a new liberal age*, ed. Brad Weiss, 294–328. Leiden, Netherlands: Brill.

Douglas, Mary. 1999. Sorcery accusations unleashed: The Lele revisited, 1987. *Africa: Journal of the International Africa Institute* 69/2: 177–93.

Evans-Pritchard, E. E. 1976. *Witchcraft, oracles and magic among the Azande*. Oxford: Clarendon.

Global University. 2006. Global University: *Undergraduate studies catalog 2006*. Springfield, MO: Global Univ.

Gutt, Ernst-August. 1991. *Translation and relevance: Cognition and context*. Oxford: Basil Blackwell.

Harries, Jim. 2005. Missions, international relations, and inter-sport language in the African context. *Jim's Journal* April 2005. http://www.jim-mission.org.uk/journal/j200504.html (accessed April 16, 2011).

———. 2006. Biblical hermeneutics in relation to conventions of language use in Africa: Pragmatics applied to interpretation in cross-cultural context. *Evangelical Review of Theology* 30/1: 49–59.

———. 2007. Pragmatic theory applied to Christian mission in Africa: With special reference to Luo responses to "bad" in Gem, Kenya. PhD thesis, Univ. of Birmingham. http://etheses.bham.ac.uk/15 (accessed January 2, 2010).

———. 2009. "The name of God in Africa" and related contemporary theological, development and linguistic concerns. *Exchange: Journal of Missiological and Ecumenical Research* 38/3: 271–91.

———. n.d. Power and ignorance on the mission field or the hazards of feeding crowds. http://www.jim-mission.org.uk/articles/power-and-ignorance.pdf (accessed April 15, 2011).

Jenkins, Philip. 2002. *The next Christendom: The coming of global Christianity*. Oxford: Oxford Univ. Press.

Kapolyo, Joe. 2006. Africans need African theology: Western theology fails to address African needs. In *WEA theological news on-line: Promoting biblical truth by networking theologians* (May), 45.

Kuhn, Marko. 2001. From African consciousness to subconscious inculturation: A study into African independent churches (AICs) in Nyanza/Kenya. Thesis, Univ. of Frieburg.

Maranz, David. 2001. *African friends and money matters: Observations from Africa.* Dallas: SIL International.

Mazrui, Alamin M. 1993. Language and the quest for liberation in Africa: The legacy of Frantz Fanon. *Third World Quarterly* 14/2: 351–63.

Melland, Frank H. 1923. *In witch-bound Africa: An account of the primitive Kaonde tribe and their beliefs.* Philadelphia: Lippincott.

Murray, Jocelyn. 1970. Interrelationships between witchcraft eradication movements and Christianity in Central Africa. Paper presented at the UCLA Conference on the History of African Religious Systems, in Dar es Salaam, Tanzania. June 1970.

Sanneh, Lamin. 1989. *Translating the message: The missionary impact on culture.* Maryknoll, NY: Orbis Books.

Schoffeleers, Matthew. 1989. Folk Christology in Africa: The dialectics of the Nganga paradigm. *Journal of Religion in Africa* 19/2: 157–83.

Sperber, Dan, and Deirdre Wilson. 1995. *Relevance: Communication and cognition.* 2nd ed. Oxford: Blackwell.

Steiner, George. 1998. *After Babel: Aspects of language and translation.* 3rd ed. Oxford: Oxford Univ. Press.

Tanner, R. E. S. 2004. The inequality of unwritten languages: Some reflections on the Christian use of the vernacular in Eastern Africa. *Nordic Journal of African Studies* 13/1: 65–75.

Turner, Harold W., ed. 1979. *Religious innovation in Africa: Collected essays on new religious movements.* Boston: G. K. Hall.

Van Rheenen, Gailyn. 2001. Money and missions (revisited): Combating paternalism. *Monthly Missiological Reflection* 13 (January), http://www.scribd.com/doc/15176981/037-Rheenen-Money-and-Missions-Revisited (accessed April 16, 2011).

Venuti, Lawrence. 1998. *The scandals of translation: Towards an ethics of difference.* London: Routledge.

Yule, George. 1996. *The study of language.* 2nd ed. Cambridge: Cambridge Univ. Press.

CHAPTER 10

Racism in Reverse: The Impact of the West on Racism in Africa[1]

1. INTRODUCTION

This chapter has been motivated through the observation that degrees of racial mixing vary between Western and sub-Saharan African contexts. Major efforts at promoting racial mixing and equality in the West have achieved a large degree of (at least apparent) success. That is, Western communities are populated by people of many different shades of colour, with similar standards of living, and working closely side by side. This does not seem to have been achieved in Africa. This chapter asks whether it is possible that policies regarding race relations in the West are antagonistic to the African context of race. It makes some suggestions on how race-relation policies could be designed on an international rather than a Western-focused basis.

The research methodology used in this chapter is modelled on that used by Blommaert and Verschueren in their study on Belgian people's attitudes to Muslim immigrants (1998). Discussion is based on implicit and not explicit communication. The difficulties of doing this in oral communities using non-Western languages have been overcome by drawing on the author's (subjective) insights acquired in two decades of exposure to rural life in Africa.

This chapter orients Western workers going to Africa to know how to most effectively engage in the cultures that they are meeting so as to achieve maximum long-term benefits for the native people. The author's experience in Africa has

---

1 This chapter was originally published as follows: Harries, Jim. Issues of race in relating to Africa: Linguistic and cultural insights that could avoid traps. http://www.civilizationoflove.org/httpdocs/archives/faceofafrica/Jim_Harries.pdf (accessed January 28, 2010; site now discontinued).

been acquired largely in western Kenya, but also elsewhere in Kenya, Tanzania, Zambia, and beyond. The African context explicitly referred to in this chapter is sometimes Kenya, at other times Africa, and sometimes Luo (the name of one of the ethnic groups originating in western Kenya). This is because sub-Saharan African countries have much in common (Magesa 1997), and also:

(1) Because much of this essay is widely applicable to much of sub-Saharan Africa.

(2) To avoid the implication that the Luo people are singularly different from other African people.

(3) By way of acknowledging that the research population has not been continent-wide.

Use of the term "black" for African people is not intended to be in any way offensive. It is applied to people of African origin wherever they are now living. The term "African" is reserved for those black people who are living in (and are assumed to have been born and raised in) Africa.

2. UNDERSTANDING THE DISCOURSE OF RACE IN THE WEST AND IN AFRICA

This chapter utilises insights in pragmatics as the basis for its research. Pragmatics can be defined as the "study of the relations between language and context that are basic to an account of language understanding" (Levinson 1983, 21). Or according to Bach, "Pragmatics is concerned with whatever information is relevant, over and above the linguistic properties of a sentence, to understanding its utterance" (Bach n.d.). Studies in cross-cultural and interlanguage pragmatics "have experienced a staggering, exponential growth over the last couple of decades," say Kraft and Geluykens (2007, 5). Researchers such as Grice (1971) discovered that the meaning of words arises largely from the context of their use. Scholars have since attempted to define the boundary in the derivation of meaning between semantics and pragmatics. That is, to define the extent to which meaning arises from words themselves, and the extent to which meaning arises from the context of the use of words. The implicit assumption in modern academics that "words mean things" of themselves has been challenged. Words have been found to have meanings only in contexts. (I have considered this in more detail elsewhere (Harries 2009, here chapter 4)

In fact human beings instinctively search for contexts that make words meaningful, and then derive relevance from them as a result. If a voice says, "Come here," my mind will consider who is speaking, where they are, whether I need to follow the instruction (perhaps not if they are a child or a mad person), how I am to travel (by bus if the person is far away, by walking toward them if they are in the room), in what time frame I need to follow the instruction, and so on. Without contexts, words are meaningless.

Comprehension of a context is therefore a vitally important part of acquiring meaning from any discourse. Because words do not have meanings apart from contexts, users of words invariably speak into contexts and expect their words to be understood by someone who has an awareness of a context. Sperber and Wilson have looked at this in depth in what they call "relevance theory" (1995a). They suggest that on receiving a stimulus (words), a listener selects from an almost infinite possible set of meanings of a given set of words (or discourse) through their understanding of context—including cognitive (their own mind), social, immediate, historical, relational, and so on. Sperber and Wilson tell us that a person will decide on the meaning for them of a particular set of words by considering that which has, for them, the "greatest possible cognitive effect for the smallest possible processing effort" (1995b).

My analysis of the discourse of "race" in this essay is modelled in part on a book by Blommaert and Verschueren (1998). In their words, "One of the basic premises of a pragmatic approach is that every utterance relies on a world of implicit background assumptions, supposedly shared or presented as shared, which combines with what is explicitly said in the construction of meaning" (1998, 32). In other words, "All forms of communication are accompanied by more or less hidden meaning systems which determine the interpretation of what is said," therefore "it is impossible to find utterances which express their full meaning fully explicitly" (1998, 32).

Blommaert and Verschueren's study examines the discourse of tolerance in Belgium in respect to Islamic immigrants. Explicit negative references to Muslim immigrants were hard to find in Belgium, but Blommaert and Verschueren found that this was because of "the majority's . . . self perception, rather than being indicative of a basically positive attitude vis-à-vis the 'other'" (1998, 54). Explicit positive references to immigrants were either dressed in the language of economic reasoning, or were very generic, they tell us. For example, some Belgian people would say that they should learn from the immigrants' way of looking after their aged. Others suggested that migrant workers were helping the Belgian economy by being willing to perform tasks that the Belgians themselves did not want to do. Blommaert and Verschueren did not find implicit positive references to immigrants. This was an ominous sign to them as in pragmatic reasoning the implicit can be more important than the explicit. They did find many implicit negative references to immigrants. For example, some people would say, "I am not a racist but . . ." (1998, 72).

Blommaert and Verschueren found a conference being arranged entitled, "Towards a liveable multicultural municipality." This conference's title implicitly indicates that the current situation was *not* "liveable" (1998, 34). What immigrants did was "culturised" by the Belgians. This contributed "significantly to the abnormalisation of the foreigner" (1998, 93). In fact, "The sense of superiority which comes along with an unquestioning confidence in 'Western' lifestyle and values is to be found even in the most magnanimous and benevolent attempts to show tolerance and to educate people for life in a multicultural society" (1998, 57). Blommaert and Verschueren concluded "the basic problem [is] . . . that the tolerant majority only imagines its own tolerance" (1998, 120).

In this chapter I want to ask what the outcome would be of applying a comparable system of analysis to "race relations" between whites and blacks (and other ethnicities) in Africa today by comparison with the West. I will focus on Kenya, drawing particularly on the communities with which I am most familiar in western Kenya. I will make practical recommendations to Western Christian mission and development practitioners by drawing on the results of my findings.

The kind of assumed desirability of interracial equality that underlies Western society today has not always been there. The years of slave trading (1502–1807; Amistad n.d.) illustrate that clearly. This does not only apply to the West. Old Testament prescriptions instruct Hebrews to have different standards for themselves than for non-Hebrews (Deut 15:3). Conquering armies have through history frequently enslaved invaded peoples. Even today notions of interracial equality are foreign to many people around the world. Inequality against non-Muslims is enshrined in the scriptures of Islam (for example, 9:29 in the Qur'an: "Fight those who do not believe in Allah . . . and they are in a state of subjection"). It is very overt in the practices and beliefs of Hinduism (known as the caste system; Ross 2010). It need not surprise us that inequality is implicitly acceptable even to those who claim to hold tightly to notions of democracy and human rights, described by Blommaert and Verschueren as "the names for a noble intention and a commendable objective" (1998, 107). What I want to ask in this essay is how Western notions of interracial equality are impacting interethnic relationships in Africa. Then, what should be done once having perceived the reality on the ground?

Parts of Europe and North America appear to be successful in integrating blacks into their communities. In my secondary school in the UK in the late 1970s there were three black children amongst the 1,500 or so pupils. They successfully started and finished the school programme. Many schools and colleges in the West these days have a smattering of black, Indian, Chinese, and other ethnicities amongst their staff. Walking up and down the road in many cities of Western Europe and North America, one can meet a mix of black, white, Chinese, Arab, and other ethnicities. The UK has blacks in parliament; the USA has a black man as president. The church seems to be leading in the promotion of interracial mixing. All Nations Christian College (a missionary training college in the UK) until recently had a black principal (Joe Kapolyo, 2001–2006). The Evangelical Alliance in the UK had a black general secretary (Joel Edwards, 1997–2008). The second highest post in the Church of England (archbishop of York) is occupied by a Ugandan-born black (John Sentamu, since 2008).

The principle of "positive discrimination," it would seem, underlies some of the above appointments. "The UK government is considering denying multimillion-pound contracts to companies that fail to employ enough black and Asian workers" says Davenport, discussing a frequently contested but widely implemented policy (2006). Many blacks living in the West are certainly supportive of such policies: "the negro's conditioning has steered him into that perpetual state of suspended tension wherein 95 per cent of his time and energy is expended on fighting prejudice in whites," explains Cruse (1967, 364). Davenport's complaining that "the idea of job quotas based on physical appearance, rather than on skills and experience, goes against how the labour market operates" (2006) does not prevent this system from continuing. Despite all this, one can be left wondering how real and how natural racial integration that is seen actually is, if it has to be legislated.

But then, what about on the African continent? Are similar policies being applied? How many of the researchers concerned with race issues in the West take time to examine what is happening outside of the West? Is interracial equality and integration part of non-Westerners' ideology; if so, is this only explicitly the case, or also implicitly? What effect is it having on communities in Africa? What about the non-Western church in places like Kenya—is it concerned to ensure that its leadership represents the ethnic diversity found amongst its people? Do African governments insist that the workforce of companies reflect the ethnic makeup of an area? Is the African church, for example, promoting whites into its leadership structure on the basis of "positive discrimination," as the Western church is doing with blacks? What is the impact on Africa of the "positive discrimination" occurring in the West?

One impact of positive discrimination in the West on Africa is the concealing of cultural differences to African people. When African-born (and to a lesser extent Western-born) blacks acquire leadership positions and employment in the West, many of African people's assumptions about the differences between blacks and whites can be challenged. Because blacks do successfully acquire powerful positions in Western nations, the difference, which makes whites wealthy while many blacks remain poor, is promoted to another level of mystery. That is, blacks holding employment and leadership positions in Western nations implicitly communicate that they are as effective in those nations as are native whites. This appears to contradict the widespread observation in Africa that whites must have some special abilities that result in their being a lot wealthier than black people. Because fellow blacks can so easily rise to it, African people can assume the wealth of the whites to arise from some source other than their unique intelligence or culture. As a result, it would seem that it is not only white intelligence or culture that must be imitated in order to acquire wealth. There is some other, less visible, missing key to success and wealth in life that African people are looking for. In many Christian churches, the assumed form of this is the "prosperity gospel."

My own experience tells me that many African communities are uniformly black. While blacks are being integrated into white communities, it is less common for whites to be integrated into black communities. Not only whites, but also Chinese, Arab, Indian, and Latin people are less likely to mix closely with African societies. Why is this? When will this change? What are the repercussions of this?

Kenya is one of the African countries that has been greatly exposed to the West. But there are many places in Kenya where one can travel for miles without meeting any nonblacks. Certainly if one meets any, they are not likely to be integrated into black communities. The black partner of mixed marriages tends to move toward a Western lifestyle. Kenyan universities, I understand, are staffed almost entirely by blacks. (I cannot be certain of this information.) This has been my observation at Maseno University in western Kenya. Despite Maseno having been a large mission centre staffed by white missionaries in years gone by, the whole academic institution now appears to be operated by locals (blacks). Apart from a small smattering of Indians, the students are black (personal observation).

I have been told that there are very few (if any) non-Kenyan students. This all seems strongly ironic considering that a very high percentage of the content of the curriculum of places like Maseno University is coming from outside of Africa (the West). (Statistics indicate that one percent of the Kenyan population is of non-African ethnic origin (About n.d.).)

In the larger townships and certainly cities, one finds people of Indian extraction running the sizeable businesses. Arabs, Chinese, and other ethnicities are economically active in smaller numbers. The mayor of Kisumu city, Shakeel Shabbir, is of Indian ethnicity (Odhiambo 2004). The reason I am frequently given for the mayor being of Indian ethnicity by people I talk to in Kenya is that when blacks are put into this office they die very quickly through being bewitched by jealous colleagues. This is an exception—most public offices are held by blacks.

Foreigners are apt to conceal themselves behind local (black) people. This is certainly the case with many NGOs. Those pulling the strings and providing finance for NGOs in Kenya are often people of European or American extraction. But because being seen as "boss" is bad business for foreigners in Africa, frontline visible personnel are usually African. This is not an objective fact for which I have statistical evidence. The whole point is that people conceal this practice. One only becomes aware of it over time. One wonders how local people get the funding to do what they do in NGOs, only to discover that foreigners are in charge, even if from outside of the country. One wonders why Africans are doing things that appear contrary to their culture and traditions, only to find that they are being directed to do them by non-Africans. On meeting foreigners, one finds that they are often not "at the coal face"—that is, not actually interacting directly with their target population, but a few steps back and having local people do the frontline work which they direct. Sometimes Africans are in charge but raise funds from overseas. Then the people overseas seek to control the Africans they are working with through accountability structures.

Many local people whom I interact with in my living in Africa recognise that these things are happening. They consider themselves to be different from outsiders. African people whom I meet are often very surprised to hear me speak their language. They tell me that someone with white skin cannot be their fellow tribesman. (To suggest that someone who is black cannot be English would be seen as very offensive. But local people in Africa do not consider that there is anything wrong with saying that a white man cannot be a member of an African tribe. I acknowledge that tribe is an ethnic description based on a common ancestry, whereas "English" is a description based on a geographic area suggesting certain linguistic and cultural traits. That in a sense is the whole point—that in much of Africa, unlike in the West, someone's key identity is rooted in their ancestry.)

People of European origin are both ashamed and proud of their origins when they meet Africa. The guilt that many European people feel for African poverty suggests that they consider themselves responsible for it. Hence Westerners hand out money or goods and "do good" in ways that they would rarely consider doing in their home communities. African people going to Europe or America are often looking to get "things." Even if they do not set out with this intention, Western people's deeply ingrained habit of understanding blacks as being poor, soon has them under pressure to do so. For a European or American person to share in the lives of Africans is seen as some kind of exciting adventure, that is usually engaged in for a short period (hence the popularity of short-term mission). The way that Westerners talk about "visiting Africa" is very different from the way that Africans talk about "visiting America."

This opening section has shown how insights gained from pragmatics have unveiled some race issues inside and outside of the West. The "truth" of a community's orientation to issues such as race often being implicit rather than explicit, and the "implicit" of Africa being largely out of reach to Westerners because it is contained in an oral discourse in non-Western languages, has meant that I have had to use considerable license arising from personal long-term exposure to languages and cultures indigenous to Africa to explain what is "actually going on" on the African continent. (More details on this below.)

3. BLACK RULE IN AFRICA

The African scene is of course complex. It is vastly different from that in Europe or America. It may be much less understood by the target readership for this chapter than the contexts of their own communities. This therefore requires me to fill in more background.

This study cannot as easily be done on the basis of written texts as has that by Blommaert and Verschueren (1998). This is for various reasons. One is that many African societies are very much more oral than is the West. Also because the dominant language for writing in many African countries is English, which is a colonial language. (Other European languages are dominant in some other African countries.) The "dominant writers" therefore are those who have had heavy doses of Western exposure and education (so as to acquire a sufficient grasp of English). What is written in English is oriented to an international readership, deeply rooted in Western ways of expression, and often designed to attract donor funds. Instead of drawing on this, my research is rooted in personal observation and learning resulting from twenty years of close exposure to African communities, interpreted through wide reading.

My experience in Africa began through living in the North-Western Province of Zambia between 1988 and 1991. Since 1993 I have lived in a village in western Kenya amongst the Luo people, but have also moved more widely amongst many different African ethnicities, including significant periods of time spent in Tanzania. Linguistically, I was once fluent in Kikaonde of Zambia, and am now a fluent speaker of Kiswahili and Dholuo. I have over the years intentionally avoided powerful positions and an identity as a donor or proponent of superior Western goods and culture. My role in the Luo community in which I live is as a Bible teacher, as someone interested in their churches and ways of life, and as someone who loves their children, some of whom stay with me in my home.

The designers of policy for Western nations are its own citizens, who therefore have a profound understanding of their own people. They also use their own language. On the contrary, policy design in Africa is increasingly determined from the outside by those who are ignorant of local conditions. That is, in the case of the church, by foreign missionaries, donors, and short-term visitors from the West. In the case of secular organisations, donors and foreign experts determine policy. In the case of governments, by multinationals such as the World Bank, IMF (International Monetary Fund), UN (United Nations, especially in the Millennium Development Project), and so on. Biased reporting of events in Africa (to the West) is widespread, as these organisations attempt to justify their interventions. Donors and project implementers over the continent are investing vast amounts of money and then are pushed into the corner to defend their reputations from ruin when their objectives are not reached. Underlying this failure is a deceptive screen of apparent "Westernisation" emanating from Africa, arising particularly from African people's use of Western languages.

Through following the research methodology described above (that I consider to be the most legitimate, although obviously with its own limitations), I can say that there is little official "positive discrimination" in favour of people of non-Kenyan origin in the Kenyan system. One reason for this is clearly that people whose ancestry is not Kenyan anyway have a disproportionately large share of economic power and influence in the country. Instead of "positive discrimination," there may be "negative discrimination"; that is, overt and implicit efforts are made in the formal sector at having enough of the majority peoples (Africans) in key positions. The powerful formal sector of the country not being indigenous, but an outside transplant, means that foreigners are (theoretically at least) the most adept at operating it. On the contrary, the problem with the informal sector is, one suspects, that foreigners have little interest in engaging in it. It would be hard to find a sufficient proportion of nonindigenous people ready to participate in informal activities to fill any "quotas" that may be devised. This being the bulk of people's occupations and activities, means that much of people's family and personal lives occur within the circles of their own and closely related African ethnicities. As foreign people rarely want to imitate indigenous languages or ways of life, the gap between locals and foreigners typically remains large.

Other related considerations can be added. Many Kenyan peoples give great esteem to their dead (Mbiti 1975). Because, as a result, it is yesterday's people who rule today's communities, "success" is considered to come to those who follow the commands and recommendations of the "living dead" (the term used by Mbiti to refer to "ancestral spirits"). That is to say that life is not guided so much by rationality and ethics, as has long been the case (at least to a large degree) in Western nations, presumably arising from the influence of the ancient Greeks through the Enlightenment. Instead, as the dead rule, so tradition rules in the informal sector, and this tradition may be of little relevance to nonlocals.

At the same time, very much of Kenyan formal society these days officially acclaims what is foreign. Hence Kenyan children are required to spend the prime years of their lives learning foreign things in a foreign language, English, in school. Constant praise and attention being given to the foreign and little understood results in its acquiring an almost divine character, as is well illustrated by the widespread popularity these days of the prosperity gospel in Christian churches. Foreigners have themselves almost become gods (i.e., pseudoancestors) in African eyes (Harries 2006, here chapter 11).

An inevitable aspect of "black rule," that I will consider again in more detail below, is its duplicity. That is, in order to acquire international recognition and respect in this day and age, and in order to obtain donor funds, countries and organisations have to be seen to be run in a Western way. It is always difficult to do something in someone else's way. Sometimes it is impossible. African governments and leaders of all kinds are therefore under intense pressure to appear to be what they are not; that is, to be less than honest. Not to be less than honest (i.e., to be honest) can be sheer folly, because it will lose them their international standing and funding. In other words, the mismatch between African and Western cultures, combined with the requirement for the former to resemble the latter, often renders honesty almost impossible.

Allow me to try and illustrate this by reversing it. I ask my Western readers to imagine that they were living in a community dominated by African culture. (This is obviously difficult for a Western readership who is not familiar with deep African culture—a difficulty that I constantly face in writing this chapter—so I can only ask for patient efforts.) How would a Westerner respond to questions or statements like:

(1) How many cows did you give in exchange for your wife?

(2) No one would disagree with the wisdom of going onto your farm in the morning before attending to your professional occupation.

(3) That was horrific—they did not even bring their dead son home (i.e., to the grounds of the house in which they live) to be buried!

(4) Any thinking man would avoid shaking hands with his mother-in-law!

(5) And so on.

One option in response to such statements is of course to deny the "objective" of the question concerned, such as to say, "I don't give cows for my wife" or "I don't see the problem in shaking my mother-in-law's hand." After a while though, it would get wearing having constantly to explain a position that is at odds with the dominant culture, so will be tempting to give the answer that pleases the questioner; this especially if the questioner's generosity is dependent on your apparently having accepted their culture. This is unfortunately a little deceptive.

4. TRAPS TO AVOID IN MISSION, AID, AND DEVELOPMENT ASSISTANCE

I have attempted to illustrate above how the current global climate *forces* African leaders of all kinds into hiding those actions and dynamics that are very different from those in the West, some of which come to be considered immoral or corrupt by the West. Because this position is *forced* onto them, in my opinion it is in the end the West and not the African leaders concerned who are to blame for this "concealment."

Section 2 above has shown how, using the research of Blommaert and Verschueren (1998) as a research model, learning about a situation through explicit communications can result in its being grossly misunderstood. This is because true understanding depends on knowledge of the context through which texts and discourses need to be comprehended. That is, "every utterance relies on a world of implicit background assumptions, supposedly shared or presented as shared, which combines with what is explicitly said in the construction of meaning" (1998, 32). Their study shows how an apparent orientation to the integration of migrant workers in Belgium was actually concealing a strong antipathy on the side of Belgian people to the immigrants. The Belgian people themselves are aware of this apparent contradiction. It is therefore not deceptive for them to share about migrant issues in the way that they do with their fellow countrymen. But it would be incorrect for an outsider to assume to have understood the Belgian people's position in relation to immigrant workers on the basis of only explicit references to them.

With respect to Africa and the West, we have a situation in which the West is exerting more and more control, especially through holding purse strings, while guided almost entirely by explicit information. The implicit remains invisible because it is in unfamiliar languages, oral rather than written, and hidden rather than public. (Maranz points out an additional reason for knowledge about African life not being widely available: "Africans readily share space and things but are possessive of knowledge . . . [whereas] Westerners readily share their knowledge but are possessive of things and space" (2001, 30).) I argue in this section that the understanding arising from such a dynamic has resulted in African and Western people respectively putting themselves and each other into traps, from which they are not later able to escape, and that act against the best interests of both.

The system under which donors control much of Africa very quickly and easily results in a serious confusion between what is "good" and what is "bad." While the basis of this may be the difference between Western perspectives on good and bad versus indigenous African ones, it very soon grows larger than this. By way of example, let us imagine a typical project that is initiated from the West. Well-meaning, conscientious Westerners begin with their understanding of "what Africa needs." They then popularise that understanding in their home country so as to raise money for it. On moving onto the African field, they begin to implement.

The implementation unfortunately does not work, but by this time it is hard to know what to do about it. The Westerner is in confusion, struggling to understand the context around them, perhaps suffering from depression, confronted with the prospect of "failure," and so on. Some Westerners will go home in despair and try to forget their bad experience. (These never, of course, get the same exposure when their "project" is quietly being buried as they had when it was first launched.) Others will plod on and continue to hope that somehow things will work out, despite the contradictory messages that they are getting. They may adjust the ways in which they are working, although such adjustments may be minimal because their course has in many ways already been set. (For example, once a purpose-built structure has been erected, it is an embarrassment not to use it for its intended purpose.) By beginning from a position of already knowing which way they are heading and investing in that, rather than putting themselves into learning and vulnerable positions, Westerners frequently put themselves into a trap. They may no longer consider what they are doing to be "good," but are forced to continue to do it to save face. Similarly, African people may be committed to a funded project, though its impact may be "bad," if the benefit of the funding outweighs the negative impact of the project.

Even those Westerners who attempt to listen closely to the African people, unfortunately usually have not sufficiently considered the latter's prior experience. Many African people in African countries already have experience of (or have heard accounts of) visiting Westerners. They therefore have considerable understanding of their culture, and likely behaviour. Many are aware that Western missionaries or project workers going to Africa frequently already have money set aside that they intend to spend. Even if a missionary is wise enough not to commit themselves too quickly, sooner or later money is bound to flow. The key for the national is to be persistent in working on relationship with the Westerner concerned so as to maximise the chances of being the beneficiary (or one of the beneficiaries) of those funds when they eventually come. Care must be exercised in the giving of advice to the missionary or potential donor. Good advice should only be given to the extent that will not encourage the visitor to choose to take their money elsewhere; for example, to a neighbouring community. The local person whose honesty will result in the foreigner's investment going to their neighbour's territory instead of their own will be a laughingstock. The reputation that Westerners on the whole already have in Africa has already put their potential advisers into a trap before new visitors have even spoken their first word.

Donors who want to make sure that there is accountability bring more traps. It is easier to make someone accountable for some actions than for others. Funds being made available for actions that are more transparent, regardless of whether they are the most important or helpful, results in these actions being the most frequently implemented, and certainly distorts many donor-dependent societies in Africa. Funding schools using English, for example, will be preferred to those using local languages that donors do not understand, no matter how badly local people understand English. Many donors prefer to cover capital rather than running costs because capital projects result in clearly visible items such as buildings, and (supposedly) do not interfere with the ongoing sustainability of what is happening. While in simplistic terms accurate, the fact that operating funds may dwindle while project balances are buoyant, can result in a serious temptation to misappropriation of the funds concerned. What is the use, after all, of a new building, if the whole school (or hospital, farm, church, etc.) is on the point of collapse? Such funding policies' giving the impression of health and wealth in situations that are strapped for funds, can certainly result in frustrations (variously vented) for employees or others who feel that they deserve a greater reward for their contributions to the apparently prosperous institution concerned. As a result, managers of such projects must either be corrupt or are trapped into an appearance of being "mean."

The fact that outside funds come to those who are familiar with foreign languages, easily traps people into choosing ignorance in preference to being enlightened. That is, foreign languages are preferred and used to engage in activities that could much more effectively be carried out using local tongues. Such self-imposed linguistic handicap anticipates that, in the end, the foreign will bring a greater reward than the indigenous could have mustered. (Like a coach who advises his team to *lose* a football match if the losers' prize is better than the winner's cup.) A country (or community) that appears to get its act together using a local language may well end up worse off (in a certain time frame) than another that accepts some chaos and a Western language. The latter "chaotic" community, both because it is higher on the scale of poverty (aid by its very nature is graduated; that is, it is more generous for poorer than for wealthier people) and because its citizens can communicate to those who are the source of aid, are more likely to be recipients of generous Western charity. Any Western charitable contributions that favour African nationals who have a good knowledge of English aggravate this. Hence organisations involved in charity that have the people's long-term interests at heart should not operate in Western languages.

By using people's own language(s), the charity may be enhancing, or at least not as seriously undermining, people's own social, economic, and instrumental capacity.

Being "trapped" into the use of Western languages creates real difficulties when it comes to discussing important issues for a certain people whenever (and this is frequently the case) the foreign language concerned cannot adequately accommodate it. For example, English is a poor language to use in discussing important issues pertaining to polygamy for at least two reasons (my comparison is with Dholuo, a language used in western Kenya).

4.1 Deficiency in terminology

Polygamy (or strictly polygyny) for the Luo people is an integral part of their traditional way of life. The name given for a polygamous household in Dholuo (the language of the Luo) is *doho*. Unlike the term "polygamy" in English, *doho* is a respectful Luo term. The same term *doho* is also used to refer to the home(stead) of an influential community leader that is the site for important community meetings. "Marriage" often being referred to as *nyombo*, which also means to take cattle in exchange for a woman, supports the institution of polygamy. This is because to *nyombo* one woman does not preclude the option of *nyombo* another if a man has sufficient cattle. *Nyombo* makes divorce more difficult than does "marriage," because divorce requires the return of cattle to the girl's parents. For various reasons, men who take a second wife usually cannot get rid of the first (unlike men in the West through "divorce"). A man's first wife may be known as *chi dala* (the wife of the family). Hence a man may marry a second woman so as to have his own wife. (*Chi dala* implies that the first wife is married by the family, so can be called *chiwa* or "our wife," which is not a familiar language usage in English.) A woman going to marry is said to *dhi tedo* ("go to cook"), which defines her role in the man's home much more clearly than does the English "she got married." There is nothing to stop two wives from cooking separately for their respective families, providing they have their own kitchens. If she goes back to her parents, a woman is known as *migogo*, a shameful term that does not even exist in English.

Another reason for either taking or not taking a second and subsequent wife is connected to *chira*—a term for a kind of curse that English does not have. Breaking *kwer* brings *chira*, but *kwer* does not translate into English except perhaps as "taboo," which native-English speakers do not use to describe their own relationships. Widow inheritance again does not translate, as an inherited widow is neither a wife, a mistress, nor a concubine in the English sense (Ojore 1995, 158). *Chi liel* ("widow") in Dholuo (literally meaning "wife of the grave") illustrates how a Luo widow is still bound by her "marriage" after the death of her husband. "Remarriage" requires an undoing of that prior relationship by the process of *ter*, often translated into English as "inheritance," but whereas "inheritance" implies an acquired piece of property, *ter* describes a cleansing process. So *jater* (the widow inheritor) actually may not "inherit" the widow. To turn to the side of the widower for a moment, he should *leko chiege* ("dream of his wife") before he remarries. But to "dream of" your wife in English probably means to have fond memories of her, whereas for the Luo *leko chiege* is to have her "ghost" revisit and sexually stimulate the husband. The landscape of English as it considers polygamy is, I suggest, so different from that of Dholuo, as to preclude intelligent discussion about it in relation to the Luo people's own culture.

4.2 Key issue considered unimportant

Because polygamy is not practiced by them, texts on polygamy will remain minority texts in the dominant English-speaking world. Hence polygamy will not be considered in depth in school or college curricula, libraries, the Internet, etc., even though it may be one of the most discussed issues in Luo households. The terms associated with it, such as "polygamy" itself, "wife inheritance," and "widow cleansing" are in English not "nice" terms, but carry implicatures of primitiveness. Those people for whom such issues are important may still prefer not to address them in English to avoid the stigma of association with such "primitiveness."

The above indicates that sensible, in-depth debate about this issue, while critically important for the Luo people, is in effect impossible using English. We may ask ourselves: What happens if an important issue such as this is simply removed from the agenda? Allow me to illustrate this by reversing the process, and assuming that Luo language and culture were dominant in the West. One effect of this would be to force debates about science, budgeting, economics, birthdays, and so on into decline, either because these topics *cannot* be discussed in Dholuo vocabulary or syntax, or because they are not considered worthy of discussion by the Luo. If native-English speakers would not want their culture to come under attack in this way, then why force the Luo into incompetence in discussing their issues by imposing a foreign language onto them?

Some may argue, because of the advantages of monogamy, that it is in the long-term best interests of the Luo people for polygamy to cease. But assuming monogamy to be a better system than polygamy does not in itself mean that discussion on issues connected with polygamy should not happen, because the very discussion may be the means by which polygamy is ended! If there are two ways of orienting a people from polygamy toward monogamy, and one is by ignoring the issues resulting from the changeover while the other is by allowing them to discuss, debate, and find resolutions to their issues, the latter route may be more helpful. This at the very least because the discussion will allow for an intelligent, well-thought-out way of altering the people's way of life, rather than the chaotic alternative that will hurt a lot of people in the process.

In other words, simply ignoring the ramifications of a move from polygamy to monogamy will leave an "incomplete way of life." It will in turn require adjustment in many areas for the family and society. For example, how will the "spare" ladies who remain single be cared for? What will happen to widows who would otherwise have been inherited by married men? How will the man live in town by himself if he has to be there to earn a wage but does not have sufficient income to pay rent and food for his whole family? Who will care for the homestead if the wife has to live in town with her husband? If (as I am suggesting is the case) issues of polygamy and the associated widow inheritance are very much discussed, this is for an important reason, and their removal from the debating table will therefore leave a critical and damaging gap. Such a gap may result in a crisis and breakdown of society. Is it good to force someone's society to a state of "breakdown"? Perhaps the best way to answer that question is to ask whether Westerners would like that for themselves. I suggest that it is more helpful to allow people to intelligently adjust and alter their own ways of life than to trip them up and leave them (metaphorically) helplessly squirming. This requires them to freely use their own language (or a closely related language), knowledgeably and intelligently.

I am therefore suggesting that overextending English and other foreign languages to artificially make them the language of "success" for African people through the use of outside subsidy is a potentially very harmful attack on the foundational sensibilities of the African communities concerned. My emphasis is here on *subsidy*. Languages and people always mix and rub off onto each other. The way this happens in much of Africa today though is unique and artificial (in a historical time frame) through the aid of technology and outside charity. For example, before the advent of the printing press, languages were spread by interpersonal contact, but nowadays they can increase in their influence, via technology, through foreign donations alone. Universal primary education using English would be unthinkable for the Kenyan government without foreign aid.

Providing foreign aid on condition that it is used to support education using English is putting Kenyan politicians into a trap that they cannot refuse. A harmful effect of the current state of international relations, therefore, is the trapping of many African peoples into the widespread use of languages that increase their incompetence in running their own lives; preventing critical issues that a people are facing from being addressed.

Another trap exists here for the foreign native-English speaker. The ease of communicating in Anglophone Africa in their own language makes it more difficult for native-English speakers to learn indigenous languages. This means that many important issues (that can only helpfully be learned and discussed in indigenous languages, see above) pass them by. This perpetuates the foreigner's ignorance, and means that the understanding of African people on the side of international academia is rendered seriously deficient. It also makes it almost impossible for Westerners to integrate closely with African communities. Because the deficiency described above is not recognised, neither are the difficulties of mixing Western and African ways of life known or acknowledged in, for example, written documents. Instead, when a Westerner attempts to live closely with an African people, he or she will condemn that which they do not understand, with apparent license from the academia (that is, in Western English).

Such difficulty in integration means in effect that, whereas the West is recruiting from Africa and elsewhere in the globe for help in discussion about its ways of life and assistance to its peoples, Africa is on its own. No one else can assist them, because no one else has the necessary knowledge or linguistic acumen to understand them. This is foundationally why African people can travel to and be incorporated into Western communities (albeit with difficulty), but the reverse does not apply, and African societies are left struggling unassisted in their efforts to adjust to twenty-first century ways emanating from the West and spreading around the globe.

This is an enormous affliction to the African people. African communities can remain exclusively black, because others are ignorant and remain ignorant as long as they use Western languages in their interactions with the African people. The great good that could arise from intercultural mixing and mutual assistance is precluded. A Ugandan can become a bishop in the (English) Anglican Church, and a black man could become the president of America, but for a white man to become a leader in black Africa in other than an "oppressive" way, is almost impossible. What a loss for Africa.

5. MORE ON "HOW TO HELP AFRICA"

I have above pointed out some very real difficulties in current efforts at intercultural communication between the West and Africa. It is also true that people in the West are concerned with the plight of the African people. This concern is a great thing. I want to say something about how, in the light of the discussion above (and see also other articles at http://www.jim-mission.org.uk), this concern can best be channelled so as to be of real "help."

I believe that God has created the world and holds it in his hands. This means that his wisdom is always greater than man's wisdom. It was the godliness of the forefathers of Western nations that got them to where they are now. The most important thing that Westerners have to share with the people of Africa is therefore their knowledge of God, in word and deed. But, cross-cultural sharing of God's word is no easy thing. As God is committed to humankind, and was ready to give his life as a sacrifice for humankind, so the Westerners who intend to share God's word with the people of Africa need to be committed and to give their whole selves. The West needs to find those young people who are prepared to devote themselves in service to God's purposes in Africa using African languages and without creating the traps mentioned above, and then support them with much wisdom in that calling.

"Helping someone" is no easy task. The people who are usually the greatest help to us in our lives are those (such as parents, spouses, siblings, and devoted friends) who stick with us through thick and thin. They are also the ones who accept us as we are. Those are the qualities needed of Western workers going to the African people. This aspect of accepting people for who they are interculturally seems to have been neglected in recent decades. Instead, the emphasis on changing people to be more Western has been a critical stand, which suggests the inferiority of those being reached who do not become Westernised. They perceive this, and that perception creates problems, including a desire for people to deny and devalue what they are while constantly desiring and valuing the foreign, that is what they are not!

God's word cannot be shared without regard for a people's culture and language. Efforts at doing so quickly hit the rocks. Love also often cannot be shown "from a distance." It must be communicated proximally. Otherwise love expressed may not be love received.

That is not to say that one does not desire for people to change. None of us are perfect, and we all need to change more and more so as to be worthy of a glorious God. But, "while we were still sinners, Christ died for us" (Rom 5:8), and so Christ's people are also to love their fellow human beings while they are yet sinners. Christ incarnated to be man. He walked and talked with the Jewish people in their language. He taught them through parables. He was ready to put his life on the line for the sake of the people whom he had come to love. He was vulnerable to the people he was reaching. He did not "buy followers" using foreign money. Missionaries need to follow his example.

What should have become clear in this essay is that helping a people includes making an effort to get to where they are. That makes it possible to come from where they are coming from. It certainly includes using their language and knowing how they use it. Then teaching them through parables, stories, and the Scriptures as Jesus did, that they too may come to a knowledge of God and salvation in his name.

The nature of the help being proffered these days is precluding many alternative options that actually have good potential. In brief, "help" being rooted in financial contributions, by maintaining the distance between African and Western peoples, leaves the latter sufficiently ignorant as to have made it impossible for them to work more closely with Africans. Hence African societies, unlike others, certainly including Western ones, are left to face their issues alone. The solution is simple, albeit difficult—to have Westerners relate to Africa using the African people's own languages and without relying on their own resources in their activities. That is, linguistically and economically not to be "set apart" in relationship.

6. CONCLUSION

Pragmatics has been used to acquire insights into the race scene in Africa, Europe, and America that would not be accessible by other means. An adaptation of Blommaert and Verschueren's (1998) research methodology has been followed, which emphasises the importance of looking for implicit rather than explicit texts. This is particularly difficult to do in an African society that is largely oral and in its informal sector operating in other than European languages. It must be done by those Westerners who have a deep, vulnerable exposure to African ways of life and languages. It is more quickly fruitful in Western nations where appearances of racism are carefully concealed by practices such as positive discrimination.

This research suggests that Western nations have been more successful in racial integration than has Africa, and that Africa's lack in this regard is due in part at least to particular Western policies that can force African rule to be rooted in deception, secrecy, and corruption. "Traps" resulting from inappropriate policy on the part of the West have been unpacked in detail in this chapter. Current practices are denying African communities the opportunity for intelligent partnerships in grappling with truly African issues, or from benefiting from the Enlightenment. Suggestions made to rectify this situation, through appropriate intervention from the West, include that at least some of the foreigners who come to the continent be determined to operate in local languages without heavy assistance from outside resources. In the long term, resolution of race as well as economic and social issues in Africa requires the use of indigenous languages. Policies originating from the West that discourage the use of indigenous African languages are found not to be in the best interests of African peoples in African nations.

REFERENCES

About, n.d. About: Africa for Visitors. http://goafrica.about.com/library/bl.mapfacts.kenya.htm (accessed March 17, 2007).

Amistad. n.d. Timeline: The Atlantic slave trade. http://amistad.mysticseaport.org/timeline/atlantic.slave.trade.html (accessed March 17, 2007: site now discontinued).

Bach, Kent. n.d. The semantics-pragmatics distinction: What it is and why it matters. San Francisco State Univ. http://online.sfsu.edu/~kbach/semprag.html (accessed April 19, 2011).

Blommaert, Jan, and Jef Verschueren. 1998. *Debating diversity: Analysing the discourse of tolerance*. London: Routledge.

Cruse, Harold. 1967. *The crisis of the Negro intellectual: From its origins to the present*. New York: William Morrow.

Davenport, Neil. 2006. Not-so-positive discrimination. Spiked. http://www.spiked-online.com/index.php?/site/article/1438 (accessed December 31, 2008).

Grice, H. P. 1971. Utterer's meaning, sentence meaning and word meaning. In *The philosophy of language: Oxford readings in philosophy*, ed. J. R. Searle, 54–70. Oxford: Oxford Univ. Press.

Harries, Jim. 2006. Good-by-default and evil in Africa. *Missiology: An International Review* 34/2: 151–64.

———. 2009. Pragmatic linguistics applied to Bible translation, projects and intercultural relationships: An African focus. *Cultural Encounters: A Journal for the Theology of Culture* 5/1: 75–95.

Kraft, Bettina, and Ronald Geluykens. 2007. Defining cross-cultural and interlanguage pragmatics. In *Cross-cultural pragmatics and interlanguage English*, ed. Bettina Kraft and Ronald Geluykens, 3–20. Munich: Lincom-Europa.

Levinson, Stephen C. 1983. *Pragmatics*. Cambridge: Cambridge Univ. Press.

Magesa, Laurenti, 1997. *African religion: The moral traditions of abundant life*. Nairobi: Paulines.

Maranz, David. 2001. *African friends and money matters: Observations from Africa*. Dallas: SIL International.

Mbiti, John. 1975. *Introduction to African religion*. London: Heinemann.

Odhiambo, Allan. 2004. Shabbir mayor of Kisumu again. *Daily Nation on the Web* (February 17). http://www.nationaudio.com/News/DailyNation/17022004/News/News1702200484.html (accessed March 17, 2007: site now discontinued).

Ojore, Aloys Otieno. 1995. Levirate unions among the Luo: A case study in Kisumu District. MA thesis, The Catholic Univ. of Eastern Africa.

Ross, Kelley L. 2010. The caste system and the stages of life in Hinduism. The Proceedings of the Friesian School. http://www.friesian.com/caste.htm (accessed April 16, 2011).

Sperber, Dan, and Deirdre Wilson. 1995a. *Relevance: communication and cognition*. 2nd ed. Oxford: Blackwell.

Sperber, Dan, and Deirdre Wilson. 1995b. *Relevance: communication and cognition*. 2nd ed. Oxford: Blackwell. http://cogweb.ucla.edu/Abstracts/Sperber_Wilson_95.html (accessed March 17, 2007).

CHAPTER 11

Good-by-default and Evil in Africa[1]

"Ka ng'ato oyudo gimoro maber giwacho ni, 'Nyasache ber.'"
"If someone gets anything good they say, 'His God is good.'"
Mboya 1997, 17

1. INTRODUCTION[2]

According to Mboya, "good" comes from "God" (*Nyasaye*). This essay attempts to explore to what extent and how exclusively this is the case for the African people with whom I have associated and about whom I have been able to learn. If good is seen as coming from God, then perhaps there is no good apart from that originating in God. If this is the case, then what are the implications of this in the Luo people's comprehension of the impact that outsiders have had on their society from the colonial period to date? If God is the only source of good, does this mean that everyone else is bad? I have found many indications to this effect.

African cosmology is a hierarchy. God is at the top. He is said to be distant, but always existing (Chirairo 2003). What then is his role?

Having lived in the North-Western Province of Zambia from 1988 to 1991, I first came to Luoland in western Kenya in 1993 where I have been mostly resident from 1993 to 2002, living with the same community in the same area. I have learned to speak Kiswahili and Dholuo fluently. Having originally come to Africa to teach agriculture, my own valuation of the agriculture I was teaching

---

1 This chapter was originally published as follows: Harries, Jim. 2006. Good-by-default and evil in Africa. *Missiology: An International Review* 34/2: 151–64.

2 Thanks to Stan Nussbaum for his helpful advice that has helped me to edit this article.

has subsequently fallen greatly. On moving with local people in Zambia, I found them to be so in the grip of the fear of evil (witchcraft) that my technically based agricultural training seemed to be entirely peripheral to the issues they were facing. I took that as God's telling me to focus more directly on Christian teaching and the work of the church, this being, in my view, at the cutting edge of the transformations going on in people's hearts.

From my arrival in Africa to date I have found myself on a fascinating exploratory journey. As a "thinking person," I came with many preconceptions, which have gradually been eroded away. My efforts at instigating development projects in my early days in Africa consistently failed, as development projects are wont to do (Clay and Schaffer 1984). I perceived what I then called a "self-destruct mechanism" that seemed to be built in to every positive, constructive venture that I initiated. The nature of this mechanism was to elude me for a long time.

In this essay much of my information comes from the Luo people in western Kenya, amongst whom I live. Through reading, travelling, and listening to people, I believe that much of what I have found amongst them also applies much more widely. I have made much use of Mboya's 1997 book throughout. This is because Mboya is a published source of many of the issues that are habitually discussed but less frequently written down by the Luo people.

2. THE STRUGGLE AGAINST EVIL

As the years went by, I gradually came to perceive some regularly recurring patterns in the speech and behaviour of my African hosts and colleagues. These patterns became evident in different ways:

(1) While in Zambia as an agriculturist, I had many opportunities to ask farmers why they did not produce more food. Patient listening revealed that they were limiting their productivity to accepted norms. In this part of Zambia there was a hungry time of year. He who has food at that time and does not share it out is liable to be bewitched by jealous neighbours. There was no point in producing more than others.

(2) Living with African people while also interacting with fellow missionaries of European origin enabled me to observe startling differences in the nature of informal conversation. Europeans take X to be "good," and occupy themselves in devising the best ways of achieving it (X could be a medical project, journey,

school, etc.). The informal conversations of African people are not so oriented. Conversations instead easily turned to identifying evil and the means (usually ritual) to overcome it. This difference is colossal!

(3) The behaviour of our (African) students at Kima International School of Theology (KIST) in Kenya is striking. The principal up to 2002, Rev. Dr. Steve Rennick, coming "fresh" from America, initially felt it would be good for him periodically to meet with the whole student body. He was amazed to find an almost total absence of positive, constructive talk from these aspiring church ministers. Meetings were instead used for griping and voicing grievances. Being my principal, this is something Rennick often shared with me as a frustration he had to face in his leadership role at the school. He eventually stopped meeting with the whole student body together.

Students themselves or the African faculty were sometimes responsible for organising an activity for students on a Saturday evening. The example they were set was of games, quizzes, and fun. Almost invariably, however, left to their own choice the preferred activity was one of worship and prayers against evil.

(4) I have been privileged while in Kenya to work with a lot of indigenous, African-initiated churches, and Pentecostal churches. The latter especially are said to be growing fast. While struggling to get by with English, it was not always easy to hear what was being said. As my knowledge of Kiswahili and Dholuo improved, I was struck by the consistency with which the theme of testimonies and sermons was the battle against evil! A valued preacher friend of mine assures me almost every time we meet that if I want to succeed as a preacher, I must use the analogy of warfare in what I say (Onyango 2002).

(5) The above and other observations prompted me to engage in recorded participant-observation research in 2000. Four days a week for five weeks I carried my notebook wherever I went. I noted the gist of what was discussed and enacted in "normal life" and during a number of church services. Again and again and again the issue attended to was cleansing of evil. So much so that this appeared to be the whole hub and focus of life (Harries 2001).

More and more my observations pointed to a widespread and commonplace perception of evil forces dominating life. There is so much that I could add to the above list of five. The tendency of leaders, including church leaders, to label fellow leaders as evil. The widely known preoccupation of African Christians with the casting out of demons or evil spirits. The persistence of rituals, such as animal sacrifice, that are designed to counteract evil forces. The way that funeral attendance seems to preclude all other activities and dominates people's lives—funerals of course being a cleansing of the evil associated with death. The conception of evil in the parts of Africa with which I am familiar is clearly very real indeed!

Paul Mboya is perhaps the most widely accepted authority by the Luo people themselves on the traditional Luo way of life. I set about translating his main text *Luo Kitgi gi Timbegi* (*The Luo: Their Traditions and Customs*) in 1996. I completed my English translation (unpublished) in 2001. This book was originally published in 1938, based on research by Paul Mboya, a Luo man amongst his own people at a time when the majority of the live population could clearly remember the days prior to the coming of the European. It has been republished many times, the most recent being 1997, and has since been widely available in bookshops in Luoland.

This account of about sixty thousand words in length is described by Bethwell Ogot as an encyclopedic source of information on Luo customs (1999, 186). Mboya himself does not claim to have covered everything in the life of the Luo (Mboya 1997, ii). He hoped that more books would be written. The tone of the book is strongly suggestive of there being a right way of doing things. "No nation can progress well with foreign customs alone if they discard their own traditions and counsels . . . the people must put their own laws and traditions that are good as foundations first. Then they can build the counsel and customs of foreigners onto this foundation," says Mboya with apparent deep conviction (1997, i; my translation). Issues concerning death and cleansing from evil recur repeatedly throughout this book.

Mboya's emphasis became focused in his latter book with the bold title *Richo ema Kelo Chira* (*It Is Sin that Brings the Curse*; 1978). The very title carries a sense of urgency that is strongly reflected throughout the text. It is written to young people to warn them to "look out" for the problems that will beset them if they do not follow their ancestral traditions. A detailed recording of the progress of the lineage of a chief (also called Mboya) in Paul Mboya's home area illustrates the tone of the book in that it takes up eighteen of the total of fifty-four pages (1978, 36–54). It maps out the family tree from Mboya, showing just how many people have died without leaving descendants. Mboya warns of an impending crisis that will not be averted while "sin" (*richo*) continues. This crisis is depicted as being one of the death and destruction of family lines. The book is a call to young people to go back to their people's "traditions" in order to avert the approaching evil.

The terms *richo* and *chira* that are much mentioned in Mboya's second book warrant close attention. *Richo* is widely used in place of the English "sin," but also to explain the badness of things and orientation to evil in general. For the Luo, very often *richo* is that which breaks "taboo" (*kwer*) or their "law" (*chik*). *Chira* is given by Capen as "sickness caused by breaking a taboo" (Capen 1998, 24) and is used to explain the state of someone who has fallen foul of harmful powers due to their failure to do what is right. Mboya uses the term to explain the problems, illness, calamity, death, and destruction that can beset family lines. For Mboya, problems and death arise from the failure to keep taboos. In other words, the taboos should be followed so as to avert these evils.

Raringo (n.d.; but almost certainly published in the 1980s or 1990s) supports a similar conclusion in his small booklet called *Chike Jaduong e Dalane* (*The Rules for a Man in His Homestead*). This contains 331 rules on how to respond to situations in home life in such a way as to avert calamity or death. In my speaking with a variety of Luo people, I have discovered that these rules are known—they are a part of the Kenyan Luo "oral tradition." This booklet is set out as a manual to be referred to in the many eventualities of home life. The rules, all oriented to eradicating or minimising the effects of evil powers, make little sense to anyone not deeply familiar with the Luo way of life.

Oryare (n.d.; published in the late 1990s) implicitly draws the same conclusion in his autobiographical booklet written in English. Oryare is not defending Luo traditions, but rather advocating that they be left in favour of Christianity. He considers the Luo, in following their traditions, to be "dancing with devils," yet his book, available in bookshops in Kisumu and other parts of Luoland that I have visited, is almost totally *negative*. That is, it is written *against* Luo traditional practices, to be replaced by a presumed Pentecostal faith in Christ.[3] In other words, it is written against what he considers to be evil practices, with almost no attention given to what is to take their place.

There comes a point at which it is difficult to identify the difference between displacing evil and actually promoting good. Is life for some Luo people really only about countering evil? Mboya's 1997 text describes fishing methods. Fishing would seem to be a positive activity. Except that is, that Mboya's description is full of detailed prescriptions on how to ensure ritual cleanness to prevent the encroachment of evil that would frustrate the fisherman's task. Preparations for fishing, making nets, and launching boats, as described, are complex and arduous

3 Oryare seems to rather naïvely assume that if only people would pray, life's complexities would cease, and as in much African theological thinking, people would become wealthy as if "by default."

processes requiring great ritual detail. Fishing is itself, in a sense, a struggle against evil—acquiring good food from a dangerous body of water that is feared almost as death itself. It is almost as if fish are caught "by default," should all the evil things that prevent them from being caught be successfully averted (Mboya 1997, 31–41).

Crop growing would seem to be a singularly positive activity. The success of cropping activities is however also only ensured by the keeping of numerous taboos. A closely specified order has to be followed in planting, harvesting, etc., according to one's position in a family (1997, 66–67).[4] Remarkably, there is a myth amongst the Luo that even the necessity to cultivate by the strength of one's own hands is only due to the rebelliousness of a newly married woman who refused to keep the taboo given her by her elders (G. Ogot 1989). Even the need to cultivate is due to evil, in this case of a newly married woman in a way somewhat reminiscent of Eve in the book of Genesis. It would appear that the attention of the people is constantly drawn toward the warding off of evil.

3. WHAT DOES IT ALL MEAN?

Mary Douglas' classic book *Purity and Danger* shows us that things that infringe the wholeness of a human body are considered "dirty" (1966, 51). Hence fingernails, faeces, spit, and hair are widely held as unclean. This being dirty also imbues those parts with special powers. Witches can take such components to prepare medicines to kill people. This is certainly as well known amongst the Luo as amongst other people (Mboya 1997, 208).

Douglas then applies this same thinking to human society. She gives the Levitical laws as an example of setting boundaries around an orderly system (1966, 51–71). Leviticus considers that bodily emissions render someone unclean, and unclean animals are those that do not fit into "normal" categories; that is, four stomached and cloven hoofed. The latter causes pigs and camels to be considered "unclean" (Lev 11:1–8).

The tendency for African independent churches (AICs) to adopt and adapt such rules suggests that such thinking is not foreign to the Luo people. Amongst indigenous churches in the vicinity of my home, the *Nomiya* church considers that only circumcised men should be at the front in church. The *Luong Mogik* church sticks to Sabbath prohibitions even more strongly than the Seventh Day Adventists (SDA) church that they emerge from (Pudo 2002). *Roho* denominations

4 This rule at least continues to be widely known and discussed, even if not universally followed by the Luo.

claim to be able to see instantly if you hide a defilement like a cigarette in your sock on going to church (Omaya 2002). Questions of social uncleanness following a woman's period, or sexual intercourse for men, greatly troubles leaders of indigenous churches in western Kenya (Kedogo 1999).

The requirement for purity described by Douglas seems to be a deep part of the lives of those people in Africa with whom I have been able to have close contact. The time at which it is particularly crucial to get things right for the people in my community, is the time of death. A dead person becomes the focus of the people in the vicinity, who strive together to ensure that the spirit of the departed be content with how the body is buried, mourned for, and generally satisfied. Various sexual cleansing rituals are necessary after the late has departed and been buried (e.g., see Raringo n.d., 17).

As scientific theories suggest about light, so evil for the people whom I mix with (and presumably other African people) is both "wave and particle." Elaborate rituals are conducted to pacify "ghosts" (*jochiende*). These generally have an identity—a particular ancestor whose life grievances were never satisfied or whose handling at death was inappropriate. In another sense evil is also like a "shadow" (*tipo*) that hangs over a person, family, or place, causing ongoing calamity. There are times when more specifically territorial spirits like *juogi* and *sepe*—for the Luo, typically lake spirits—are invoked or held accountable for evil. All these things together are these days often given the label "Satan," from the Hebrew word for "devil" that has come to East Africa via English.

It should be clear at least that the fact that Satan is considered to be an *individual* source of evil in Western and/or biblical lore, does not mean that his identity is so restricted in East Africa. Here the word "Satan" covers many things such as witchcraft and evil powers in general (Omari 1993, 90). This allies with my experience in Luoland, where witchcraft power and ancestral spirits are almost synonymous and rooted in the word *juok*.

Okorocha from West Africa tells us, "It is true that Igbo gods keeled over at the advance of the British gunboats, but their demise did not indicate a rout" (1987, 279). This seems to apply to East as well as West Africa. Major spiritual battles rage in Luoland today. The association between cleanness of living and ritual functions, with health and prosperity, runs very strong in people's psyche. It is a fallacy to think that one can understand what is happening in a society by only listening to the eloquent (in English) and young and healthy who may claim that "all those things are gone." Pressures to conform to one's community's notions of "clean and unclean" are in reality enormous, and usually effective.

A widely discussed and greatly troubling issue is that of the inheritance/cleansing of widows. Until inherited, which involves the building of a new house and usually four days of cohabitation with a selected man, a woman in Luoland is considered to have *okola* (a spirit of death that renders her unclean). In my eight years in Luoland, I have seen many women widowed. Many of these have said that, because they are Christians, they will not be inherited. All those whose cases I have followed have been inherited despite such resistance. A noninherited widow, having limited social contacts and being liable to be blamed for calamities that arise in the community, will usually not stand up to the pressure.

There are various present-day responses to such restrictive practices. Christians claim the power of Jesus to be greater than that of the ancestral spirits, and to my observations are freed from the need to participate in certain practices. "Modern" life brings a confused message of liberation, all too often closely followed up by meaninglessness, yet apparently brings some freedom from spiritual aggression to taboo breakers. The conservative camp is quick to blame the people's current problems on the speed with which they have ditched age-old practices. The Kenyan legal machinery appears often vainly to try to bring order to an environment to which it barely fits. So the battles rage.

4. ASSUMED GUILT

"Guilty until proven innocent" seems to be the legal maxim people operate on in their day-to-day lives. This is a shock to discover for those accustomed to "innocent until proven guilty" that operates in Western nations. In what sense is guilt then assumed?

This "assumed guilt" seems to have a widespread effect on the African way of life. My colleagues in Zambia years ago frequently explained to me that any African owning a car must be a liar or a thief. It is hard to imagine that someone could be sufficiently good as to deserve such "foreign" wealth, so it is rather assumed that it was acquired through corrupt means. This means that the wealthy are particularly likely to be accused of evil. I am personally aware of a bishop of a small group of churches who managed to curry favour with some Christians from Britain, who agreed to buy him a personal vehicle. The local version of events—that he bought the vehicle using money intended for distribution in the churches—has since often come to my hearing. This bishop, as so many church leaders before him, has been branded a thief by those under him in a case in which I know he is innocent. People's respect for this leader is by this means severely diminished. "Evil" is assumed.

The situation in present-day Kenya is such that "immoral" behaviour pays dividends, to the extent that the morally upright may even be mocked for his naïveté (I take "moral" here as being that behaviour that follows the mores of one's people, and not rationally derived, ethical understanding). There are two parallel economies operating in Kenya, as elsewhere in Africa, being the "formal" and "informal" sectors. In the informal sector, which includes subsistence farming, craftsmanship, and small-scale trading, many people make a living but seldom much more. Large amounts of money circulate only in the formal economy. This is largely in the hands of people of foreign ethnicity. A local person wanting to draw from this economy requires good English and the ability to elbow his way into places. A chronic level of misunderstanding, due amongst other things to cross-cultural miscommunication, means that corruption is rife in this sector. The person who will benefit from it must fit to those corrupt ways, and then may suddenly become rich out of all proportion to his colleagues sweating in the informal arena. In this loose sense then, evil pays. It follows that he who has much wealth is assumed to have used evil means to get it.

This clearly puts Christian churches into a difficult predicament. Many foreign-planted churches maintain links outside of Africa. Much of what they do thus becomes identified with the formal sector, with all the above implications of immorality and evil. When the church is so heavily involved with money as it often is in Africa, particularly because outsiders see it as a convenient conduit for their aid and projects, the identity of God and the devil easily become confused. The church, supposedly the harbinger of good, is often the means by which people come face to face with immorality arising from windfalls of money, televisions, scanty dress and long trousers for women, widespread use of the language of exploitation and corruption (English), advocating "courting" of prospective marriage partners that is considered taboo in traditional Africa, and so on.

Whatever its origin, the concept of "guilty until proven innocent" is extremely far-reaching in its social consequences. In short—no one can be trusted. It is not easy, perhaps often impossible, to prove one's innocence. So all are assumed to be guilty. The implications of this on business and other social organisation is profound.

It could be argued that it is the kind of trust sometimes found in Western nations that is unusual, and that it is not unusual on a global and historical scale for people not to trust one another (Fukuyama 1996). If this is the case, then unfortunately the West is not succeeding in spreading its ethic of trust to Africa.

Failure in business is widely attributed to incursions by evil entities. Hence I was struck some years ago on being asked to lay hands on and pray for a lathe used in the business of a member of a particular church. The business in fact failed, as he explained to me some years later (Otieno 1999). Otieno takes his failing in such worldly exploits as a calling to serve God, and is gifted in the pastoral field, although hindered by his having two wives. Such directing of people into his service by the Spirit of God is reminiscent of the traditional African practice of pacifying possessing spirits by agreeing to be a medium for them to speak through. (e.g., see Lan 1985, 49 on Zimbabwe and Kirwen 1987, 91 on the Kenyan Luo).

This brings us to the vexed question of the evil in possessing spirits and by implication the activities of the "witch doctor" (Luo: *ajuoga*), who is typically guided by such (Kirwen 1987, 91). Discussion with students at KIST has often revealed that the witch doctor is widely considered by them to be a valuable person to have around, as he is responsible for doing away with evil, saving people from death, etc. Ironically the "evil" is needed (insofar as people also recognise the social damage done by witch doctors) in order to bring good. In my own experience, Pentecostal churches with strong links to the West are inclined to cast out such "evil," possessing spirits. Truly indigenous churches, such as those of *Roho* and *Legio Maria*, may interpret spirits as being God's Holy Spirit and encourage those with such spirits to prophesy to the church (see also Ndiokwere 1981, 90).

In this way indigenous churches have often appropriated the role previously held by the witch doctor. Their being active in healing and preventing death is well known (Wambugu 1995). Preventing death has been the preoccupation of Luo magical practitioners in years gone by, such that according to their tradition the Luo people know that they should not die (Obondi 2000). The pastor of my local *Luong Mogik* (indigenous) church concedes that all men are destined to die, but sets out to prevent "unnecessary death" (Pudo 2002). This is death caused by evil forces that can be turned away through prayer and a variety of rituals such as throwing water over someone, hopping around them, hitting them with a Bible, finding herbs for them as given by God in a dream, and so on.

Aging to the Luo is not a "natural" process as we understand such in Western nations. The infirmity associated with advancing years is caused by an accumulation of evil attacks, in turn leading to a gradual decline of the body's well-being. The upright person is able, by closely following the right as against the wrong way of life, to avoid the circumstances where evil attacks are many and strong. Careful communication with the divine realm helps to counter specific attacks.

Again and again we have seen wealth and progress arising from people's success in countering evil forces. What I have perceived increasingly is that being wealthy, and even eternal life, are the default position that would be everyone's if it were not for recalcitrant spiritual forces of evil.

This goes a long way to explaining the power of the prosperity gospel in Africa. The products of the "civilisation" that the white man has brought to Africa have been identified as those things that every person should have, but for his inadequacy at countering evil. The past ideal of much land and many cattle, children, and wives has been replaced in many people's minds by a new one of brick houses, vehicles, televisions, phones, and graduation robes that would all be theirs *if only* people were able sufficiently to purify themselves and keep evil forces at bay! This is, to them, evidently what has happened elsewhere in the world, or the wealthy Christians from America wouldn't always be such staunch advocates of prayer. Complex, traditional rituals are temporarily put aside as the young African Pentecostal immerses himself in his attempt to imitate the West (in language, dress, even social behaviour) and follow cleansing ceremonies as interpreted from the Bible by Pentecostal Christianity—such as fasting, all-night prayers, emphatic confession and repentance for sins, etc.

The Anglican churches in my vicinity are another striking illustration of people's tendency to concentrate on fighting evil forces. The Anglican Church is divided into the saved, or redeemed (Dholuo: *jomowar* or *jomokwo*), and the unsaved. A retired Anglican minister, given opportunity to speak at a wedding at Ulumbi (St. John's) Anglican Church, said, "*Ji mangeny wacho gin jomowar, to kanisani ok oger gi jomowar*" ("Many people say they are saved, but this church was not built by the saved"; Odera 2002). The "saved" these days resemble an indigenous church within the Anglican Church. They favour meetings that the Luo call *lalruok* ("fellowships"), at which people are required to confess their sins (Olanga 2000). These fellowships are often beyond the control of the official hierarchy of the church, who are themselves likely to be considered as *mogak* (i.e., unclean or in some way corrupted by evil and in need of cleansing; Obondi 2002).[5] This strong and, according to the church hierarchy, somewhat subversive movement within the Anglican Church is illustrative of a tendency within the Christian church in Africa as a whole to a domination by an active struggling against evil.

5 According to Obondi (2002), the formal church leaders cannot participate in these *lalruok* meetings, because it is inappropriate and would result in an inordinate amount of gossip should the church hierarchy have to "tell all" where their members are present.

The African has finally viewed the actual source of prosperity that he has been so desiring. Although not easy for him to understand, it now appears that there is "good" in the universe. The teaching brought by the white man confirms that this good comes from God. It appears to the African that this god is indeed the white man himself. Hence I have often heard people say that "*Jarachar en Nyasaye mar ariyo*" ("The white man is the second God," or more literally, "is God number two").

There is a lot of evidence that this is the conclusion being drawn. The acclaim of the white by African children is widespread; in Kenya, Tanzania, and Zambia it is much the same—where the white person walks, throngs of children are likely to gather shouting, "*Mzungu.*"[6] In casual conversation people are enthralled by the white man's achievements—the greatest of all to their minds perhaps being his construction of aeroplanes.[7] This acclaim of the divinity of whites has widespread repercussions for the life of my neighbours and colleagues.

"Worship" of whites is especially evident in Christian churches. Prominently displayed pictures of a white Jesus accentuate such. Those church leaders that are widely respected are those who have travelled in the white man's lands. Seminars, conferences, and teaching sessions are rendered respectable by the presence of whites. Photographs of Africans with whites are put on prominent display in people's houses. A calendar produced by one particular African church for its members is resplendent with pictures of their leaders sharing close fellowship with whites.[8] The white man's language, English, is coveted as the language of power. Compared with the white man, the African often sees his own standards falling far short.

While few would dispute that whites are held in great awe in Africa, some will deny my above association of whites with "gods" and "worship." I suggest that such a debate may be academic. Given the African traditional conception of good and evil plus his holistic world view, it is hard to escape the conclusion that whites are seen as "superhuman" (where "human" refers to his fellow Africans), which seems to come into the English category of "divine." In the old days, Mboya tells us (1997, 17), people used to say, "*Nyasache ober*" ("His God is good"). Perhaps people did not know good apart from God. They only knew that if they could succeed in defeating evil, then one day good would come, via God. "Good" has

6 I understand that this term is used in praise and awe of a white man.

7 I have noticed this mentioned as the pinnacle of the white man's achievements by a number of people in conversation.

8 I saw such a calendar produced by the Voice of Salvation and Healing Church in a pastor's home in rural Luoland in June 2002.

come, albeit in a confusing array of styles and colours, so those who brought it must be god(s).

This coincidence of identities gives present-day missionaries an extremely difficult task, that they in practice rarely want to engage. That is, to point to a God who is other than themselves, and thus avoid the strong undertones of idolatry that otherwise emerge. This is extremely hard to achieve in practice. In a place where a holistic worldview holds sway, as in Africa, God is the source of good. At the same time, the white person claims to be the source of good. He will bring "good," and sometimes claim that it is not God's but *his own* or that of his people. He will confirm people's suspicions as to his divinity through being able to hold his wealth to himself even in the face of great need amongst the people around him.[9]

This topic is a large and complex one. It would hardly be true to claim that white men have brought only good to Africa. Many problems come in their wake, such as the increasing poverty, rampant death, disease, and overpopulation affecting many parts of western Kenya today. Some would say, it appears that not everything has as yet been got right. That is, in their efforts at imitating the ways of the whites they are clearly still making (ritual) errors. Others will want to throw out the ways of the new "gods" and go back to their old ways.

5. WHY IGNORANCE HAS RULED FOR SO LONG

If this account is right and, in my various contacts' ways of thinking, good is the absence of evil, why does this have to be announced afresh, and why is it not already widely known?

The expectation that the African is capable and aware of "good" is clearly widespread. Much "development aid" and financial support is regularly sent to Africa to enable people to use these resources in order to build and develop their nation and economy. Such plans frequently fail to work as envisioned. Resources are diverted from the supposed achievement of good (as ascertained

9 In "traditional" Africa, claims to personal ownership were limited. Land, for example, was never someone's own, but belonged to the ancestors or to a man's clan. Food was there to be shared with the whole extended family. The use of tools, chairs, etc., was either restricted by laws given by the ancestors (Dholuo: *chike*), or they were available widely to the whole community. Good things that come from God, like animals hunted and large amounts of wealth, were to be distributed. Hence on coming to power in Kenya in 1963, Jomo Kenyatta said, "*Nimeshika ng'ombe kichwa. Kazi yako, kamua*" (Kiswahili for "I am holding a cow by its head. Your job is to milk it") (Kenyatta 1963). The cow refers to the wealth left to Kenya by the withdrawing British colonial powers. In Africa he who fails to make wealth available to the community acts contrary to accepted norms. One of the ground rules of Western economics is contrarily the holding of finance to enable the building up of productive capital.

by the Western donor) into uses that are countering evil, as valued by the African. Examples of the latter may include money invested in funerals, building of houses (in Luoland often built for ritual purposes as well as with use of the house in mind), and other investments that demonstrate one's "purity" and confirm one's victory over evil, such as motor vehicles, mobile phones, etc. Some resources of course go into escape from evil—by means such as moving overseas or studying foreign things to link in with the international sector. What is "good" is foreign, whereas indigenous uses of money and resources are against evil.

English words that presumably once referred to ritual levels of cleanness have gone into at least two directions. Many, such as "clean," "pure," and "dirty," or "infectious," have been appropriated by the medical profession and are nowadays widely presumed to refer to the presence or absence of microorganisms (see Harries 2000, 488; here chapter 12, 204). Others, such as "holy," "sanctified," and "repentance," have become specialist terms used by the "religious" fraternity, often with specific meanings derived from Christian theology. The man on the street in the West may talk of feeling good, or refreshed, or confident, but will not say he is holy. The Swahili equivalent (*mtakatifu*) and also the Luo (*maler*) are, on the other hand, common terms (or in the case of Swahili, at least roots of terms) that are used frequently in the course of normal life.

Steiner (1998, 375) sets the rhetorical question: "Are there 'untranslatabilities' caused by the remoteness from each other of . . . cultural contexts?" My answer to him is—yes there are! Steiner looks at numerous translations made from Chinese to Western languages. He finds they are remarkably similar and concludes: "Each translation in turn appears to corroborate what is fundamentally a 'Western invention of China.'" (1998, 378). Is the same thing happening for Africa?

If there are things that are hard for a Westerner to perceive about Africa, with all the sophistication in research techniques he has at hand, is the reverse not even more likely to be the case? The African is taught English in most cases with only a minimal and almost certainly distorted view of the culture from which it arises. Such a language taught in a kind of cultural vacuum "is like a thin wash, marvelously fluid, but without adequate base" (1998, 494). This is hardly a medium through which to communicate the intricate details required to imbue the worldview that allows the building of a positive good, as practiced in the West. Instead, the African person can learn the language and recall the words associated with financial management, economic growth, technical advancement, etc., without ever grasping the use intended by the originators of such terms. Rather, the new concepts will be: (a) considered to have a pseudomagical force,

(b) discarded as irrelevant, or (c) reinterpreted into a familiar framework. In the same way, a Western reader has a number of options as to how to comprehend Levitical laws, such as those considering certain animals as unclean to eat (Lev 11:1–7) or those considering a woman unclean after giving birth (Lev 12:1–4). Westerners often either: (a) stand in ignorance but awe of some Levitical laws, (b) ignore these laws as irrelevant, or (c) reinterpret them in ways that make sense to their current understanding, such as in terms of the need for hygiene.

Therefore, carefully put together English instructions intended to lift the African out of his "superstitious fear of evil forces" are so distorted in the process of communication that they simply become a part of the same original African worldview. "Western activities" going on in Africa could be compared to (the way a Westerner might understand) rituals conducted repeatedly by a priest in a temple as long as they are effective in bringing him wealth and possessions. Because the purpose of the knowledge held by teachers, doctors, lawyers, etc., is not *deeply* appropriated, changes in circumstances defeat the "professional." Things grind to a halt when the state of affairs is transformed.

"Twisted communication lines" continue to be the order of the day. Massive cultural exchange, as is being attempted to Africa, does not work as is all too often expected in the West. Effective communication with someone is only possible insofar as one understands his way of life. This is learned by living with him. Such proximal living between Westerners and Africans is rare, so the African is left trying to learn from someone who is distant.

My colleagues in Kenya and Zambia are left seeing good occurring by default in the absence of evil. Its positive manifestations are brought by white men, standing in the place of God. The people's preoccupation is countering spiritual sources of evil and attracting as much of the good that whites bring as they can.

6. CONCLUSION

Life in parts of Africa has been found in this essay to be a constant struggle against evil forces. "Good" is the default position achieved if these evil detractors are successfully averted. The belief that good comes from God has been strengthened and supported by the coming of the gospel to Africa. "Good" was at one time defined in terms of number of cows, wives, and children that a man had. It is these days increasingly perceived as the possession of Western goods and a Western lifestyle. Hence the strength of the prosperity gospel, and the frustration of the

African man that prompts him to pray all the more vigorously should he fail to prosper in this way.

The ability of European people to acquire and even "be" good is sufficiently startling to many African people so as for the white person to be considered to be a god. Such confusion of the human and divine is all too often naïvely ignored or incredulously misunderstood by the West, yet its ramifications are many and widespread. An embryonic theology arises out of the African worldview regardless of whether or not the bringers of what is good claim a divine origin for their products. Westerners' communications with people that supposedly ignore good and evil powers easily come to be, as heard by local people, loaded with divine connotations. Secular language does not exist amongst the people I have lived and worked with on the African continent over the last fifteen years. The failure of many missionaries to separate their own identity from that of the divine himself, by claiming to be or acting as if they are good, has been a root cause of the idolizing of the West that continues to encumber Africa.

The perception of "good" as the default position that is prevented by evil in the form of bewitchment and spirits is a key to unlocking the African worldview. It is implicitly assumed in the teaching of many African churches. Theologians who understand this and can communicate the gospel through this worldview are desperately needed.

REFERENCES

Capen, Carole A. 1998. *Bilingual Dholuo-English dictionary*. Tucson, AZ: Carole A. Capen.

Chirairo, Lillian Dube. 2003. Cosmologies and independentism. Lectures presented at Birmingham Univ. in Birmingham, England.

Clay, E. J., and B. B. Schaffer. 1984. *Room for maneuver: An exploration of public policy planning in agricultural and rural development*. London: Heinemann.

Douglas, Mary. 1966. *Purity and danger: An analysis of the concepts of pollution and taboo*. London: Routledge and Kegan Paul.

Fukuyama, Francis. 1996. *Trust: The social virtues and the creation of prosperity*. London: Penguin.

Harries, Jim. 2000. The magical worldview in the African church: What is going on? *Missiology: An International Review* 28/4: 487–502.

———. 2001. Ghosts and cleansing amongst the Luo people of Kenya in 2000. http://www.jim-mission.org.uk/articles/jochiende-gi-puodhruok-2000.pdf (accessed April 18, 2011).

Kedogo, Ayub. 1999. Lecture presented at Kima International School of Theology in Kima, Kenya. (Title and date not known.)

Kenyatta, Jomo, 1963. Presidential inauguration speech. Quoted in Francis Kiboi, lecture presented at Kima International School of Theology in Kima, Kenya.

Kirwen, Michael C. 1987. *The missionary and the diviner: Contending theologies of Christian and African religions*. Maryknoll, NY: Orbis Books.

Lan, David. 1985. *Guns and rain: Guerrillas and spirit mediums in Zimbabwe*. London: James Currey.

Mboya, Paul. 1978. *Richo ema kelo chira*. Nairobi: East African.

———. 1997. *Luo kitgi gi timbegi*. n.p.: n.p.

Ndiokwere, Nathaniel. 1981. *Prophecy and revolution: The role of prophets in independent African churches and in biblical tradition*. London: SPCK.

Obondi, Boniface. 2000. Immortality in the African context. Lecture presented May 24 2000 at Kima International School of Theology, in Kima, Kenya.

———. 2002. Becoming all things to all men for the sake of the gospel context. Lecture presented June 27, 2002 at Kima International School of Theology, in Kima, Kenya.

Odera, Aggrey. 2002. Speech presented at a wedding at Ulumbi (St. John's) Anglican church, July 6, in Ulumbi, Kenya.

Ogot, Bethwell A. 1999. The construction of Luo identity and history. In *Building on the indigenous: Selected essays 1981–1998*, ed. Bethwell Ogot, 179–204. Kisumu, Kenya: Anyange.

Ogot, Grace. 1989. *The strange bride*. Nairobi: Heinemann.

Okorocha, Cyril C. 1987. *The meaning of religious conversion in Africa: The case of the Igbo in Nigeria*. Aldershot, England: Avebury.

Olanga, Dan. 2001. Personal conversation.

Omari, C. K. 1993. *Uchawi na ushirikina*. (Witchcraft and superstition.) Mwanza, Tanzania: Inland.

Omaya, Abraham. 2002. Personal conversation.

Onyango, Tom. 2002. Personal conversation at his rural Luo home in Gem, Kenya.

Oryare, Owlar. n.d. *Luo traditions and Christian warfare: Dancing with devils*. Ruiru, Kenya: Ofra Christian.

Otieno, Paul. 1999. Personal conversation.

Pudo, Aluoch. 2002. Informal conversation.

Raringo, Jacktone Keya. n.d. *Chike jaduong e dalane*. n.p.: n.p.

Steiner, George. 1998. *After Babel: Aspects of language and translation*. 3rd ed. Oxford: Oxford Univ. Press.

Wambugu, Nyeri et al. 1995. African-instituted churches' contribution to the wider church. In *Report of the proceedings of the consultation: Building bridges between African traditional churches and the historic mission churches*, ed. P. A. Kalilombe, 31. Unpublished report.

CHAPTER 12

The Magical Worldview in the African Church: What Is Going On?[1]

1. INTRODUCTION

The Christian world rejoices over the phenomenal growth of the church in Africa. Yet at the same time many voices lament over its immaturity and lack of depth. We struggle to rectify the latter deficiency. Numerous programs for education and training of African church leaders are set up to that end. This paper suggests that one of the causes of the weakness of the African church is an error in the conception of one of the fundamental ways in which African culture is seen to relate to Christian doctrine. That is, it is wrong to think that Christian belief provides immunity to witchcraft attack and the curses that result from the breaking of taboo. This misled belief arises, I believe, from a misconception regarding the nature of magic.

2. WHAT IS MAGIC?

While in Western nations these days secularism appears to be a powerful, rampant force, much of the world continues to be directed by what I am calling the magical worldview. This presumes that physical and social reality originate from the good or bad will of people (dead or alive) and/or the gods. In turn, that success and prosperity or poverty and failure in life then depend on maintaining appropriate relations with the above. It seems that the English language is very poorly equipped to explain the nature of magic. In British English, Paul Daniels has confused

1 This chapter was originally published as follows: Harries, Jim. 2000. The magical worldview in the African church: What is going on? *Missiology: An International Review* 28/4: 487–502.

magic with trickery.[2] Although there may be trickery involved, it is not all trickery. The word "medicine," which no doubt used to describe magical substances, has been co-opted by the scientific biomedical fraternity. Although some traditional medicine may be scientific, much of it certainly is not. Words like "spell" are simply no longer in use. "Cursing" is considered to be merely the uttering of expletives. "Ghosts" are found primarily in children's stories, etc.

Yet contrary to popular opinion, I would like to suggest that magical worldviews do not simply disappear on exposure to Enlightenment thinking or to Christianity. Magic is not primitive, unsophisticated, and confined to the uneducated and the dull. It can be extremely sophisticated. And it works.

It is found in the West as well as elsewhere, although of a different nature and under different names. Examples of acceptable magical practices in the West include the following:

(1) Making use of a counselor with whom to share difficulties. Very often, we can be helped without receiving any direction or physical benefits from the counselor. Just having him or her listen to us is already of assistance.

(2) Placebo, as a recognised effect, even in biomedical circles.

(3) Positive thinking as an approach to life, whose advocates claim that thinking positively brings positive outcomes.

(4) Some day-to-day use of language is designed to have a magical impact. A typical example of this occurs if someone comments that he or she is not feeling well that particular day. A friend may reply, "You will be all right," as if that in itself can bring healing, and, of course, in a way it does.

It could be argued that these are not examples of magic but of the power of suggestion. Then one would need to ask whether there is a legitimate category called "power of suggestion" that is distinct from "magic" in the magical worldview. I suggest that there is not.

A friend of mine (a Luo pastor named Thomas Ogoda) often tells me that a "word has power" (*wach en gi teko*). It would appear that he has observed how positive words can build up someone's confidence and ability, how negative words

2 Paul Daniels is well known in the UK for his televised magic shows. He is very happy to admit that the "magic" he uses is no more than clever trickery.

can be depressing, and how, in a sense, telling someone something makes it come true (see examples above). Then he has also observed that sometimes people can be more or less encouraged or move in different directions without first hearing any audible words. It is only a small extrapolation to presume that such mood swings or changes in direction are nevertheless due to words of affirmation or condemnation which were uttered or even only thought, whether or not the person affected is consciously aware of this having happened.

It is clear that magic in the magical worldview as we are defining it overlaps with practices that in the West would not be deemed as magical. We could therefore begin by drawing the tentative conclusion that we have magic type A, which includes acceptable practices that are given different names in the West, and magic type B, which includes practices that are not recognised in the West but are found in Africa. For example, the power of suggestion would fall into type A, whereas the ability to make someone's crops fail through being jealous of him or her (a typical witchcraft case) falls into type B. To explore this issue further, we can go back to asking whether indeed a "word has power." I must acknowledge that if a family member came into my room and said with obvious, serious intent, "I wish Jim Harries would get sick and die," then this would trouble me. But if the same person stood in an empty field and said the same thing, then it would not trouble me. Or would it? If I were to admit honestly that the latter would also trouble me, then I would be conceding the power of magic type B over my life. In fact, in my understanding of the nature of human beings, we are inclined to acknowledge type B. In other words, I do not like having enemies, even if they do not appear to be in a position to do me any physical harm, and it makes me unhappy to know that some people do not like me. There is a deep inclination within me to consider such a person or people responsible for a misfortune should it befall me.

The above examples and explanation show that both types of magic still have roles to play in the West, even though much of the lives of Westerners and their understandings are rational. In traditional Africa, magic has much more of a hegemony over people's lives while rational understanding, such as scientific understanding, has a much smaller part to play.

In many African societies, events are often understood as happening due to magic, including especially good and bad fortune. When somebody gets sick, it is due to sin, a curse, or bad magic (i.e., bewitchment) (Mbiti 1975, 165). When that person recovers, it is because the curse has been undone or good magic has been brought to counteract the bad. Similarly, if someone becomes wealthy or has a good or bad harvest, it is due to magic.

It is only natural (although this is often not considered) for African people to assume that Westerners are fundamentally the same as they are and also to consider that prosperity arises due to magic of one sort or another. Hence, many people are preoccupied with trying to decipher the magical secret to the prosperity they see coming from the lands where the white man lives.[3] The question of whether or not magic "works" is in the African context a very heavily loaded one. A negative answer would seem to condemn the African people to being stupid. If it does not work, then why do so many people in Africa and elsewhere around the world pay so much attention to it? Yet if it does work, then some people in the Western missionary and secularising force should have egg on their faces because they have been saying that it does not.[4] The social reality of magic is of course beyond doubt. While perhaps not real in the scientific sense, it is as "real" as friendship, or as the love of parents for children, or as the team spirit of a group of boys playing football. As each of these has critical roles to play in life, so does magic.

Understood in this way, magical forces are a normal, powerful, and necessary part of social relationships and normal human existence. According to the magical worldview held in Africa, they are also primary, whereas physical forces are secondary.

For example, a likeable person (someone with a particular magical power) is often a person who prospers (a physical occurrence). The suspicion that a wife is committing adultery (magical insight) is what causes her husband to beat her (physical event).[5] Having an attitude of love for a co-wife (magical property)

---

3 This preoccupation can take many forms. It can be a primary motivation to the acquisition of further education. It can result in imitating the behaviour of whites without first understanding the motives that underlie their actions. Turner points out that it can result in suspicion that the African people have not been given the whole Bible (1979, 271–88)!

4 Just as an example to illustrate this: There is a poster that has been widely circulated in Kenya which reads, "AIDS is not witchcraft. AIDS is real."

5 Western readers may rather suppose that someone will not act on the basis of the suspicion of his wife's behaviour, until he has some evidence. This may not be the case in those living under the magical worldview. Hence even in the Old Testament there is a procedure instituted to ensure that women are not mistreated on the basis of ungrounded suspicion (Num 5:11–31). This example is comparable to one that happened at an African-led church in my home area in Kenya recently. A group of young men were very active in this church, working as elders and deacons. Then one day they told me that the pastor had forced them all to resign temporarily from their duties. I later discovered from the pastor that this was because he had received a word from a church in Malawi (which does not even share a border with Kenya) to the effect that his elders were visiting women in the church with ulterior motives. Having heard this divine word, there was no need for seeking "evidence."

will result in the two wives being able to cooperate in a task together (physical occurrence).[6] If positive thinking brings a positive outcome, then it would seem obvious also that negative thinking can be held responsible for a negative outcome. Hence, to take this one step further, if there is a negative outcome, then there must have been some negative thinking somewhere. As we are saying that the "magical property" precedes the physical outcome, somebody is hence held responsible for every negative outcome. This is where the magical worldview, when not centred on the sovereign God, gets to be extremely destructive. A culprit is sought for having caused every calamity; hence, suspicion, hatred, and jealousy between people are propagated. Someone who in this way is held responsible for every negative outcome has an extremely destructive effect on the whole society. The person who brings the negative outcome upon others or upon the whole society has become the enemy of society and the root cause of the evil that troubles it. This person is known as a witch.[7]

3. MAGIC AND THE BIBLE

It seems that magic is found in the African Bible. At least African people seem to find it there, according to our understanding of magic as described above. Theological educators may try to convince their African students that it is not there, but the enormous growth of Pentecostal churches in Africa, plus the presence of numerous spiritual indigenous churches of many varieties (Barrett 1968), show that the old orthodox teaching has been seen as having something lacking.

I have come across magical claims so often in churches in different parts of the continent (and in African-led churches in Europe) that I would not know where to begin to give references. Just today, as I write this on May 2, 1999, I was worshipping in a Revival church, and the pastor was assuring us that a truly godly man will not suffer illness or death until he reaches old age. Here is the best in magic, tied in with prosperity theology. Parts of Africa suffer enormously high mortality among youth and people of all ages because resources are simply inadequate to go around. In those areas, such claims are simply misleading lies from a Western, rational perspective. Yet here there are plenty of takers; the Revival church and other so-called spiritual churches are growing at incredible

6 Polygyny is common in this part of the world.

7 We have here focused on the nature of witchcraft in magically based societies. Yet it is rare to find a society oriented entirely to witchcraft. The latter tends to rise to particular prominence in times of instability. We have not yet mentioned the role of spirits of the dead or of gods that also have a part to play in ascertaining someone's prosperity. Their role falls within the same magical framework.

rates. There is plenty of fuel for the prosperity theology fire in the Scriptures. Much of the Scriptures indeed do follow the same magical worldview that Western nations seem to have rejected. Proverbs furnishes us with many examples; for example, Proverbs 12:21 and 22:9. Perhaps Deuteronomy 30:1–3 is one of the plainest explanations to the effect that prosperity does not come through careful planning and rationality, but by obeying the laws of (and this is where the Bible is strikingly unique) the one God:

> When all these blessings and curses I have set before you come upon you and you take them to heart wherever the LORD your God disperses you among the nations, and when you and your children return to the LORD your God and obey him with all your heart and with all your soul according to everything I command you today, then the LORD your God will restore your fortunes and have compassion on you and gather you again from the nations where he scattered you.

The uniqueness of the Bible is not in its denial of the power of magic. It is rather in its acknowledgment that ultimate power is in the hands of one God.

4. THE EFFECTS OF MAGIC

The effects of living under the magical worldview are many, wide-ranging, and deeply penetrating into a society and its people. Below are effects that I have found in nine years in total of living among rural people in Zambia and later Kenya.

Many of them will appear to be negative. This is almost inevitable because the evaluation is from the Western viewpoint where the magical worldview has been devalued for generations. For a Christian, this devaluation is right only insofar as the magical worldview falls short of the way of life that is lived under a genuine acceptance of the all-encompassing power of the great, mighty God and acknowledgment of the cleansing power of his son Jesus Christ. In other words, Christians brought up in the West need to be careful to ensure that they distinguish the critique of magic that arises from their inherently secular lifestyle from that arising from the Scriptures.

4.1 Complex codes of conduct govern the lives of people

Life governed by the magical worldview is extremely complex, as numerous rules and traditions are likely to be devised to maintain order and prosperity in society.

It is worth pointing out that rational legal and economic systems,[8] such as are operated in the West, are unknown in magically led societies. Whereas rational law supposes that living human beings functioning as responsible decision-making individuals are the only significant participants in a community, this presumption is totally contrary to a society governed by the magical worldview. In the latter, as we have mentioned above, the good and the bad wills of gods and of other people, whether dead or alive, must be taken into account if some issue arises.

For this reason, rational aims and objectives cannot form the guiding principle for life as they do in Western nations. Many Western governments are heavily committed to understanding how their national economy functions so as to prime and to maintain it at a high degree of efficiency for maximum productivity guided by indices such as the GDP (Gross Domestic Product), etc. Even at the household level, people are calculating how, with the most efficient use of time and other resources available to them, they can best please their families.

From within the magical worldview, such a mere predisposition to physical efficiency is far from adequate. Many more things must be kept in mind. One of these is the critical importance of following the examples laid down by one's forefathers, whose spirits often remain responsible for maintaining one's peace and prosperity (Mbiti 1975, 73). Another is the extreme necessity, whenever possible, to be friendly and accepting to everyone through fear that, should you upset them, their magic may prove to be of harm to you. Hence, the avoidance at all costs of face-to-face confrontation mentioned by Hill (1996, 327).

The combination of the above two, especially the former, results in oral (or sometimes written) traditions being developed that need to be adhered to as meticulously as possible in order to prosper. Anyone who fails to follow these laws or does so only half-heartedly is like a rebel in society who must be forced to comply for the good of the whole group. Such matters are no joke! To deny or to ignore these traditions is dicing with death. Therefore, people are bound hand and foot through their lives by numerous stringent regulations. According to Sayer (reporting on Max Weber), there is a "deep repugnance to undertaking any change because supernatural evils are feared" in societies governed by tradition and magic (1991, 14).

---

8 The discussion regarding the meaning and significance of "rationality" continues. It revolves especially around the interpretation of the writings of Max Weber. For comments on the relationship between traditional authority (such as that found in many non-Western and certainly African societies) and the economic order, see Weber 1947.

It is not easy to give up in a stroke the very things one understands as having brought life and prosperity to one's people for generations. The magic by which people are bound in Africa is not an inconvenient side issue in the way of the gospel or even an issue of development. It is *the* issue! Some of the aspects that propagate these traditions and help them to survive include the following:

(1) They give identity. What makes one a member of a particular tribe is that one follows the customs and traditions of that tribe. Giving up one's magically based traditions can result in losing one's identity.

(2) They give order and purpose to life. Simply removing people's traditions can leave their lives chaotic, meaningless, and purposeless. Here one must be careful.

(3) They give authority to the elders who authoritatively interpret the traditions. While some people may prefer to curtail the authority of old men over their society, few want anarchy.

(4) They make fascinating conversation. There is never a lack of interest in life as long as the latest speculations on the identity of witches, or on the way people's lives accord with traditional customs, can be discussed and disputed.

(5) The fear that failing to keep the traditions will bring problems (which is often shown to happen in practice[9]) means that people will continue to keep them.

It is these reasons and others in addition that account for the sheer persistence of customary beliefs.

4.2 Witchcraft beliefs flourish

Witchcraft beliefs and practices are almost inevitable companions to the magical worldview. In fact, the two terms, "magic" and "witchcraft," are indistinguishable in many African languages. For example, in Swahili "witch doctor"[10] and "magician" are both translated by the same word, *mchawi* (Johnson 1939, 271). (I would personally suggest that a more correct translation for both these words might be

---

9 This is seen to be proven in practice because it is on these lines that events are interpreted. Hence there is plenty of evidence, in people's eyes, for the advisability of following tradition.

10 I have avoided the term "witch doctor" in favour of "diviner" in most cases in this chapter because of the stigma attached to it in some circles. The term used by the Luo people is *ajuoga*, where *juok* is "witchcraft." The Bantu people (in the Swahili and Kaonde languages) use *mganga/muganga*.

mganga, which is also used to translate the English word "doctor"). Within this worldview then, when misfortune or illness strikes, there is always the possibility that this has been caused by someone's evil intent or thoughts; that is, by evil magic or witchcraft.[11] Let us take the example of a death occurring. This may be interpreted as being due to the person's failing to keep some particular law or tradition; that is, by breaking a taboo. Yet to assume this is to degrade the character of the person who has already died. Family and friends, especially of someone who has been popular, will not want to spoil that person's name when he or she is dead.

Instead, they are likely to assume the dead person to be innocent of causing his or her own death, but then the death must still be explained. The explanation will be that someone else has killed him or her! A killer is sought out, usually with the help of a magician who specialises in such discernment. This killer may be understood to have functioned as a sorcerer who kills by prepared magic, or the killer may have been a witch who killed unwittingly or even unknowingly; for example, by harboring evil thoughts, as discussed above.[12] It should be realised that illness and death are never neutral, incidental, or primarily physical events (Mbiti 1975, 165). They inevitably have a magical cause. Illness must then be dealt with by countering the attacking power, and death must be avenged. This is often done by arranging in turn (through magical means) the death of the one who is considered to have been the killer. In this area, we find one of the most horrific side effects of the magical worldview. People who believe in witchcraft—in blaming another person for any misfortune that one meets—propagate jealousy, suspicion, distrust, and hatred within a community. So Shorter tells us that where witchcraft is rampant, "evil is always on the verge of victory and must be constantly held at bay . . . It is a topsy turvy nightmare world" (1985, 96). But what I hope will also be apparent is that witchcraft cannot be dealt with in isolation. It is one of the outcomes of having a society run on the principle of magic, in which the power of Almighty God is not recognised. Another important point that needs to be made is that bewitchment and the breaking of law or tradition are terms that are used as almost synonymous in meaning with illness, misfortune, and death.[13]

---

11 This understanding is certainly not confined to Africa, but has been found in many parts of the world, including in early Greek religion, where according to Parker, "it seems almost inevitable that human malice must often have been diagnosed or at least suspected as the cause of a particular misfortune" (1983, 251). See also Mbiti 1975, 165–66.

12 There is a recognised distinction in anthropological circles between witches who have innate, destructive magical powers and sorcerers who concoct magic. For example, see Mbiti 1975, 165–166.

13 For example, in the language of the Luo the word *chira* refers both to the breaking of traditional laws and to the wasting illness that results.

Too many Western missionaries have been mistaken for generations in perceiving witchcraft and its allies as being in some mysterious, upper spiritual realm. In that realm, it is assumed that the greater spiritual power of God has already totally defeated them. Yet if the above is true—that the terms "witchcraft" and "illness" are almost synonymous, as the latter is always thought to be caused by the former—then to say that a Christian is not affected by evil magic is in effect to say that a Christian is always happy and wealthy and does not become sick or suffer misfortune![14] Through an inadequate understanding of the linguistic semantics of the magical societies they have been working in, missionaries have been inadvertently propagating the prosperity gospel. They have taught in effect that Christians do not have troubles and do not get sick. This teaching is unbiblical and in the end unhelpful.

We need to admit that Christians can still suffer from witchcraft and curses for our teaching to make sense to people. Our focus must be somewhere else! In effect, for Christianity to give immunity to magic reduces the Christian faith itself to being no more than a brand of magic. I do not believe that this is the case, as I believe that in salvation through Jesus Christ there is something different and new. Jesus is not only the latest and most powerful diviner!

Where should the focus of our teaching instead be? This is a big question. One answer is the Christian teaching that God has a purpose even in suffering (e.g., see Heb 12:1–13). This even goes so far in the Scriptures that in some way, albeit in a limited way, our suffering completes the work of Christ (1 Pet 4:13–14). To suffer is a privilege. It is not something to be avoided or to run away from at all costs, whether through magical means or other.

4.3 Western institutions flounder

Western institutions have been set up all over Africa and elsewhere in the non-Western world. Many of them are founded and function with the aim of bringing good with the aid of science and reason. These include hospitals, numerous varieties of schools and colleges, businesses, leisure societies, aid and development projects, even political parties, etc.

Yet how do these fare in magically based societies? The foundations and underlying principles of these organisations are generally foreign and unfamiliar. Local people therefore inevitably try to understand them by comparison with

14 I am considering the term "sickness" in its broad sense, as explained by De Rosny (1985) as including unemployment and general misfortune.

familiar institutions. They then adapt them to more closely resemble something that makes sense to them. Typically these are the extended family-, age-, and male-ordered village hierarchies, and the preexisting network of magical practitioners.

The above assumes that there has been a degree of ownership. Other institutions are just so foreign that they remain no more than the purveyors of mysterious rituals. After all, local people in most cases do not understand them, did not design them, and did not ask for them.[15] If they do want them, it is generally because they are evidently generators of funds.

This was illustrated clearly to me in recent years by a cloth-dying project that was introduced to my area.[16] Being a project run by a white person, and with money to back it up, it could not be refused as there would certainly be advantageous side benefits for the community. The local person hosting the project conceded openly that he did not understand what the project was supposed to achieve or how it was supposed to work. Three years later, the initiator's hopes that this project will continue in his absence look less and less likely as he has had to realise that those who were encouraging him by telling him that he would succeed were in effect reasoning magically. That is, they took words as having power and projects as succeeding if only everyone believed that they would succeed, and anyone expressing doubt was at risk of being accused of causing the resulting failure. As a third party talking with people about the project, I learned very early on that only a few of them had any genuine hope for success.

Hospitals have their particular difficulties. They deal with the symbols and objectives of good health and life, which are very familiar to African people. Many modern medical practices have a remarkable resemblance to traditional medical rituals.[17] Yet in other ways they remain extremely foreign.

Their major weakness from the perspective of the magical worldview is their failure to deal with the root cause of a problem, the root cause being magical. Instead, the focus in Western hospitals is on dealing with symptoms.

The enclosed and regulated style of hospital management is also difficult for people to cope with. People from different tribes and backgrounds are simply mixed. Nonfamily members are expected to carry out intricate patient care,

---

15 That is not to say that no verbal desire for something was expressed, but that there was no deep, heartfelt urge that would motivate people to put themselves out to achieve it.

16 I am not revealing the true nature of this project, as it remains a sensitive issue locally.

17 Such as the diviner purporting to remove an evil substance from the body, and an appendix removal in a modern hospital. Similarly the swallowing of various substances which are oriented to alleviate particular bodily disorders.

such as dressing, washing, and changing bedpans for the sick.[18] This gives ample opportunity for the administration of bad magic or for the nurses to be affected in turn by whatever magic is troubling the patients. Numerous taboos may be broken, even unwittingly, such as exposure of nakedness or sleeping on a bed previously slept in by one's mother-in-law.[19]

Western institutions are usually founded on an understanding of cause and effect in the physical realm in which human activities and finance are perceived as essentially physical. This is contrary to the magical understanding. The physical realm functions by planning; the magical realm by protecting and securing relationships, sacrifices, incantations, spells, medicines, and the following of traditions.

Attempts by individuals or sectors of the population at following planning and rational procedures are frequently frustrated by the pressures of the extended family. Pressure from relatives can be difficult for anyone to overcome. For example, when someone is wanting funds from a relative who has access to money which is earmarked for another use, the difficulty of standing up to such pressures is enormously magnified when the failure to cooperate brings destructive magical retaliation.

4.4 Tribalism is underpinned

Tribalism is considered a major problem in Africa, and along with racism, in much of the world. One cornerstone of a people's distinctiveness that underpins this great partiality to others is their particular set of traditions which are often supported by magical beliefs. Certain rituals are considered to have great magical significance. For example, male circumcision is not primarily valued due to any improvement in hygiene or sexual pleasure. Circumcision brings a blessing and bars a curse. It also acts as a mark of group identity. In other words, it is an essentially magical ritual (Mbiti 1975, 93–97). Reading the Scriptures reveals that circumcision is not a new issue, yet it seems to remain as much a divider of people in Africa as it did in the ancient Middle East. As long as the distinctions that people seek to maintain between their group and another group are magical, it is extremely difficult to find an acceptable unifying ritual. This is because of the nature of the foundation that underlies magical taboos and traditions, which are

18 In many African hospitals, nurses are not expected to do these duties for the reasons here being explained.

19 This is thought by some tribal traditions (for example, that of the Luo people in Kenya) to result in death (personal communication in 1997 with Isaac Odhiambo, pastor to a Pentecostal church in western Kenya).

not required to be logical.[20] This foundation may in some instances be extremely nonrational. Its origin may be almost arbitrary, which means that there is a very good chance that it will be different for one people than for another, which can in turn make cooperation among people very difficult to achieve.

For example, the law of the Luo people states that sons must build their houses in order of seniority. That is, older sons must build before younger sons can build. This is justified by saying that this is a way of showing respect. The law is underpinned by magical powers, which will bring misfortune or a curse should it not be upheld (Mboya 1983). This customary law continues to be much debated and variously upheld among the Luo of western Kenya today. Yet its reasoning is sufficiently shallow, or as I have said above, nonrational, for people from many other tribes in Kenya simply mock those who feel obliged to uphold it. Hence, the magical underpinning of a customary law continues to aggravate intertribal tensions.

4.5 Language has different bearings

We are accustomed to the need to expect different degrees of relationship between language and the world it describes. For example, we know that journalists sensationalise and politicians use words in careful ways that seem to make problems disappear.

We have mentioned that the modern positive-thinking school in the West is making use of a form of magic. They hold that by thinking of things greater than they are, the reality of the world tends to follow where their thoughts have led (Peale 1948). There may be truth in this. Yet it also helps to know when dealing with such people that they are following this line so as not to be misled by what is happening.

Language is very much of this nature in the magical worldview. What is said may not be a description of the reality as it is recognised by someone from a realist's vantage point. Things are rather described in the way that they ought to be in the hope that on having been described in that way, that which ought to be will come about.

We can also examine here the question, "Will it work?" In the rational worldview, this is a matter of weighing pros and cons, checking out a budget, or

20 A contrast can be drawn with some legitimacy with the relations between Western nations. In the latter, interflow of resources, personnel, finance, etc., is possible due to the high degree of rationality found in the reasoning of many institutions, even across national and cultural boundaries. For example, a bank in France functions on the same principles as a bank in Japan.

examining forecasts that are based on an extrapolation of previous experience. The answer may come out as "yes" or "no" or "it depends." In the magical worldview, if the thing being asked about is desirable, then there is a strong bias to answer "yes," regardless of the lessons of previous experience.

The widespread assumption of those in the magical worldview that the West is operating on the same basis as they are has already been mentioned. The magic that the West employs is evidently more powerful than theirs. They may therefore have more faith in Westerners than they do in their own people!

4.6 Jesus is the greatest of diviners

In any society, the unknown can only be understood by relating it to the known. This applies to people's understanding of Jesus. For someone in the magical worldview, the person whom Jesus most resembles is often the magician or diviner (sometimes known as a witch doctor). Jesus is understood as being the great magician ancestor! (See also Schoffeleers 1982.)

To some extent, the understanding of Jesus as the greatest diviner is very useful, but somewhere along the line, it must also fall short. That is because no magician that this world has known has succeeded completely. Illness does take hold despite the magician's efforts. The normal thing then for many African people is to move from one diviner to another until their resources run out or death or the severity of the disease finally defeats somebody. This then is the way Jesus can come to be treated by those who consider him to be the greatest diviner. He is still only a diviner.

A diviner is evaluated by the extent to which he can help people with their (usually immediate) problems. Yet Jesus did not come only to solve our problems. In fact, he admitted that he was also bringing us some (Matt 10:34). He taught us rather to live through our difficulties and that they could even bring reward (Heb 12:11). While it may be right to classify Jesus as a great diviner, he was also much more than that!

5. IMPLICATIONS FOR MISSION STRATEGY

Once we have a grasp of some of the widespread effects of what we are calling a magical worldview, on the whole, of a people and culture, then this needs to influence the way we carry out mission. Below are just a few suggestions of practical implications.

5.1 Magic and religion

The dichotomy between magic and religion has often been discussed. Much of James Frazer's thinking about this distinction has fallen into disrepute. However, Frazer's evolutionary-based definition is still widely accepted among many anthropologists; that is, that religion is petitioning and worshipping a great sovereign being, whereas magic is the attempted forceful manipulation of occult powers that are assumed to exist by "less advanced" people. Hence, magic is relegated to the realm of the backward and the ignorant (see Grunlan and Mayers 1988, 228).

Definitions are often unhelpful when they impose a false limitation on the breadth of meaning which words otherwise carry. This is certainly a case in point. The relegation of magic to the realm of backward people has blinded academia to its deep roots and its persistent hold on society.

The Enlightenment tendency to create a dualism between the physical and the spiritual has lead to a further demise in the understanding of magic. Not only is it now considered dated, but it is also considered to be found in that "other" realm often considered unreal and imaginary by secularists (Hiebert 1985, 158).

We must take a renewed look at magic if we are going to make progress in understanding those peoples around the world who visibly labor under it. We are not going to make progress with such a dualistic model. I suggest that magic must be seen as a normal part of human existence. It is deeply rooted in the human psyche. The mystery should be removed from it. This will begin to happen when we recognise that there are Western equivalents to some of the magical practices and practitioners found in the non-Western world (see above).

Hill gives us a good start in suggesting that we begin to see magic as neutral powers, something like the psychic (1996, 337). Such can be used for good or evil. It is not their presence that is the problem, but their abuse. I suggest that it is not their abolition that we are aiming for as Christian missionaries, but their orientation to God in the place of spirits of the dead. It would appear that when working with people who are functioning within a magical worldview, the Christian missionary may have much to learn from diviners before he or she begins to suggest changes to their practices. Hence, also Kirwen tells us, "The more a Christian Priest takes on the role of the diviner . . . the more effective and meaningful he becomes in the lives of the Africans" (1987, 106).

5.2 A revised understanding

It seems that even today all too many Western observers look down upon the African way of life as lazy, inefficient, etc. It is not so common to try to investigate why this may be. The reason I suggest is the deep and widespread belief in the efficacy of magic. Examined from a secular or physical point of view, some of people's behaviour may appear illogical. But when all the magical beliefs are taken into account, this is no longer the case.

Magical beliefs are powerful and penetrating. They underpin whole ways of life and do not simply disappear in the face of modernity and material prosperity. Rather, an understanding of the latter is intricately incorporated into the preexisting worldview.

5.3 No immunity to witchcraft

I suggest that missionaries and those church leaders and commentators in Africa who publicly follow their example are wrong to depict salvation in Jesus Christ as giving immunity either to witchcraft attack or to tribal curses that arise from people's failure to follow their tribal traditions.

This conclusion was originally drawn by dualistic thinkers. They imagined that magical forces were unreal—existing only in the mind—or otherwise in a spiritual realm that we as Christians consider to be already totally defeated by the power of Jesus Christ. For the latter, we need to remember the "already and not yet" thinking on the kingdom of God. For the former, our missionary forefathers considered that if these forces could only be ignored, they would go away. The difficulty lies in ignoring them when they have had such a consuming hold on people's lives. There is nothing "only" about magical beliefs being in the mind. The mind after all is the very seat of human consciousness and the core of our being.

Perhaps the most damaging effect of the immunity-to-witchcraft-and-curses view in Africa has been the mushrooming of prosperity teachings. This is because those who have brought such teachings have not realised to what an extent in people's understanding disease and suffering are synonymous with bewitchment and curse. To say that Christians are immune to the latter is in effect to say that they are immune to problems. It is also to say by simple implication that those who suffer or have problems have backslidden or have lost their faith. Here there is no assurance of salvation, no resting in the arms of Jesus, no acceptance of the purifying and upbuilding role of trials. Instead, there is an incessant fear of making a false move lest the protection of the greatest diviner, Jesus, should be removed.

We need rather to teach that while the kingdom of God has already come, it is at the same time not yet here. Witchcraft can indeed take a hold on us. Then it is not ours to avenge. Breaking of a taboo can hurt us, yet traditions need to take second place. We do not force Gentiles to be circumcised, but neither do we deny the Jews their ancient rite. We trust in Jesus through all, we claim him as a great diviner, but also much more! A recent incident helped me to understand Jesus' role as diviner.

Luo tradition dictates that, should a man take a second wife, he should continue to give the first wife senior status. A neighbor of ours married a second wife but then, contrary to Luo law, built a larger house for her than he had built for the first wife. The man subsequently became ill. He went to the diviner, who told him that in order to get well he must rectify his error and knock down the newer largest house. He did this. He still did not get well, so he called some Christians from a spiritual church to pray for him. They did pray for him and told him that he must be saved in the name of Jesus Christ. I later asked the same Christians about this, and they told me what had happened. On inquiring whether the diviner had given good advice, they said that, yes, of course he had. The Christians agreed that he was right to have knocked the second house down, but now he needed to be saved in the name of Jesus in order to be healed.

5.4 The basis of teaching

Too often our theological education is comparable to that of giving someone in a cheese store instructions on how to cook beef. Unless there is a way of getting him or her some beef, little benefit is obtained. He or she needs to know how to prepare cheese if unhealthy dependence on meat is to be avoided.

What does all this mean in practice? Below are three very practical points that need to be taken seriously in further research and practice.

(1) The current Protestant emphasis on critical Bible study for all believers must be recognised as relatively recent. The Reformation did not occur until the sixteenth century after all. This means that God was prepared to allow his church to exist for 1,500 years without the modern biblical studies' insights that it brought.

We need to be careful that the baby does not disappear with the bath water. However, we also need to think carefully about our attempt at transferring a product of sixteenth-century European thinking into an African society that in many respects more closely resembles biblical culture as it was at the time of Exodus. A rational, systematic approach to the Bible may seem to have little point to those whose lives are neither rational nor systematic but continue to be governed by magical interpretation in their approach to life in general.

It is necessary to investigate what is an appropriate approach to biblical interpretation from within the magical worldview, such as I did with the thesis I wrote while engaged in postgraduate study (Harries 1995).

(2) Closely connected to the above is people's deep desire for release from spiritual oppression, and not primarily for understanding in an apparently abstract way. The latter appears to be a particularly Western trait. Liberation theologians would seem to agree here, hence their major focus on praxis (Gutiérrez 1983).

While going along with the liberation theological analysis of recent Western theology to some extent, I differ with them in the proposed alternative direction. Some appear to have falsely reified the magical powers that Paul describes: "For our struggle is not against flesh and blood, but against the rulers, against the authorities, against the powers of this dark world and against the spiritual forces of evil in the heavenly realms" (Eph 6:12). Liberation theologians on the other hand are over inclined to interpret these powers from a Marxist perspective instead as being political and economic forces. Is this effectively throwing people "off the scent" of their real oppressors who are witches, sorcerers, the gods, and/ or the dead?

The section of the church that has taken the latter powers the most seriously in recent times has been the Pentecostals. There is considerable evidence that a Pentecostal approach even originated and certainly continues to be especially strong among African and non-Western people.[21]

Pentecostalism indeed does speak to the hearts of non-Western people in a way which classic Reformation theology does not; hence, the enormous growth of Pentecostalism in many parts of the world.

The great danger that I perceive here is the confusion that is occurring as a result of the leadership of many Pentecostal movements being in the West. The connection is stark between Pentecostalism arising from the West, whose material prosperity has arisen following the Enlightenment and the Industrial Revolution, and a grossly misleading prosperity theology. While Pentecostalism has much to teach us, its effective spread and its remaining true to biblical teaching requires its divorce from many of the misleading symbols of specifically Western

21 Hence, for example, William J. Seymour, who was active in the birth of Pentecostalism at the great Azusa Street revival in the USA, was an Afro-American (Nichol 1966, 32).

prosperity that often accompany it.[22] Failing this, it is all too easily perceived as the brand of Christianity that legitimises magic to an extent which far surpasses biblical precedent.

(3) Following on from the above is the desperate need for a theology of suffering that makes sense in the non-Western context. This theology must arise in the context of a clear recognition of the power of the magical forces of evil, but also, to borrow a term from the liberation theologians, out of praxis.

The vast gap in material prosperity in many parts of the world between Westerners and the majority of the non-Western population makes it extremely hard for a presentation of a teaching on suffering by the former to be heard by the latter. Such teaching can all too easily be seen as a mockery or aiming to try and pacify those who could otherwise see themselves as being the oppressed in a Marxist sense.

For such a theology to take root, a contribution from academia is required. More importantly, what is required is the giving of lives in sacrificial service in ways that are understood by symbols comprehensible to the non-West. And such sacrificial lives must continue to be ones of joy. Maybe there is no other way out than that of the cross and of sacrifice. Sometimes this may mean that a Westerner will consciously refuse comfort and protection that is offered to be sufficiently vulnerable to share in the suffering with which local people can identify.

6. CONCLUSION

To relegate magic to backward people and bygone years is to misunderstand its nature and to underestimate its power. In Western nations, what was once known as magic now goes under different headings, yet when carefully examined, its roots are evident. Reading from an African cultural perspective reveals a lot of magic in the Bible.

The much more central role of magic in African societies has widespread and profound effects on Africans' ways of life. Complex codes of customary laws govern the whole of life. Witchcraft beliefs flourish, Western institutions flounder, and even tribalism is underpinned by magic. Jesus' life as depicted in the New Testament is easily seen as being that of a great diviner. Very often this

22 Such as the use of an American accent, black shoes and suit, public address system, and wealth in terms of access to cash rather than locally grown food, cattle, etc.

widespread prevalence of magic is hidden from view to the West by the use of English, which is poorly equipped to explain it.

The distinction between magic and religion set out by Frazer in the nineteenth century is proving to have a blinding effect on current scholarship. A greater appreciation of the role of magic would improve understanding by missionaries and others for the reasons that many African traditions seem so nonrational and resistant to change. It can also go a long way in explaining why we now find such a rampant prosperity theology in Africa.

This essay throws light on a number of critical missiological issues. First, prosperity theology is reinterpreted as an almost inevitable misunderstanding arising from different aspects of Western and African thinking meeting in the way that they have. Second, and a closely related conclusion, is that the magical worldview has not been and is not as easily defeated by Western rationality as was once thought. What often appears to the Western observer as a widespread or even wholesale adoption of Western thought forms, on closer viewing transpires to be a Western veneer on a confused but otherwise vibrant magical system.

The above conclusions do not mark the defeat of the gospel so much as what has been an almost inscrutable victory. The very existence and power of the magical worldview is also one reason why the gospel of Jesus Christ has taken such a strong hold in Africa. Unlike secular Western prescriptions for progress, problem solving, and development, the gospel strikes a beam of light and hope to the heart of African culture and values. "The stone that the builders rejected has become the cornerstone" (Luke 20:17b).

REFERENCES

Barrett, David B. 1968. *Schism and renewal in Africa: An analysis of six thousand contemporary religious movements*. Oxford: Oxford Univ. Press.

De Rosny, Eric. 1985. *Healers in the night: A French priest's account of his immersion in the world of an African healer*. Maryknoll, NY: Orbis Books.

Grunlan, Stephen A., and Marvin K. Mayers. 1988. *Cultural anthropology: A Christian perspective*. 2nd ed. Grand Rapids, MI: Zondervan.

Gutiérrez, Gustavo. 1983. *We drink from our own wells: The spiritual journey of a people*. London: SCM.

Harries, Jim. 1995. Silver or gold have I none: The good news of Jesus Christ in relation to witchcraft in Africa. MA thesis, Brunel Univ.

Hiebert, Paul G. 1985. *Anthropological insights for missionaries*. Grand Rapids, MI: Baker Book House.

Hill, Harriet. 1996. Witchcraft and the gospel: Insights from Africa. *Missiology: An International Review* 24/3: 323–44.

Johnson, Frederick, ed. 1939. *A standard Swahili-English dictionary*. Oxford: Oxford Univ. Press.

Kirwen, Michael C. 1987. *The missionary and the diviner: Contending theologies of Christian and African religions*. Maryknoll, NY: Orbis Books.

Mbiti, John. 1975. *Introduction to African religion*. London: Heinemann.

Mboya, Paul. 1983. *Luo kitgi gi timbegi*. Kisumu, Kenya: Anyange.

Nichol, John M. 1966. *Pentecostalism: The story of the growth and development of a vital new force in American Protestantism*. London: Harper and Row.

Parker, Robert. 1983. *Miasma: Pollution and purification in early Greek religion*. Oxford: Clarendon.

Peale, Norman Vincent. 1948. *A guide to confident living*. Greenwich, CT: Fawcett.

Sayer, Derek. 1991. *Capitalism and modernity: An excursus on Marx and Weber*. London: Routledge.

Schoffeleers, Matthew. 1982. Christ as the medicine-man and the medicine-man as Christ. *Man and Life* 8/1–2: 11–28.

Shorter, Aylward. 1985. *Jesus and the witchdoctor: An approach to healing and wholeness*. London: Cassell.

Turner, Harold W., ed. 1979. *Religious innovations in Africa: Collected essays on new religious movements*. Boston: G. K. Hall.

Weber, Max. 1947. *The theory of social and economic organization*. London: Collier Macmillan.

CHAPTER 13

Biblical Hermeneutics in Relation to Conventions of Language Use in Africa: Pragmatics Applied to Interpretation in Cross-cultural Context[1]

1. INTRODUCTION

Discussions on hermeneutics have rarely considered one very important factor. That is, *how* words are *used*. Such is the bread and butter of the academic disciplines of pragmatics and discourse analysis. I would like to consider the implications of this in today's "shrinking" world, especially in relation to biblical interpretation and Christian teaching and mission in Africa.

The Summer Institute of Linguistics (SIL) and its associates in Bible translation have undoubtedly done an impressive job in taking the Scriptures into diverse languages around the world. Somewhat in close sequence to possession of Scriptures in mother tongues, we also however find emergence of new religious movements or, in the African context, African indigenous churches (AICs). We can ask ourselves why such apparently non- or marginally orthodox movements are so quick to emerge if the translation process has been so successful? It would seem that indigenous people do not always come to understand or apply (i.e., use) the Scriptures "as they should."

---

1 This chapter was originally published as follows: Harries, Jim. 2006. Biblical hermeneutics in relation to conventions of language use in Africa: Pragmatics applied to interpretation in cross-cultural context. *Evangelical Review of Theology* 30/1: 49–59.

2. SCRIPTURES BOOST TRADITIONAL BELIEFS

A good clue as to why this should be is given by Sanneh, who points out that, far from the translation of Scriptures being a means of oppressing "traditional cultures," it very often results in their revival (1989, 83). On careful consideration this should not surprise us, as Bible translators into mother tongues are of course "forced" to use terms that already have deep and wide roots in the preexisting way of life. Finding such in written form in a book said to have originated in God himself is likely to be a boost to traditional rituals and practices, now given official Christian legitimacy and sanction. It is ironic that churches and their Bible teaching, often considered to be destructive of traditional cultures, are shown by Sanneh as being rather the refuge for the latter.

A few examples of how this works in the Luo language of western Kenya, written from an indigenous African perspective, may illustrate this point:

(1) "Holy Communion" is a new, foreign, and no doubt powerful white man's ritual but becomes *sap ruoth*—a memorial celebration for a departed Luo chief.

(2) "God" who was a mysterious, ambivalent fellow originating in distant parts of the globe, whom one can barely fathom, is now clearly identified as *Nyasaye*—the very life-force that has guided our people for generations.

(3) That strange-looking, nuclear family need no longer be our model for Christian living, as the Old Testament is replete with examples of big men having multiple wives.

(4) Confusing teachings on science and physical causality need no longer be taken seriously, as numerous biblical examples make it clear that at the root of suffering and misfortune is no less than *ketho kwer*, which we (i.e., the Luo) know to be breaking the laws handed down by our ancestors.[2]

3. LIP SERVICE NOT MATCHED BY ACTION

Some of the above discussion is old hat to missiologists. Although it must be said, such discussion is deceptive in its penetration and power. That is, while

2 The above four examples are drawn from personal understanding after an extended period of sharing in the lives of African/Luo people.

a missiologist may give lip service and recognition to the above, their mind gravitates back to their own roots when giving a morning devotion or preparing a message to share at the Sunday service. (Such "gravitating back" can, in my view, be avoided to some extent if a non-Western language is used.) The same of course happens in our theological seminaries that are dominated by Western texts and inputs. In other words, even the degree of recognition of what happens once the Scriptures are indigenised has much less impact than it "ought" when it comes to their mainstream interpretation and application in the church.

The question is being asked as to why theological education around the continent of Africa continues to be in English, French, and Afrikaans despite the fact that living churches on the continent mostly operate in African languages (Maluleke 2004, 164). This is an important question. Its answer, at the moment I suspect, has more to do with economic power than reasoned theology. Seminaries will continue to be in cloudland, considering sets of questions foreign to people's experience, until this question is addressed.

Teaching in cloudland may not be so bad in itself. But we need to remember that students at such seminaries are trying to *apply* what they are taught. Being unfamiliar with deep lexical and cultural implications of even commonly used English words, our African students assume "new" English words to be equal to African equivalents. (There are, of course, also many other reasons as to why what is taught in seminaries may not be very practical for the African context. This much-discussed area is not the major focus of this essay.) As a result, applying seminary knowledge becomes at least disruptive, at worst catastrophic, for the church.

As in many areas of cross-cultural activity, lip service is these days often given to vast, existing cultural differences. Implementing what has been lip service becomes the difficult next step that is rarely taken, especially by monolinguists (or monoculturalists). More serious issues lie under the surface. Scholars have recently become astutely aware of issues concerning language *use*. This is considered in detail in the discipline of pragmatics, which is an important theoretical foundation for this work (Levinson 1983, Leech 1983).

4. THE FOLLY OF INTERSPORT LANGUAGE

A good illustration to help a monolingual person understand the dilemmas that arise when we take account of pragmatics is to think of sports. The English-speaking world knows of many sports and games. Each one has its own vocabulary!

In cricket we have *out, over, run,* and *innings*. In football (known in America as "soccer") we have *goal, defence, shot,* and *free kick*. In tennis we have *set, match, racquet,* and *serve*. Now imagine that these games represent different peoples with distinct languages. One people and language of tennis, one of football, and one of cricket.

If a football player says to a cricket player that he scored a goal, the cricket player won't have a clue what he is talking about. So the football player must learn the language of the cricket player. Instead of reporting that he scored a goal, the football player must say that he got a run. But hang on, you may say, a goal is not the same as a run. And that is exactly the problem.

Then it comes to be the turn for the cricket player to explain to a football player that the ball hit the wicket and thus he was out. Football fields do not have wickets but do have goal posts, and players are not knocked out, but the ball can go out. So from saying the ball hit the wicket and the player was out, we understand that the ball hit the goal post and went out—in other words, a corner was awarded. Having a corner awarded in a football match is quite different from a batsman walking out at the end of his innings. And that is exactly the problem!

In tennis a powerful serve that hits the net has to be retaken, as it is counted a failure. In explaining this to a football player, the tennis player is forced to say "powerful shot" instead of "a powerful serve." When the football player hears that the powerful shot has put the ball into the net, he may rejoice at this, leaving the tennis player askance.

Those examples (that could be multiplied many times) are powerful illustrations of translation blunders which I face constantly here in Africa. Such things happen when English and African people converse. They are also what I find in the essays written by African students using English. African students using English write like a cricket player who is used to describing a cricket match but is using the terminology of football. When I mark the essay using my knowledge of football, I see all the familiar terms being used. The terms do not seem to be used in the right way, but I give the writer the benefit of the doubt and give him a grade as I hardly want to be accused of being biased.

But does this analogy of sports hold up? After all, one person can learn to play many different sports and adjust accordingly. If I play football, I say "good goal," whereas if I play cricket, I say "good run," and there is no confusion.

We would of course never be so foolish to teach someone the language of a sport without also teaching them how that language is used and the rules of the game. There is no "intersport" language. Every sport has its own language. Note that even if the same words are used in different sports, the way they are used and their meanings vary significantly. A football player, a rugby player, and a cricket fielder can all "catch the ball," but for the football player it is a foul, for the rugby player it is very normal, and for the cricket player it means that the batsman is out.

Anyone inventing an "intersport" language would be laughed out of town. So why don't we laugh when English is used as an international language? Perhaps we ought to laugh more, or cry. In fact, the impracticality of such "intersport" sharing of wisdom illustrates why Western theology introduces confusion into the African church and why it is actually often best for an African theological student to learn *not* to apply what he/she has been taught.

5. LANGUAGE IS MEANINGFUL ONLY IN USE

We are now beginning to delve below the tip of the proverbial iceberg in terms of language usage and hermeneutics. A mass of issues regarding daily language practice now needs to be unearthed.

The ongoing concealment of issues is rooted in false conceptions of the nature of language. These conceptions that have spread around the world, helped by Western economies, appear to be rooted in notions of Greek philosophy and of the Enlightenment. The misconceptions suppose that language is a bridge between a person and a physical and social world "out there." Because, barring a few variations in climate and skin colour, the physical and social worlds appear to be the same around the world, and so also language. As a result, it is supposed, that as I talk to my mother about issues affecting my neighbours and friends, I am doing what young men do the world over.

But do they? In this instance, clearly not in today's world. Many urban dwellers have little clue as to the lives of their neighbours. They are caught up in media presentations of what should be live issues and networks of friends rooted less and less in geographical proximity. But what then are friends?

"She is my friend" is a phrase all men know to use with caution (except of their wives), even within the confines of Western English. Men need to be very careful how they even express themselves regarding fellow men, as "we had a friendly time together" can be quickly misunderstood, and men holding hands as they walk is similarly quickly interpreted to mean something that Africans who do this habitually are shocked by. "My friend" I am often called in the African use of English as a prelude to an uninhibited, blunt request for funds by a complete stranger. "He is my friend" is stronger than "he is a friend of mine," and then we have, "he is just a friend." A "good friend" implies that you have been helped, but there is presumably no "bad friend." A husband and wife can be "friends of mine," but the wife is definitely not "my friend," although I "am friendly" (in moderation) whenever I meet her.

There are clearly acceptable and unacceptable, advisable and ill-advised, ways of *using* the word "friend." To give a definition of "friend" is far from adequate to enable understanding of the *use* of the word. In fact, appropriate, detailed knowledge of *uses* of the word "friend" clearly arises from a comprehension of all factors pertaining to relationships within a community! How often does this apply?

"Christians do not greet each other by saying, 'How are you?' but by saying, 'Praise the Lord,'" an old lady told me in a Luo village (translation from Dholuo). So on meeting a fellow Christian, while being unsure as to whether one has already greeted them, one can ask, "*Ase pako kodi ruoth?*" ("Have I already praised with you the Lord?"), meaning, "Have I greeted you yet (this morning)?" Again, knowing the *meaning* of *ruoth opaki* will give an Englishman little idea of its *use*.

The common Western conception that words are there to *prepare for* a doing, well illustrated by the widespread use of behavioural objectives in educational curriculum planning (Davis 1983, 305–29), seems to fly in the face of Austin's realisation that we do things *with* words, and that applies really to *all* words (1962, 52). What are the implications of such a discovery, if indeed it is true that the role of words is not primarily in *meaning* but in *doing*? Why should I pay attention to a word anyway, if it is not going to do anything for me?

The reason the relationship between meaning and doing seems to be confused in the Western worldview would seem to be connected to the preeminence of a mechanical perception of the world. A carburettor by itself does nothing, but knowing its place in an engine and knowing where to put other similarly "useless" bits, results in a powerful driving force. So words are taken as meaning things that only "do" something when correctly combined with other words.

6. RINGING BELLS IN THE AFRICAN THEOLOGY DEPARTMENT

What would be the implication of the absence of such a mechanical worldview (that is, of a worldview where there is no perception of postponed doing)? In a sense we are here referring to Mbiti's much maligned suggestion that in Africa there is no future (1969, 15–22). Instead of taking words as meaning things which later in some elaborate complexity do some doing, every word is expected to be unpostponed doing. An accumulation in the doingness of many words is what results in the desirable way of being.

Some bells should here be being rung in the African theology department. In many African languages someone who is sick, if asked how he is, will say "a little bit," thereby acknowledging that his life-force level is low. In African thinking, salvation is a boost or guarantee to that life-force. This is why a saved person cannot possibly get sick, and why salvation is considered an ongoing or frequently repeated experience. (I am aware that in saying this many Westerners will consider me in theological error. Yet I am saying that this is a natural and logical conclusion if the Bible is read in many African languages.) Again, African people are noted for their liking of long church services, as those many words continue to add to life-force levels. Any absence of a morality identified in African Christianity[3] clearly arises through words being valued for what they *do*, and not in constructing an understanding that can later be considered to be moral.

Examples of profound differences in word usages between cultures can easily be multiplied. I can put my finger at random in a dictionary to find words, and explain how usage of those words differs between African (Luo) and Western (British) cultures (I have used Capen 1998):

(1) I find the word "mistrust." This word is often used to malign a fellow Westerner but in the Africa that I know this word is "normal." People's hearts being by default guided by "bad" forces,[4] makes mistrust the default position.

(2) "Bullet" is in English a thing that hits another, hence a bulletin board brings information, and an innocent person can be found (killed or injured) by a bullet from a gun. A bullet (*lisasi* in Dholuo, from Kiswahili) in Africa implies that your fate has caught up with you. The bullet wouldn't have hit you if you hadn't erred in your relationship with the forces of the universe; for example, by saying the wrong thing to someone or breaking a taboo. Many scholars have pointed out that in Africa death, as also suffering, is always caused by sorcery, spirits, or a curse (Mbiti 1991, 117).

(3) "Self-love" is a desirable feature necessary for being able to love others in Western thinking, but must be bad in the Luo way of thinking as it implies a

3 See, for example, Ferdinando 1992, 284.
4 Note the popularity of Anon 1996.

reduced investment to the common good. Mbiti goes so far as to suggest that love is a rarely used word in Africa (1969, 38).

In conclusion we can say that in a different culture every word is *used* differently!

7. CONVENTIONAL HERMENEUTICS FALLS FAR SHORT IN THE CROSS-CULTURAL ENVIRONMENT

So what is the relation of the above to the discipline of hermeneutics? In the cross-cultural sense, I hope I have made it clear that the numerous detailed considerations dealt with under the heading of hermeneutics, even though they may all be important, are only a small part of the interpretational differences one is faced with in a cross-cultural environment. Ignoring differences in language usage has been a primary cause of unsuspected shocks, causing AICs to emerge from mission churches.[5]

Two further examples can serve to emphasise the point. Take the words of Ezekiel 31:6a: "All the birds of the air nested in its boughs." I think of the words of an old lady who is my neighbour in my African village home. Her late husband liked trees, and therefore preserved many of them and planted others on his land. This has resulted in our having many songbirds all around us. I rejoice in the dawn chorus, but "*Winyogo goyona koko*" (Dholuo), said the old lady (literally translatable as "Those birds hit me with their din," or "These many birds disturb me with their unpleasant noise"). I have at times spotted the old lady chasing away owls from her house at 5:00 in the morning, as owls are said to bring death to the home. She is cutting down trees as fast as she can, partly so as to reduce the bird population. Her use of the term "bird" shows that to this lady "birds" are akin to devils. Understanding this remarkable change of use of a common word can be ascertained only by attention to use of language or knowledge of culture.

Turning to 2 Chronicles 36:18a: "He carried to Babylon all the articles from the temple of God, both large and small." The picture that this brings to my mind is that of an ornate Anglican church with numerous crosses, candlesticks, and items of historical interest; this of course being informed by my having seen numerous illustrations of "temples" in various contexts over many years, as well as having visited various churches of this type. I suspect that an informed African interpretation could go in one of two directions. First, "temple" could

5 Application is of course much wider to many fields of human knowledge that are communicated cross-culturally.

be associated with "shrines" that some African people are known to have as sites for making peace with their ancestors. Thus ancestors have come strongly into the picture. The "articles" have now become those of African shrines—wooden carvings, perhaps skins, stones, etc. For those African people for whom the priest is the household head, the shrines are small, and the articles correspondingly few. Alternatively (and perhaps simultaneously) is the notion of "temple" (in many East African languages *hekalu*, a loan word from Arabic via Kiswahili) as a foreign thing understood by outsiders. Those outsiders have things that are very powerful, understood of course in holistic African cultures as a peculiar power of the gods. So we have an implicit African understanding here that appears in some ways closer to the ancient Near Eastern one, in which the "articles" (in the quote above) being carried away imply a severe reduction in power. Although, given African people's meeting with modernity, this "power" now resembles what we in Western English call "technology" and could be computers, cameras, and video machines.

I believe that these examples fall outside of the breadth of conventional hermeneutics. They can be discovered only by exposure to language in use, that is of course inherently related to culture.

Many stark differences in language-use conventions arise between the West and the non-West. The church is disadvantaged in its understanding of the non-Western world insofar as it has been swept into the Western worldview. It would be supposed therefore that a church that has maintained a "traditional" theology or ecclesiology may be more able to integrate into the African way. The "pure Westerners" who work in Africa, such as experts in development who work as consultants around the world, can be supposed to be much more seriously disabled in their understanding than church workers.

8. BIBLICAL INTERPRETATION IN THE LIGHT OF LANGUAGE-USE CONVENTIONS

Such differences in language usage have wide implications for biblical interpretation—that are these days all too often simply glossed over. Scriptural passages can be examined for these differences. I selected Psalm 100:1–3 pretty much at random. I believe that comparable differences in interpretation according to language-use conventions will be found throughout the Bible. I look at these verses in comparing an African with a Western language-use convention:

Verse 1. *Shout for joy to the Lord, all the earth.*

African people are widely known for their overt expression of emotion, used as a means to bring spiritual or heart power, that may seem senseless to "rational" people.

Verse 2. *Worship the Lord with gladness; come before him with joyful songs.*

The Luo have a long tradition of *pakruok*, praising someone, almost as a pastime. A musician can be given a gift in order to sing in praise of someone. God's seeking praise in this way implies that those praising him are doing so in direct return for favours.

Verse 3. *Know that the Lord is God.*

God in the West is he who "fills the gaps" which are not filled by science, whereas in much of Africa this is God taking the credit for nature and science. The latter can be known as *hono* (Dholuo), often translated back into English as "miracles."

It is he who made us, and we are his;

Acknowledging that "we are his" is a way of asking for help and support in exchange for obedience and service in the patrimonial system widespread in Africa. In Western use of such language, this is more a statement of fact.

we are his people, the sheep of his pasture.

The shepherding notion in Africa is seen as provision in every sense, but in the West primarily restricted to the spiritual realm. This is because Western society has many of its own mechanisms for physical provision.

The doing power of words is important in people's relationship with the superhuman or metaphysical realm. God is clearly not dependent on our "doing," but does value our adoration (Deut 5:9–11, Ps 150, etc.); that is, our heartfelt words. Traditional healing practices clearly make much use of the doing power of words by using incantations, encouragement, and repetitions of key terms for calling on deities and for healing. Healing, it will be noted from the above, is a restoring of vital-force levels, and not foundationally a biophysical realignment of the body or its parts. Herein lies the nub to much confusion between whether God "heals" or not in African churches. The word "heal" is clearly used differently according to cultural context.

9. THE CONTEXTUAL PRESENCE OF "SPIRITS"

In the above examples and more widely, the presence of bad forces or evil spirits associated with ancestors who have some grudge must be remembered. Turning to God can have a danger equivalent to that of being "teacher's pet" in my memory of my secondary education. Playing up to the teacher gives considerable advantages, but the wise pupil always has his classmates (in this case, the departed) in mind because, if he is not careful, they can come to trouble him should "teacher" not be looking. In practice, offerings and other due respect must continue to be given to ancestors.

It is this constant presence and presumed activity of those who were once members of our (extended) families that is perhaps the most difficult for Westerners to understand in terms of its effect on biblical hermeneutics. In my conception as a Westerner, my departed ancestors are gone. Even should I dream about them, this will not trouble me in the slightest. This does not apply to the Luo, or many other African people. Imagine having your late grandma watching you lie in bed, your late aunt making your child sick because you have not yet sacrificed a chicken for her, or your great uncle stopping your son from getting a job. Every time you read your Bible, you must be thinking how what you read will help you avoid those troublesome spirits. Whenever you talk to someone else, you must be careful as to what you say, because the spirits are listening. Every dialogue is in effect a "polylogue," with all that this implies (Kerbrat-Orecchioni 2004).

The same applies to Bible expositions. It is impossible to tell whether what is said is in response to you as living respondent, or whether it is said to please some overhearing deceased predecessor, or both. Taking the answer given to the latter as if it is meant for you can be, to say the least, grossly misleading. What if the ancestor has left the command: "Always agree with the Europeans"? A European would, in such an instance, be wrong to conclude that someone who "agreed with them" actually considered them to be correct.

We could take another illustration. Picture the conversation between yourself as pastor and your church member whom you meet in town. Imagine what would happen if you were to start chatting with him, but unbeknown to you he is sitting within earshot of his mistress, who up to this time has been unaware that he has a wife and children.

The situations are not helped by the currently widespread perceptions of these "ancestors" as being evil. In Dholuo they are often referred to as *jochiende*, which is also the translation for "devils."

Egner is amongst those who find a routine deceptiveness in language use in Africa. She found her Ivorian friends regularly making promises that they could not possibly fulfill (2002). Southall tells us that among the Alur people in Uganda there is a "divergence between stated rules and observed or even recollected behaviour and . . . great verbal stress by the Alur on regularities which do not obtain in practice" (1970, 238). The Alur's description of their way of ruling their people was found by Southall to be there to impress and not to be truthful. That is, they use language to create (political authority by impressing people with their words) and not to describe (what actually happens).

10. UNIQUE LANGUAGE USAGES

Certain uses of language may be taboo and unsustainable by local people. Foreigners making such uses may be tolerated, but not imitated. As pregnant women will even avoid speaking of their pregnancy and hide it for as long as possible in cultures such as that of the Luo of Kenya, pastors may also do the same regarding issues in their churches. Open sharing is making oneself vulnerable to mysterious evil (witchcraft) powers.

Mismatches in vocabulary and terms very easily arise cross-culturally. On first arriving in Kenya, I was told that there is hardly any witchcraft around these days. As the years went by, I found it to be very prevalent. Perhaps it was a condemnation of practices such as witchcraft from the West that encouraged people to redefine their practices so as to fall linguistically outside of this much-maligned category. A preacher's condemnation of witchcraft may meet with approving nods and smiles, while the very thing he is condemning may be practiced but under a different name.

The example of different types of snow, often associated with discussions on Sapir and Whorf's theory of language determinism, illustrates the possibility of whole realms of meaning and value being lost in the process of translation (Chandler 1995). The language of the Eskimos apparently has many distinct terms referring to different types of snow. How does one deal with these distinct terms in a text if translating into English? Devising English equivalents for Eskimo terms for snow will hardly solve the issue, because English people will see no need for the use of such a bewildering array of terms. Thus vast and critical realms of life's key functions can be omitted by well-meaning hermeneuts who are ignorant of language-use conventions. (In the same way that, in the above example, any importance attached to reference to different types of snow will be lost, so also important conventions of language usage can be lost in the course of translation.)

11. CONCLUSION

Ignoring differences in language-use conventions is no longer acceptable in today's world. The apparent dominance of Western culture may have concealed these differences, but it has not done away with them. It may give the deceptive impression that they are no longer there, but they are! They will not disappear overnight, if ever. Language *usages* are not picked up in classrooms or even from textbooks but from participation in people's lives. We need a hermeneutics of language usages, or we need to put hermeneutics on the shelf for a while as we explore the impact of the Scriptures on people's living cultures. Translating the Bible into African languages has been a valuable exercise. Now we need Christian scholarship *in those languages*. Only thus can conventions of language use, with their manifold implications for hermeneutics, begin to be taken account of in the derivation of non-Western theologies.

REFERENCES

Anon. 1996. *Moyo wa binadamu.* (*The heart of man.*) Arusha, Tanzania: Kituo cha maandiko habari maalum—Kimahama.

Austin, J. L. 1962. *How to do things with words.* Oxford: Clarendon.

Capen, Carole A. 1998. *Bilingual Dholuo-English dictionary.* Tucson, AZ: Carole A. Capen.

Chandler, Daniel, 1995. The Sapir-Whorf Hypothesis. http://www.aber.ac.uk/media/Documents/short/whorf.html (accessed May 21, 2011).

Davis, Gary A. 1983. *Educational psychology: Theory and practice.* London: Addison Wesley.

Egner, Inge. 2002. The speech act of promising in an intercultural perspective. SIL International. http://www.sil.org/silewp/2002/001/silewp2002-001.pdf (accessed January 8, 2003).

Ferdinando, Keith. 1992. Biblical concepts of redemption and African perspectives of the demonic. PhD thesis, London Bible College.

Kerbrat-Orecchioni, Catherine. 2004. Introducing polylogue. *Journal of Pragmatics* 36/1: 1–24.
Leech, Geoffrey H. 1983. *Principles of pragmatics*. London: Longman.
Levinson, Stephen C. 1983. *Pragmatics*. Cambridge: Cambridge Univ. Press.
Maluleke, Tanyiko Sam. 2004. African Christianity: The Bible and theology. In *Bible translation and African Languages*, ed. Gosnell L. O. R. Yorke and Peter M. Renju, 161–76. Nairobi: Acton.
Mbiti, John S. 1969. *African religions and philosophy*. London: Heinemann.
———. 1991. *Introduction to African religion*. 2nd ed. Nairobi: East African Educational.
Sanneh, Lamin. 1989. *Translating the message: The missionary impact on culture*. Maryknoll, NY: Orbis Books.
Southall, Aidan W. 1970. *Alur society: A study in processes and types of domination*. Oxford: Oxford Univ. Press.

CHAPTER 14

Language in Education, Mission, and Development in Africa: Appeals for Local Tongues and Local Contexts[1]

1. INTRODUCTION

Negative outcomes arising from the use of European languages by African people in African contexts are perhaps the least visible to the Europeans themselves. To them, all seems well—their languages are the best thing that ever happened to Africa, and because they are the ones paying the bills, things continue as they are. Many African people on the ground know no different having been born and bred on the same system, so they fill gaps in understanding from the magical background of their own culture. Life goes on, and the power of international languages grows—but what damage is being done in the process? More precisely—what progress that might have been made is not being made? To what extent are language policies making it impossible for people to take responsibility for their own lives?

This chapter raises logical questions as to the desirability, practicality, morality, and sustainability of such use of European languages in sub-Saharan Africa. What are the implications for the African continent of continuing to (supposedly) self-govern on the basis of that which is not locally rooted? What is actually happening when cultures and legal systems are transported *en masse* from point X and dumped wholesale onto country Y?

---

1 This chapter was originally published as follows: Harries, Jim. 2007. Language in education, mission and development in Africa: Appeals for local tongues and local contexts. *Encounters Mission Journal* 19 (August), http://www.redcliffe.org/4134.

Short as it is, this chapter can only survey the issues. But the author's message is clear—the current rate of linguistic globalisation, added to the colonial foundation on which African nations are already founded, is handicapping the building of stable, productive African societies. Urgent action is advocated to transfer genuine self-responsibility to African governance, churches, NGOs, and political rule as a whole.

2. CROSS-CULTURAL SELF-DECEPTION AND ITS OUTCOME

Cognition is a prerequisite for communication to lead to understanding. Inference determines the way in which this happens; that is, how a stimulus will be understood as having meaning. That is, words do not of themselves carry meaning. They evoke meaning through their peculiar impact on someone's cognition and context (Sperber and Wilson 1995, 2).

That this process of cognition is largely subconscious is evident, because we do not need to overtly "think about it." That is, when someone speaks to me, it seems *as if* meaning is encoded in their words. This apparent ability of words at carrying meaning can be very convincing, and so very deceptive. Whether it be through long habituation, or whether it is innate, I do not know. But my mind tells me that words carry meanings.[2]

Differences between people of different cultures and worldviews are reflected (or contained) in the complex, cognitive stimulus-response mechanisms of the mind. The cognition systems of people of the same "culture" (loosely defined) share many similarities, thus enabling them to understand one another sufficiently for many practical purposes. The more distant the cultures of origin of the communicators concerned, the less alike are their inferential cognitive networks.

Recognising the tendency of the mind to self-deception is key in comprehending what goes on in "cross-cultural communication." To some extent consciously, but even more subconsciously, the mind works to make sense of whatever stimuli it receives. (My mind will automatically correct and make sense of something that seems wrong. Someone telling me, "I have come tomorrow to help you," I correct as meaning, "I will come." If someone tells a cook that the toasted "wickens" are overdone, then the cook will assume the person to have meant roast "chickens," and so on.) One result of this is that translation of the

2 This "code model" of meaning has, according to Sperber and Wilson, been extant at least since the time of Aristotle. It is widely believed to date (1995, 2).

words of people of a very different way of life (culture) into a familiar language will give an impression of understanding the whats, whys, and hows of their lives, whether correct or not.[3] This impression gains currency with the passing of time as the complexity of linkages in the mind accommodates what was foreign. The undermining of such supposedly orderly relationships is known as *culture shock*.

Unfortunately, because of the deception mentioned above, a person's use of their innate stimuli responses in attempting to comprehend what is foreign, has limited accuracy. Because there is, I suggest, an instinctive or at least very deeply ingrained tendency for the human mind to expect to be functioning in only one culture and *not* cross-culturally, the mind domesticates the foreign (Venuti 1998, 5).

There is no objective map of the mind's stimulus/response combinations. Unlike a landscape with predictable physical features that can be ascertained/perceived from a distance, even by different people simultaneously, the cognitive landscape of stimuli responses resembles a four-dimensional, multitextured, multicoloured jungle.

The complexity of this pattern is such as to be beyond human capabilities of accurate description, rather as it would be impossible to describe a three-dimensional scene if restricted to the language of only two dimensions (e.g., up and down, left and right). We do not know what electrons are, physicists tell us, or what they look like, or exactly where they are—but we know that they exist because of the impact (charge) that they have. Examining our own minds is more difficult than examining electrons, because whereas electrons are "out there," we are our minds, and there is no vantage point other than from within them.

Translation (between cultures), explaining one kind of four-dimensional jungle to another, is fraught with impediments. We do not know what the "foreign" *is*, but only the impact that it has on us. Part of that impact will be on our subconscious, which is beyond our understanding (never mind explanation). When someone explains what he or she felt or experienced in response to the foreign, they are in effect, I suggest, drawing on an unfathomable depth of their person that is closely linked to the cognitive subconscious.

A person moving from Hombone to Ndere (taking Hombone as the name of a European country and Ndere as the name of an African country) will have impression Z of Ndere. While Z may resemble the impression of another person visiting Ndere from Hombone, it must be realised that *Z is not by any means equal*

3 Readers will assume language to have "cohesion" and "coherence" (Yule 1996, 140–41).

to what Ndere actually is, and neither can it ever be. Hence, a person from Ndere moving to Hombone or from anywhere else to Ndere cannot be expected to reproduce or even necessarily recognise or understand Z (a Hombone person's description of Ndere). A person from Ndere may be able to offer only very limited help to someone from Hombone in their understanding of Ndere, that is Z, if the person from Ndere is not familiar with Z (the Hombone person's implicit understanding of Ndere). The explanation of Ndere by a person from Hombone (i.e., Z) may be as foreign to someone from Ndere as would be the Hombone person's explanation of country D, E, or even F or G—that is, different cultures altogether.

As a result, the notion that a native of a country such as Ndere (i.e., an African country), that is foreign to a particular people such as those of Hombone (i.e., a European country), is going to be particularly effective at *enhancing* the understanding by someone from Hombone of Ndere, that is Z, may be misguided—in the same way as a description of a view of a mountain is aided by someone sharing the same view (or a similar view) and not by someone in a cabin on the mountain, looking the other way *from* the mountain. The reverse also applies. In terms of relations between the West and Africa, this means that the person who can most "helpfully" tell the West about Africa is likely to be a Westerner, and vice versa.

This can also be explained the other way around. The view of a country/culture and context such as Ndere will be different between a resident of Ndere called Mr. Ndere and a nonresident of Ndere called Mr. Hombone, resident of Hombone. Mr. Hombone will invariably be struck by the *differences* between Hombone and Ndere, which the resident of Ndere (assuming he has no, or limited, familiarity with Hombone) will not even be aware of. Mr. Hombone will, in the course of living in Ndere, initially not know how the language use of Ndere's residents interacts with their culture. Instead he will have to assume that the language of the Ndere is used in interaction with the culture of Hombone. (No other alternative is available to them.) That which will help Mr. Hombone to know how Mr. Ndere uses the Ndere language in relation to Ndere culture, is knowledge of Ndere language and culture. Insofar as the Ndere language will be learned without a knowledge of Ndere culture, it can very easily be mislearned.

The use of an international language does not resolve this issue, as the same language must be learned in the context of a culture. If language L is common to Hombone culture and Ndere culture, then members of the Hombone culture will know how to use L in Hombone's way, and members of Ndere culture will know to use L in Ndere's way. Hombone's and Ndere's cultures are likely to be relatively close if the use of L arises because people have a common origin—such as English used in America and Australia, and Kiswahili used in both Kenya and Tanzania. Understanding difficulties will be more serious between unrelated cultures that use the same language, such as African as against European cultures that use English. The use of a common language can conceal rather than reveal differences.

The implications of this should be becoming clear. That is, that teachings and governance in order to take account of local conditions and avoid making cultural blunders, should be of local origin.

The reasons for this not happening these days is that half of the equation is ignored. That is, it is *falsely* assumed that a person from the country of Ndere (i.e., an African country) will be the most effective in guiding Hombone's people (of European origin) as to how to operate in Ndere. This even though the person from Hombone falls far short of knowing what people of Ndere want to do and how and why. The answer to the question of how to help Mr. Hombone operate in Ndere's culture that I am suggesting is *not* that the advice of Mr. Ndere not be sought, but for it to be realised that it must be sought in the context of (or at least with a close knowledge of) Ndere's culture using Ndere's language.

The most natural and helpful way to assist these learning processes is for Mr. Hombone and Mr. Ndere to have different languages. Hence Mr. Hombone's understanding of Ndere will develop in Hombone's language, while Mr. Ndere's understanding of Hombone will develop in Ndere's language. Those who will most helpfully add to Mr. Hombone's knowledge of Mr. Ndere are people of Hombone's country who are closely exposed to the language and culture of Ndere, and so also those who will most helpfully add to Mr. Ndere's knowledge of Hombone's people are the people of Ndere who are closely exposed to the language and culture of Hombone.

In other words, it is vitally important for workers from Hombone (representing Western nations) interested in doing mission or promoting development in Ndere (African nations) to do so in the language of Ndere only after having learned it in the context of the culture of Ndere.

Cross-cultural communication is in today's world of shrinking boundaries more and more important inside and outside of the church. I would here like to describe the nature of such communication in what to me is a simple but very helpful way, and from that description proceed to consider the practical possibilities of it occurring.

The practical way in which cross-cultural communication causes difficulties, I suggest, arises from differences in nuanced meanings and *implicatures*[4] of words used. This applies even if (and this is the case that I consider here for the sake of simplicity) one language, let's say English, is being used by both (or all) parties. I illustrate translation differences that I am referring to through Table 1 below.

English term	Implicature in the use of this term in the UK	Implicature in the use of this term in East Africa
Rain	Bad	Good
Fat (person)	Bad	Good
Pension	Good	Bad
Courting	Good	Bad
Tree	Scenic object	Firewood
Paraffin lamp	Rare object	Common object
Table	Everyday item	New and relatively rare item
Bread	Staple diet	Luxury diet
Shoes	Keep feet warm	Required to look modern
Wedding	Ceremony to initiate life together	Ceremony performed for stable couples
Water	Comes from tap	Comes from spring or stream
Chicken	Meat bought frozen	Sleeps in our sitting room

Table 1.

Implicatures of English usage in East Africa as against in the UK

That the above may be generalisations, I think, does not detract from their validity. If someone considers my examples to be "wrong," I nevertheless ask them to bear with me in considering implications that are illustrated by them. In addition to having different implicatures as above, the meanings themselves of some words can be different in English in different parts of the globe. An example is "courting," where the same word, that is in East Africa often used to describe a process of preparation for marriage, is vastly different to the one used in Western countries such as the UK.

It is possible for people, as presumably the readers of this chapter, to gain some understanding and appreciation of the above differences. Description of

4 That is, meanings that are implied in the use of a particular word in a particular context.

such differences has been the bread and butter of traveler's tales, anthropological accounts, and ethnographies for decades, if not centuries. The question I would however like to ask is: How easy is it for someone to have all such differences in mind in the course of cross-cultural conversation, planning, decision making, and discussion? That is, does my having a knowledge that such differences exist enable me to make plans regarding the lives of a foreign (to me) people in which I can truly take account of many (or all) of the ways in which they use language, even if the language is English? Or will I, in directing my mental activities in other directions (such as planning or conversation, etc.), return to a default understanding of language that is likely to be rooted in the kinds of implicatures familiar to my own people? In other words, even though I may be able to appreciate the educational value of having information such as that in Table 1 above available, will I realistically be able to learn sufficiently the implicatures of the breadth of a second (and even third or fourth) living vocabulary/culture/context so as to be able to intelligently engage in communication with or about a foreign people? How is such a set of implicatures effectively learned? Surely it is only through a long-term exposure to a people by living closely with them. That is assuming it is possible at all. Another question that arises is: Once having understood the importance of being able to grasp the implicatures as well as "meanings" of words so as to be able to effectively use them in a foreign culture, is it most helpful that the language to be used with that culture be the same international language, or is the learning of a foreign language advantageous in that such will provide a separation in the mind between meanings and implicatures of "equivalent" words?

But does all the above really matter? Is it not sufficient to communicate internationally in a language in which meanings and implicatures simply approximate? Is lack of attention to such detail important? I suggest that it is important, and that it is vital that we consider depths of language use and not assume language to be merely a crude tool for engaging in surface-level interactions. Many examples could be drawn even from the above small table. A European text saying that a "fat man came" is not implying (as it would in East Africa) that he is happy and successful, but that he can't control his eating habits. Not having a pension may not in Europe imply that one has chosen to spend all one's income in culturally appropriate ways on the extended family as it might in Africa (Maranz 2001, 16), but more likely that one has not used sufficient foresight.[5] "He lit a paraffin lamp" is an everyday statement in places not

5 Maranz points out the importance amongst African people of meeting immediate needs, thus suggesting that savings, such as for a pension, are immoral.

connected to electricity, but conjures up very different thoughts where people are accustomed to operating with electricity. Such implicatures that are bread and butter to normal communication are, I suggest, vitally important, and a failure to grasp them results, in many respects, in communication failure.

My suggestion on the basis of the above is that any cross-cultural communication at any depth (and human beings tend to like to communicate at depth) requires both a deep knowledge, by at least one part, of the culture of the "other," plus an ability to keep two language categories (those of the two cultures concerned) separate in the mind so as to be able to communicate using one of the two categories (Mazrui 1993). I suggest also that such language understanding as is required *cannot* be learned either in a classroom or through professional contact over short periods. The human mind's ability at self-deception (see above) is too great for that. It requires a long-term, vulnerable exposure to the daily life of the "other" people. I suggest also that such different understandings of words are best achieved when the language in question is different. That is, that it is helpful to have language barriers in places where there are cultural barriers so as to prevent texts (of all sorts, including written and oral) that make little sense from one culture swamping another in an untranslated (i.e., not transformed so as to be appropriate) form.

The above, if correct, has important implications. I suggest that the cultures of many people within the Western world are sufficiently similar to be able to benefit through communication using a common international language such as English. But also that the differences between "Western" and "non-Western" cultures are sufficiently great for their sharing in communication via international Western languages such as English without translation (from Western English to say African English or Arabic English) to be more harmful than helpful in the long term. I suggest rather that a translation process is a helpful (vital) middle process, and that this translation should be done by people with great expertise and a high level of exposure to both cultures. Translation on the basis of word-for-word conversion, or even dynamic equivalence, is insufficient. This translation needs to take account of pragmatics so as to translate implicatures, such as recent translation models based on relevance theory (Gutt 1991). I suggest that it is in the long term more helpful to translate between different languages (for example, from English to Kiswahili) than between the same language (for example, between American English and East African English). I suggest that what is at stake in the current globalising world is great. Failure to attend to the above concerns is going to severely handicap the functional abilities of non-Western societies who are "under attack" by Western tongues. This may lead to the disastrous collapse of whole societies. Or the invention (or perpetuation) of racial boundaries leading toward a global "caste system," perhaps akin to that known to exist in Hinduism today. Or at the very least the rise of fundamentalisms that are linked to the preservation of distinct aspects of "threatened" cultures that have come to be misunderstood by powerful neighbours. Already it certainly leads to widespread corruption.

3. CULTURES THAT ARE NOT "PRISTINE"

One failure, I suggest, of many missiological writers (and that of others who attempt to make in-depth descriptions of peoples in the non-Western world) is that of not realising that the "errors" of previous generations of missionaries (or colonialists or development workers) have already had a lasting impact. In 99 percent of the African "mission field," one is not converting people from pure "animism" into Christianity, but neither is one assisting (in whatever way) "normal" Christians of the ilk that are found "in the West." In addition to the foundational impact resulting from their own culture of origin, the contours of Christianity in Africa have also been profoundly influenced by the particular strategies of previous generations of Western missionaries. Hence we are no longer in a situation of *preventing* people from becoming dependent on and misunderstanding the West. They are already dependent, and have already misunderstood (the West, as the West has misunderstood them). Amongst the important questions that should now be asked is how to *correct* gross misunderstandings that have already occurred. This, I suggest, may be more, and not less, difficult than the original missionary task!

The obvious approach to take to a prior imbalance is to redress it. If someone has been having too much F and not enough G, then we would normally say it is time that they be given more G and less F. The actual response being widely expressed on the "mission field" today though, it seems to me, is that because someone has already got used to having too much F, his supply of it should be further increased to meet the growing appetite. If it is prosperity teaching that people have had too much of, then what should the response be? Should it be that the rate of provision of prosperity be stepped up? This seems to be what is happening in East Africa, and presumably also much further afield today.

I have already argued above that consulting the "target" people themselves will *not* be sufficient to provide guidance to the development and missionary agenda. It seems that they are these days being *overly* relied upon. Amongst the reasons for this is the fear of non-Africans (Europeans) of sharing too closely in ways of life taken as being of poverty, ill health, and even mortal danger on the African continent. As a consequence, "missionary" activity is a *pulling* of people from the African way of life into a European way of life, even when on the African person's home territory. (For example, mission stations are outposts of Western activity, and this is often where the Westerner likes to engage with the African.) This is a situation that needs urgent attention—for African people (as others in the world) to have education and assistance to live their lives in a way that fits with how they live. The only way that I am aware of to effectively achieve this as a Westerner is to be vulnerable to African people and to reach them in their *own* languages.

More recent communications occurring on the basis of prior experience of relationship reminds us of the kinds of tensions that arise in families as against meetings of strangers. While relationship can deepen love, it can also breed bitterness, suspicion, distrust, and even hatred. Family disputes are known to be complex and difficult for outsiders to assist. Hence nurturing of intrafamily relationships takes much more time and wisdom than those with workmates, the person who drives the bus that takes you to town, your neighbour whom you greet over the fence, and so on. As asking family members "What do you want?" and giving it to them is often far from adequate to nurture good relationship, the same applies increasingly in the globalising world.

This is the situation that needs urgent attention. Yes, of course, the African people will ask for "more money." Who wouldn't? In fact, offering it is putting them into a trap.[6] They have learned from experience that European people anyway have no patience to learn their language and culture. Is anyone prepared to prove them wrong on that score?

4. ENGLISH: THE FALSE PROPHET

A new missionary (or development worker) coming to Africa is quickly faced with a difficult language question. In many Anglophone countries on the continent, people find they can "get by with English," so few see the importance of learning an additional tongue. What are the consequences of this decision to "get by," spread over thousands of foreign workers and many decades?

6 This is clearly recognised in Western societies themselves where many people fall into the trap of taking credit that they end up not being able to repay.

Personally speaking, if I share of my experience amongst the Luo people[7] and my fluency in Dholuo (the language of the Luo people), it is extremely debilitating. That is, it makes it impossible for me to interact "normally" with Luo people in Luoland, except for the few who already know me well. Wherever I mix in different social settings, I am surrounded by whisperings of "He knows Dholuo," groans, laughter, and other expressions of amazement over my familiarity with this "tribal" language. The Luo people are surprised, taken aback, and even shocked, to find a white man who is fluent in their vernacular.

I may be the only white person in Kenya (?) who is the exception to the Luo people's underlying understanding that "white men are ignorant." I mean—how can one be considered intelligent (in the colloquial sense of that term) if one does not understand a people's language? I am sorry—but this does cut both ways. As on my being brought up in the UK, we considered anyone who did not know English as backward, so also with Dholuo in Luoland. The notion that "whites are ignorant" being almost constantly perpetuated (every time a white visitor comes to Luoland, which is rather frequently) means that people's initial assessment of my likely "intelligence" is "very low." I can get talked down to like a child, and people will not expect me to understand their real issues. I suppose you could say that the Luo take me as *primitive*.

This is an interesting turn of circumstances. Whatever term or turn of phrase the Luo use for "primitive" (perhaps *jamwa*), they can use it with impunity, because Dholuo is not an international language. (Not being an international language, its use does not have to be sensitive to how other people who are not of the same ethnicity will understand it.) Here is yet another reason why the Luo people are much freer to use their own language in place of English. (English is carefully hedged because many people of many different cultures are capable of reading it and therefore of misunderstanding it.)

Something is wrong when, after one hundred years of colonialism, there is (perhaps) no other Westerner who is a fluent speaker of Dholuo in Kenya, despite this being a language of 3 million people. This while at the same time the English-speaking Western world is an enormously powerful influence in the life of every Luo person today. This means that while British/American-rooted international policies have almost entirely taken over much of the lives of the Luo people—there is no one able to intelligently comment on their impact. What does this say of efforts to overcome racism?

---

7 Of western Kenya.

"Hang on," I can hear people thinking. "What about the Luo people themselves and the international research community that surely has people operating in Luoland?" To begin with the Luo people themselves, careful thought should make it clear that one cannot rely on the expressed views (especially in the foreign—to them—language of English) of the victims of an intervention to guide its continuity. "You don't bite the hand that feeds you." How can someone refuse money on which their whole extended family has become grossly dependent? How can the West hope to begin to understand African uses of English in the first place, rooted as they are in a very different and little-understood culture? Much of the same critique (only outlined in summary form in this paragraph) can be applied to short-term researchers from Western universities and institutions. They misunderstand, and then share their misunderstandings and limited insights with others in the West who often believe them.

A brief reference to India may not be out of place. The movement of Aryan people (of the same stock as Western Europeans) in early history to India resulted in the caste system.[8] We are heading toward a similar circumstance in Africa. Severe marginalisation and oppression of the Luo language (and many others in Africa) is denying people groups the means (briefly—self-understanding) with which to progress. Instead, their own languages, through being totally ignored in the formal sector of life and economy, while remaining the foundation for all the important social parts of people's lives, are stuck in a time warp. The more the West forces its presence into all corners of Africa, the more the people's own development can be hindered as a result.

"Hang on a minute," I can hear my reader objecting. "The whole point is that an international language will *enable* development." So indeed the theory seems to run, although this kind of development is very much one of "dependence," usually on charity. Visionaries imagine an African continent, in decades ahead, being divided into English, French, and Portuguese sections, with local languages pretty much forgotten. I suggest that the attempt to do this is seriously debilitating millions of people. Another problem with English for use in Africa is quite simple—it doesn't belong to Africa. Perhaps it could belong, if a big wall was put up to keep Westerners out. Recent trends in international relations are moving in the opposite direction.

This means that (constant!) attempts at indigenising English, are as constantly being thwarted. African uses of English are marked as "wrong" in the formal

8 Wallbank indicates that the caste system in India has "certain commendable features," especially as it helped "many [immigrants/invaders] with various levels of culture . . . to live together." Unlike, he tells us, in Europe where "backward peoples . . . were either exterminated or enslaved" (1958, 27–28).

educational and governance system in a country such as Kenya. But, whether through ignorance or frustration, African countries, far from putting up a fight, are, figuratively speaking, rushing into the jaws of the lion. That is, throughout much of Africa, the standard for English being given is British or American. Hence African issues, conditions, and problems are ignored, while African people are making guesses and building elaborate structures in their ether in order to attempt to line up their English with "international" standards. Not only has the African person's own language got struck in a prior eon, but the language that they are forced to use, through official orientation and ever-increasing links to the West, cannot be their own.

Trying to use someone else's language in their way in trying to explain things your way is intellectual suicide. Too much of this is found in African universities and education and the wider society below them. It is sad. The connection between language and the "real" world that native-English speakers so value is almost nonexistent. English words are said to mean Luo things. "Lying" is just the norm—the only way to get by. Corruption is a normal part of life. The spreading of this mantle of Western hegemony spells disaster for the African people, who are at the same time silenced through their own dependence.

The solution to this looming disaster is at once simple and difficult. Advice for the Westerner who wants to intervene to help the people is this: *Depower yourself* (i.e., be poor) and *use the language of the people you are reaching*. Those wanting to perpetuate cognitive incoherence by promoting the use of European languages in Africa should be aware of the disaster looming on the horizon.[9]

5. IMPLICATIONS FOR THE INTERPRETATION OF SCRIPTURE

Having reevaluated many of the interpretational processes going on between Western and non-Western nations, particularly in Africa, we are left to consider the implications for biblical interpretation, and with it the belief of Christians and the running of the church.

Kuhn (2001) made an observation regarding the self-understanding of African-founded churches. It is widely appreciated that these are churches that have rooted their beliefs in local-language interpretations of the Scriptures. There is a popular view that these churches have made a conscious decision to move

9 Note that the above is not necessarily advocating the saving of every ethnic language on the continent of Africa. I believe that regional languages such as Kiswahili can be used and promoted to great advantage.

away from biblical orthodoxy to accommodate aspects of their own culture. But I suggest along with Kuhn (2001, 89–90) that this view is, at least in most cases, incorrect. On the contrary, these churches (African indigenous churches, or AICs) see themselves as following genuine orthodoxy, but now *interpreted through their own languages* as they read it in their own Scriptures. The singular beliefs and practices of these churches frequently arise from their being true to the language used in their translation of the Scriptures.

In saying this, I am implying various things:

(1) The need for a language to be Christianised in the course of time as it comes to be used in Christian ways (Tshianda 2005, 46).

(2) The importance of Christian tradition in guiding a new church. I am hence differing with the idealist Protestant belief of *sola scriptura* ("by Scripture alone") and suggesting that following the Bible without having a historical church to learn from is an inadequate basis for the Christian faith.

(3) Following on from the above—the importance of having Christian education and debate occur in the language of a people, so as to enable the language and its use to develop in Christian ways (see also Harries 2009, here chapter 1). If this fails to happen, a church will continue either to be foreign or unorthodox in the true sense, in order to be true to the language that it uses.

What is foreign in a church can take on a "godly" character. The sound of Latin has for centuries reminded people in the Roman Catholic Church of the holiness of God. In the same way nowadays English, as the language of international relations and the Christian church, has taken on a divine character for many in Africa and presumably elsewhere around the globe. Much that is culturally European—the wearing of shoes and clothes in general, formal education, clerical garb, and the drinking of tea—is being interpreted as Christian activities or rituals. This is an embarrassment for a member of the original culture who finds that processes, perhaps of rational foundation, in their culture of origin have become religious rituals in another. It can certainly make it difficult for the foreign visitor to feel at home in the new, foreign, but all-too-familiar setup.

It is extremely difficult for natives, especially of poorer countries of the world, to get a sufficient grasp of English to be able to use it at a formal, or an international, level. This severely limits their capabilities of interacting with their wider community, and therefore leads to idleness and thoughtlessness. (The only way is simply to allow others to do things for you.) The English that dominates their lives remains out of reach. It is easier to just accept what some foreigner has said than to try and correct them, just to be mocked for your lack of linguistic acumen. It is especially difficult to be inventive and innovative in a language that you barely understand. This difficulty of course becomes exaggerated if the owners of the language, who are particularly likely to find fault, enter the proximity. The use of a language such as English in Africa has a stultifying effect and encourages laziness in the church and in life in general.

Christian teaching (i.e., words), as other teaching, does not easily move across cultural and linguistic barriers and remain intact. Invariably such movement *transforms* it. It is in effect impossible to know just what will "come out in the wash." What may be highly orthodox or commendable teaching at the point of origin may be something quite different when assimilated at its "foreign" destination. The way to ensure that teaching "strikes home" is to move the teacher with the teaching. That is, the only way to effectively transfer the orthodoxy of Christianity from one culture to another is to have the person who is familiar with this orthodoxy in the culture of origin become as familiar as possible with the target culture. This is why missionaries (and development workers) must learn the language of the people they are reaching and be immersed in their culture.

6. CONCLUSION

The way that the human mind responds to stimuli so as to produce meaning or understanding is here shown to be such as to result in deception in crossing cultures. That is, the mind instinctively corrects "abnormalities" in stimuli arising from foreign cultures so as to fit its familiar scenery, rather as it can instinctively correct "wrong grammar." This kind of self-deception that results in the foreign appearing familiar is one reason why the close governance or control of a people by those foreign to them is often unhelpful.

The same difficulty arises if we consider language use across cultures in terms of implicatures instead of only meaning. Examples given illustrate that the implicatures of words with the same meaning can be vastly different between cultures. Implicatures being central to communication, or even the sole objective of communication, shows that familiarity with language (meanings) may not enable someone to either communicate meaningfully or understand clearly. A case is again made by this consideration of implicatures for caution in cross-cultural communication, and for the advisability of language barriers corresponding to cultural gaps.

Increasing rates of globalisation resulting in few, if any, cultures being "untouched" by "the West," means in turn that the people's response to the West will be affected by their prior experience of it. This frequently being an experience of dependence has many implications that certainly reduce the options for straightforward honesty in communication with them. Simply asking, "What do you want?" being often far from wise means that the prerogative is on the side of the one intervening to draw sufficiently closely to situations (cultures) so as to have adequate understanding to guide his/her intervention.

English invariably being accompanied by money in its spread around the globe can give the misleading impression that the impact of the language is that of the wealth that accompanies it. In fact, wherever English appropriates power in a non-English community (especially a poorer community), it condemns non- (or nonfluent) English speakers to increasing ignorance over things that are vital for their own lives. The spread of English, making it in turn more difficult for native-English speakers to discover "what is really going on," adds to the recipe for disaster that should be evident to thinking people. Vulnerability and language learning should be the starting points for cross-cultural intervention.

The language difficulties explained above are found to be *as*, or even *more*, pertinent for the missionary task of planting and nurturing churches. The church should be heading the field in ensuring the vulnerability and linguistic prowess of her servants in cross-cultural service.

In conclusion, I trust that this chapter has laid out a clear case for intervention outside of the West by Westerners, for whatever purpose but especially in church and evangelism, to be conducted in non-Western languages and with sufficient vulnerability.

REFERENCES

Gutt, Ernst-August. 1991. *Translation and relevance: Cognition and context*. Oxford: Basil Blackwell.

Harries, Jim. 2009. "The name of God in Africa" and related contemporary theological, development and linguistic concerns. *Exchange: Journal of Missiological and Ecumenical Research* 38/3: 271–91.

Kuhn, Marko. 2001. From African consciousness to subconscious inculturation: A study into African independent churches (AICs) in Nyanza/Kenya. Thesis, Univ. of Frieburg.

Maranz, David. 2001. *African friends and money matters: Observations from Africa.* Dallas: SIL International.

Mazrui, Alamin M. 1993. Language and the quest for liberation in Africa: The legacy of Frantz Fanon. *Third World Quarterly* 14/2: 351–63.

Sperber, Dan, and Deirdre Wilson. 1995. *Relevance: Communication and cognition.* 2nd ed. Oxford: Blackwell.

Tshianda, Josée Ngalulu. 2005. Quest for theological lexicons in African languages. In *Interacting with Scriptures in Africa*, ed. Jean-Claude Loba-Mkole and Ernst R. Wendland, 40–54. Nairobi: Acton.

Venuti, Lawrence. 1998. *The scandals of translation: Towards an ethics of difference.* London: Routledge.

Wallbank, T. Walter. 1958. *A short history of India and Pakistan: An abridged edition of India in the New Era.* New York: New American Library.

Yule, George. 1996. *The study of language.* 2nd ed. Cambridge: Cambridge Univ. Press.

GLOSSARY[1]

Africa: For the purposes of this book, "Africa" refers to sub-Saharan Africa.

African: A dark-skinned person who has been born and brought up in Africa.

AIC: Either African Indigenous Church or African Independent Church.

Black: A person whose skin is of dark complexion who is ethnically of African origin.

***Chira*:** An illness arising from the breaking of taboo (Dholuo).

Dholuo: The language of the Luo people of western Kenya.

European: A light-skinned person who is ethnically of European origin.

Implicature: The implication of the use of a word, or what a word implies in its use in a particular context, as opposed to the "meaning" of a word.

Kiswahili: The language of the Swahili people, widely spoken in East Africa and national language in Kenya.

Luo: Name given to people considered to be of the same ethnic origin who share many similarities in their language, found particularly in Tanzania, Kenya, Uganda, Congo, Sudan, Ethiopia, and in smaller numbers elsewhere. In this book "Luo" unless otherwise specified refers to the Kenya-Luo.

Magic: A term that is difficult to define. It is used to refer to powers, or apparent powers, that are or appear to be outside of or beyond scientific explanation.

Missionary: I use this term in the sense widely understood in sub-Saharan Africa as referring to a Westerner who has come to Africa with the overt intention of spreading the gospel of Jesus Christ.

Native English: English as used by a person whose underlying philosophical presuppositions are the same or similar to those that are prominent amongst native English people.

Polylogue: A conversational engagement involving more than two people at the same time.

---

1 Note that some of these definitions reflect East African uses of common translations of these terms in indigenous languages. This applies especially to terms relating to ethnicity.

Rational: An intelligent way to think, say, or do something, which varies according to the culture of the people concerned. Hence we have "British (Western) rationality" and "Luo (African) rationality."

***Roho*:** A translation often given for "spirit" in English both in Kiswahili and Dholuo. Originally a loan word from Arabic in Kiswahili.

Tradition: Living faith that reflects the desires of those who are already dead.

Vulnerable Mission: Mission or development intervention carried out by a Westerner in the non-West using the language(s) and resources of the people being reached in ministry.

Westerners: People of European descent and those who have similar philosophical presuppositions to them, including their communities and societies.

White: A person of European origin who is light skinned, usually a Westerner.

Witchcraft: Untoward impacts on individuals or society that arise from unfriendly orientation(s) of the hearts of others.

RECOMMENDED READING[1]

Allen, Roland. 1960. *Missionary Methods—St. Paul's or Ours?* London: World Dominion Press.

Corbett, Steve and Fikkert, Brian. 2009. *When Helping Hurts: How to Alleviate Poverty Without Hurting the Poor . . . and Yourself.* Chicago: Moody Publishers.

Grigg, Viv. 2004. *Companion to the Poor: Christ in the Urban Slums* (revised edition). Milton Keynes: Authentic Media.

Gutt, Ernst-August. 1991. *Translation and Relevance: Cognition and Context.* Oxford: Basil Blackwell Incorporated.

Harries, Jim. 2011. *Three Days in the Life of an African Christian Villager.* Lancaster, Pennsylvania: Jim Harries.

Horst, Willis, Ute Mueller-Eckhardt, and Frank Paul. 2009. *Misión sin Conquista: Acompañamiento de comunidades indígenas autóctonas como práctica misionera alternativa.* Buenos Aires: Ediciones Kairos. chacofrank@gmx.net.

Jennings, J. Nelson. 2007. *God the Real Superpower: Rethinking Our Role in Missions.* Phillipsburg, NJ: P & R Publishing.

Maranz, David. 2001. *African Friends and Money Matters: Observations from Africa.* Dallas: SIL International.

Paul, Frank and Ute. 2010. *Begleiten statt erobern: Missionare als Gäste im nordargentinischen Chaco.* Schwarzenfeld: Neufeld Verlag. (The English version of *Mission Without Conquest* will be published soon. Please contact frank.paul@ojc.de or chacofrank@gmx.net.)

Pennycock, Alastair. 1994. *The Cultural Politics of English as an International Language.* London: Longman.

Reese, Robert. 2010. *Roots and Remedies of the Dependency Syndrome in World Missions.* Pasadena: William Carey Library.

Schwartz, Glenn J. 2007. *When Charity Destroys Dignity: Overcoming Unhealthy Dependency in the Christian Movement.* Milton Keynes: AuthorHouse.

1 Not all these books advocate vulnerable mission. Some cover important ground parallel to vulnerable mission concerns.

INDEX